DOWN THE ROAD IN THE
Carolinas

Day Trips and Weekend Vacations

by
Dawn O'Brien

Published and distributed by:

Becklyn Publishing Group,
Inc.
P.O. Box 14154
Research Triangle Park, NC
27709
(919) 467-4035
(800) 777-4843

•

First Edition
First Printing

•

Copyright 1994
by
Becklyn Publishing Group,
Inc.

•

•

ISBN 0-9623690-8-X

BPG
BECKLYN
Publishing Group, Inc.

Publisher/Manging Editor
Carolyn Clifton

President
Barbara C. King

Director of Sales and Marketing
Pamela Bell Myers

Management Consultant
Nancy Kitchener

Editorial Consultant
David McNally

Account Executives
Annabelle Lee Gates
Theresa Y. Graham

Administrative Assistant
Kristen Heir

Acknowledgements

Cover Color Photos
Courtesy N.C. Travel and Tourism

Cover Design
Angela Miller

Maps
Fraser VanAsch

Foreward

I don't remember a time when I wasn't ready to hit the road. My grandmother couldn't understand why anyone would want to "go" as much as I did. At age 11 I read everything I could find on India because it sounded more exotic than West Texas. My grandmother rolled her eyes to the heavens praying for divine intervention. Some prayers concerning me were never answered to her satisfaction.

Before such hifalautin' entertainments as drive-in movies and miniature golf hit my home town, Snyder, Texas, we went down to the train depot to watch the Roscoe, Snyder and Pacific train come chugging through at dusk. Townspeople wanted to see if anything other than a mailbag showed up. I didn't care who was coming. I was only interested in going! When I saw that train pull away from the station, I wanted to hop aboard and keep on going. I knew it would take me to those exotic places I'd read about.

In high school my favorite song became, "Those Far Away Places With Strange Sounding Names." They called to me in high school. They call to me today. Now is better—I can answer them.

Ramblin' Man Coleman Collar explained me best when he said: "I never saw a road I didn't want to take, a bus or a train I didn't wish I were on, a photograph of a faraway city I didn't long to visit."

I'm writing this book because there's a general misconception that you have to have big bucks to travel. You don't. Particularly in the Carolinas. Because of my travel addiction I've paid some pricey tabs for expensive trips and never thought the money could have been better spent. I've traveled out of the country and also from state to state for next to nothing and enjoyed that, too. Sometimes more. The old saying, "Rich is better" isn't always true. When I wasn't so well-heeled but wanted to go, I've loaded my car with coolers of food and camped at good parks which enabled me to pay admission to museums, tours, theaters and events that I couldn't have otherwise afforded. Or sometimes I've spent sight-seeing time for hiking, tubing, skiing, climbing mountains, crawling through caves, horseback riding, picnicking and singing around a campfire with fellow travelers who, like me, had more interest in experiencing something fun and different than staying home with creature comforts.

Although travel is thought of as relaxing and having fun, which it is, travel is really about learning and not just what we discover on tours, and in museums. We can get that out of guide books, like this. The learning comes in finding out that we like, love and hate things that we didn't know existed. And, we might never have found these latent interests if we hadn't left home.

When tackling a white water rapid, it's finding courage we didn't know was there; when visiting a Revolutionary battle field, it's giving us a clearer understanding of what freedom means; when driving a stake through the ground, setting up a tent and then catching dinner, it's a reinstatement of independence and resourcefulness.

Travel is also about pampering, like finding a chilled bottle of wine and fruit beside your bedroom Jacuzzi when all the muscles in your legs are angry with each other. It's "laying out" on the beach with your watch left behind. It's rocking on a porch with a mountain view while reading that trashy thriller and knowing that you don't have to get up, go in and cook dinner. You can go out or order up. It's about tasting new foods and wines that aren't in your town. It's about not caring whether you shoot par or not, the scenery more than makes up for your score. It's meandering through sleepy towns and passing the time of day with folks who still enjoy taking the time to talk; it's barreling down the water chute at a theme park or sampling the night life in a jazz bar. It's being humbled by such scenery as waterfalls and remote barrier islands. It's catching a blue heron on film and seeing a ruby wink up at you from your sifting pan. It's letting dolphins eat out of your hands that sends a trembling sensation straight through you.

And what's good (educational) about all this? You tune in to new things. These newly discovered interests, whether it is period architecture or hang gliding, can reshape the way you think and spend your leisure time. It may even change the direction of your career.

In this book there's plenty to see and do in the Carolinas throughout the year, all within two to three hours driving time of your home. Parts of West Virginia have also been included because it is accessible to both Carolinas, but primarily because West Virginia has the best snow skiing and white water rafting in the Southeast.

You can sketch it out—a day trip, a weekend or longer. Read to see what each area offers, then make reservations. It's absolutely true, you don't have to have a hunk of money to experience great places, but if first class is affordable, the following are a few wonderful options: Richmond Hill Inn in Asheville, North Carolina (this pampering inn does everything but unpack your clothes), Greystone Inn at Lake Toxaway, North Carolina (understated elegance in a lake setting with water sports and golf), Earthshine Mountain Lodge near Brevard, North Carolina (upscale rusticity with empowerment and fun activities—great for families), Sanderling in Duck, North Carolina, (creme de la creme at the beach), 1790 House in Georgetown, South Carolina (superb restoration and breakfasts), Bay Street Inn in Beaufort, South Carolina (beautiful, on-going restoration where *Prince of Tides* was filmed), Lodge Alley Inn in Charleston, South Carolina (traditional beauty with hotel services). The Willcox Inn in Aiken where you are treated so well you don't want to go back home.

If lavish B & B's and resorts are still a dream, then don't stay home until your wallet is fatter. Go to the area **now**. You can have a good time camping out or staying at budget hotels for several trips. Then you can save money for a once-in-a-while splurge.

Where you stay will depend on your pocketbook and the time of year. In each area, I've tried to provide a price range of choices. For instance, in Hilton Head, South Carolina (one of the more posh resorts), off season you can stay in a nice budget motel that has a good continental breakfast for around $35. And, choose from a variety of popular priced food restaurants as well as play tennis and golf at favorably reduced rates. Or, during the season, you can camp out and add the beach and water activities to other recreation choices. You can also stay in four star hotels and five diamond resorts on Hilton Head's plantation complexes for several hundred dollars a night.

For those on a strict budget with children, Raleigh, North Carolina, offers more free history, art and historic home tours than any city in both states. You can stay in the downtown historic district at a moderate priced bed and breakfast that serves a full gourmet breakfast, or a more expensive motel, or camp in the park downtown for a modest fee.

Directions, price guides, telephone numbers, street addresses and days of the week open have been listed, but some hours have been omitted due to frequent time changes from peak seasons to off seasons. A good rule of thumb on operating times: museums, galleries, historic sites and battlefields are generally open from 10:00 a.m. to 4:00 or 5:00 p.m., Monday through Friday and Saturday, and from 1:00 p.m. to 4:00 or 5:00 p.m. on Sunday.

Lodging accommodations, telephone numbers, a price code and description of what you can expect have been listed. Where possible, I've tried to include all price accommodations as well as a good price range for dining.

Acknowledgements

Putting a travel guide together that covers such a wide scope of interests is a collaborative effort. I could not have known about all the gems and back road goodies without the help of South Carolina,

North Carolina and West Virginia state and local Visitor and Convention Agencies. I have a special thank you to those who kept me from getting lost, which is a big time loser in this business, alerted me to certain safety precautions and lent tireless support and enthusiasm.

My thanks in South Carolina go to: Amy B. Blythe, Director, Media & Public Relations, and Karen Cofino, Assistant Executive Director, Charleston Trident Convention & Visitors Bureau, Charleston; Katherine Bricey, Director of Tourism at Hilton Head, South Carolina's Chamber of Commerce; June Murff, President of The Greater Aiken Chamber of Commerce, Aiken; Gina Nevius, Administrative Assistant, Lowcountry & Resort Islands Tourism Commission in Hampton; Bruce Earnshaw, owner of Cassina Point, Edisto Island; Jane Scarborough, Executive Director of Olde English District, York; Tim Todd, Executive Director of Discover Upcountry Carolina Association, Greenville; Miriam Atria, Executive Director and Karen Thompson, Lake Murray Tourism and Recreation Association, Irmo.

In North Carolina, thanks to: Sam Bass, Executive Director, Highlands Chamber of Commerce, Highlands; Karen Baker, Information & Group Tour Specialist, and Melody E. Heltman, Executive Director, Henderson County Travel & Tourism, Hendersonville; Sue Bumgarner, Executive Director, Cashiers Chamber of Commerce, Cashiers; Oren Coin, Executive Director, Smoky Mountain Hosts, Franklin; Cindy Mihok, Tour Coordinator, Colonial Guides of Hillsborough, Hillsborough; Tom Moshier, Director of Sales, Winston Salem Convention & Visitors Bureau, Winston Salem; Gail C. Murphy, Director of Marketing/Communications, Greensboro Area Convention & Visitors Bureau, Greensboro; Kim C. Myers, Assistant Director of Communications, Greater Raleigh Convention and Visitors Bureau, Raleigh; Jane Peterson, Executive Director of Cape Fear Convention & Visitors Bureau, Wilmington; Elizabeth Wall, Assistant Site Manager, Historic Spencer Shops, Spencer; Esther Wesley, Executive Director, Brevard/Transylvania Chamber of Commerce, Brevard; Beverly D. Wilson, Sales Manager, Pinehurst Area Convention and Visitors Bureau, Pinehurst; and the whole gang at High Country Hosts, Boone.

In addition, thanks to the following Chambers of Commerce in North Carolina: Beaufort, Brunswick, Hickory Nut Gorge, New Bern, Outer Banks as well as the West Virginia Chamber of Commerce.

About The Author

Dawn O'Brien did her undergraduate work at Stephens College in Missouri and at the University of North Carolina at Chapel Hill. She received her master's degree in communications from Wake Forest University.

Ms. O'Brien produced and directed "Scrunch," a syndicated teenage television program for Multi Media and was the host and creative force for the PBS series, "A Taste of Adventure," and has worked as a television reporter, anchor and host. A free-lance writer for numerous magazines, she has authored or co-authored seven cookbook/travel guides on historic restaurants in the southeast and is co-author of *The Insiders' Guide To Charlotte.*

Table of Contents

Directory of Maps

PRICE CODES

ACCOMMODATIONS

    For purposes of comparing prices, we have categorized accommodations with one to four dollar signs (based on the typical daily rates charged for a standard room with two double beds.

    $ 31 To $ 50 = $
    $ 51 To $ 75 = $$
    $ 76 To $100 = $$$
    $101 And Up = $$$$

DINING

    Restaurants have been given one to four dollar signs, in order for you to have a general idea of how much dinner for two, including appetizer, entree, dessert and coffee will cost.

    Under $ 20 = $
    $ 21 To $ 35 = $$
    $ 36 To $ 50 = $$$
    $ 51 And Up = $$$$

State of South Carolina

Office of the Governor

CARROLL A. CAMPBELL, JR.
GOVERNOR

POST OFFICE BOX 11369
COLUMBIA 29211

GREETINGS

On behalf of the State of South Carolina, I invite you to experience the rich heritage, beautiful scenery and enticing charms which are the essence of the Palmetto State.

From South Carolina's Upstate to the Palmetto Coast, you can enjoy it all. Our beautiful countryside, a variety of cultural entertainment, and premier sporting opportunities are just a few of the amenities awaiting your enjoyment. As an international playground, the Palmetto State speaks the language of recreation and hospitality you are sure to understand. I am certain you will be anxious to return once you have experienced our special brand of Southern hospitality.

All South Carolinians join me in welcoming you to our home.

Carroll A. Campbell, Jr.
Governor

STATE OF NORTH CAROLINA
OFFICE OF THE GOVERNOR
RALEIGH 27603-8001

JAMES B. HUNT JR.
GOVERNOR

Dear Friends:

As Governor of the State of North Carolina, it is indeed my pleasure to invite you to explore the Tar Heel State through day trips and weekend vacations.

Join us on a journey that starts high in our mountains, through our foothills and heartland, and on to our coast. You can visit 43 mountain peaks that reach 6,000 feet, including Mount Mitchell, highest peak in the Eastern United States. You can see breathtaking valleys, powerful rivers, cascading falls, and enjoy the largest natural habitat zoo in the world, museums, planetariums and festivals. We have worldclass golf courses, parks, and forests, and sand dunes that would qualify as mountains elsewhere. Some of our beaches have wild ponies, some of our islands have no roads, and our lighthouses are second to none. There are caves to explore, trails to hike, and secret treasures to find.

Welcome to exciting North Carolina!

Sincerely,

James B. Hunt Jr.

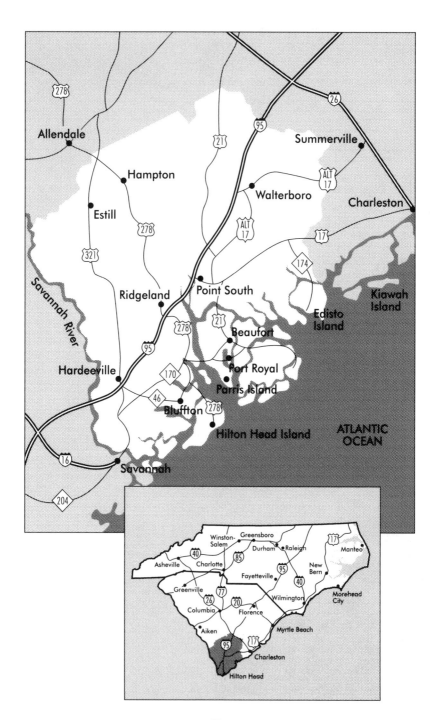

Lower Coast

LOWCOUNTRY

The Lowcountry's horizontal landscape seems to stretch into forever. The fragile sea oat-covered dunes, mystery-filled swamps and dirt roads of live oaks necklaced with Spanish moss coincide to give the feeling that you've stumbled into a Virtual Reality video game.

Turbulence from the Civil War, boll weevil, hurricanes and earthquakes has provided dramatic transitions for South Carolina, and the Lowcountry has borne the brunt of this unpleasantness. Yet, when you watch the migration of waterfowl at Cape Romain National Wildlife Refuge, see folks harvesting oysters in the salt marshes, hear children shout as they run along the wide beaches, or listen to the putt-putt of an angler's outboard motor on one of the many interlocking rivers, you see how man is making strides toward balancing nature and commerce.

HILTON HEAD ISLAND

To Get There:

Take exit 28 from I-95 to S.C. 278. From Beaufort, take S.C. 170 south to S.C. 278 east.

Hilton Head Island is small, dignified and discrete. Don't look for the friendly Colonel's face or the big golden arches because, even though both fast food places are here, the signs are small, designed to blend with nature, and unobtrusively positioned at street level. From the beginning,

Hilton Head was developed through very strict building codes. Nothing upstages nature. That's why you'll see most buildings and homes stained brown or gray to blend with nature's landscape of live oak, pine and palm trees.

Wise planning disallows neon signs, overhead lights or flashy advertising on the 42-square-mile, foot-shaped island. Due to this restriction, even the Red Roof Inn's motel roof wasn't permitted its signature color.

Hilton Head offers visitors a variety of activities to suit the most diverse interests. Nature lovers will enjoy feeding the dolphins or observing a 200-pound loggerhead turtle depositing her eggs on the beach. Those interested in more active pursuits may prefer parasailing or windsurfing over the warm ocean water. Hilton Head's 12 unblemished miles of beach are distinguished by hard, tight-packed sand, strong enough to support bike riders and joggers along with the sun lovers. Biking, whether along the beach or along the numerous paths and trails that wind throughout the lush forests and marshlands, has become one of the island's most popular activities. With 27 golf courses (7 of them public) and 300 clay, grass or hard surface tennis courts, it's easy to see why sports are a year-round opportunity here.

Things To See and Do _____

TOURS
Hilton Head is also an island with some intriguing historical sites. Located in Plantation Center, near the entrance to Palmetto Dunes Resort, the new **Museum of Hilton Head Island** hosts tours of the remaining island ruins of Native American significance. One tour takes a look at the remains of what is believed to have been a ceremonial structure measuring 240 feet across and 9 feet high. If you look closely, you can see remnants of unusual shell rings erected by the island's first inhabitants, Yemassee and Ewascus Native Americans. Tours, including the ruins of a Civil War fort, guided beach walks and ecological programs can also be scheduled at the museum's headquarters.

THE BEACH
A bit past the island's center lies a traffic circle that divides the island into quarters. You can find public beach access at 9 different locations, although parking is sometimes a problem. Two of the easier public accesses to the beach, Folly Field Road and Bradley Beach Road, lie to the island's north off Hilton Head Boulevard (U.S. 278). At the end of Bradley Beach Road you can park your

Photo courtesy Hilton Head Island Chamber of Commerce.

A lazy day at Hilton Head beach.

car, and take a short hike to the beach (about 1 1/2 blocks).

The third best public access is at Coligny Circle. Nearby restaurants and facilities can be found on Pope Avenue, just off the traffic circle. Metered parking spaces are located adjacent to Holiday Inn off Coligny Circle, and there is the Town parking lot off Lagoon Road for half-day or all-day parking.

FISHING AND BOAT TOURS

The Vagabond (803-842-4410) sails out of Harbour Town. It offers a tour that lets you watch dolphins jump out of the water for their twice daily feedings. This partnership-with-nature experience is one you'll remember for years to come. Bring your camera.

The Drifter (803-671-3060), departing from South Beach Marina, takes you out to the gulf for deep sea fishing.

TENNIS

As one of the country's Top 50 tennis destinations, the good public tennis courts are an attractive lure for many players. You can also attend tennis schools for all playing levels at the **Van Der Meer Tennis Center**. (803-785-8388)

Other popular tennis facilities include the **Hilton Head Island Tennis Resort** on Folly Field Road (803-785-6613) and **Palmetto Dunes Tennis Center** at Palmetto Dunes Resort

(803-785-1152). **Port Royal Racquet Club** at Port Royal Plantation (803-686-8803) is an exceptionally attractive racquet club near Westin Resort, and rated a five-star club by *World Tennis Magazine*. It provides the only grass courts on the island.

GOLF

Although the first golf course wasn't built on the island until 1960, recent construction has made up for lost time. You'll find some of the most beautiful courses in the U.S. here, many located at the private resorts, but there are many good public and semi-public courses, too. We have listed a few of them.

Old South Golf Links
Par 72   *$40 to $65*

This course, designed by Clyde Johnston, has a terrain of tidal salt marsh, forest of oaks and open pasture. Located off U.S. 278, across from Moss Creek, it is open to the public. (800-257-8997 or 785-5353)

Hilton Head National
Par 72   *$40 to $68*

This course was designed by Gary Player and is rated one of the Top 50 courses in the country by *USA Today*. Number 17 is perhaps the best Par 3 in the Lowcountry, with seven tees and a variety of challenges. (803-842-5900)

Sea Marsh
Par 72   *$42-$69*

The broad fairways amidst heavy forests of live oaks, pines and palmettos make this a visually pleasurable course. It's not considered a difficult course, but will test your skills. Sea Marsh is located at Sea Pines Resort and is open to the public. (803-842-8484)

Harbour Town Golf Links
Par 71   *$160*

Also at Sea Pines Resort, Harbour Town is a beautiful course designed by Pete Dye. The MCI Golf Heritage is played here each April. The course has a par-four 18th hole that is one of the most feared in golf, especially when the wind is blowing off Calibogue Sound. (800-845-6131)

Ocean Course
Par 72   *$63 to $72*

The Ocean Course at Sea Pines Resort is Hilton Head's oldest golf course. The 15th hole is said to rival any on the island for challenge and beauty. The green slopes steeply uphill and gives a knockout view of the ocean. (800-845-6131)

BIKING

You can see the island, which is essentially flat, a lot better from a bike or roller blade skates than you can from a car. Miles of good bike paths exist, and you can ride up and down hard-packed beaches during low tide. If you don't bring your own bike, you can rent one by the hour or the day at **Bike Rentals**, which also rents canoes and paddle boats. It is located at 77 Queens Folly Road (803-785-2021). **Bicycle** (803-842-5522) at 71 Pope Avenue has rentals for $5 a day. **The Fun Center,** (803-785-5517) rents bikes, roller blades and jet skis.

Accommodations ___

Although sometimes difficult to spot, hotels and condos, which are called villas, bloom in abundance on Hilton Head. By winding back through long curving drives and lush vegetation you'll find plenty of accommodations including luxurious resorts and authentic Southern plantations. Most of the major chains have a presence here, along with budget hotels costing a whole lot less than you would expect on this upscale island. Weekly villa (condo) rentals make up a big portion of the island's accommodations. Accommodations along William Hilton Parkway (U.S. 278), Folly Field and Forest Beach tend to be less expensive, while still offering access to many activities.

RESORTS

The **Hyatt Regency** ($$$$) is a full resort with a pool

overlooking the ocean. The resort, located at 1 Hyatt Circle in Palmetto Dunes Plantation, also has three restaurants. (800-233-1234)

When you're away from home, getting to sleep is sometimes a problem, but the slap of the surf against the sandy beach at the five-diamond **Westin Resort** ($$$$) can lull you to sleep in no time. In the morning you can perk your own coffee and enjoy breakfast on your balcony watching folks play volleyball on the beach or following sandpipers scurrying toward the curve of the island's heel.

Important extras include tennis and golf, with special packages to include your whole family. The resort's 16 tennis courts and three 18-hole golf courses offer a diversity of challenge surrounded by beautiful landscapes.

The resort has three restaurants and guests' children are served free at all three. Following a few days of delicious food, you may want to join one of the hotel's pool aerobic workouts.

Each guest finds his or her own favorite activities, but after a day of relaxation, the ultimate indulgence for some is a midnight whirl in the courtyard Jacuzzi. The Westin Resort is located at Port Royal Plantation. (800-228-3000 or 803-681-4000)

VILLAS

If you choose to rent a Palmetto Dunes' Villa, call **Trident Villa Rentals** (800-237-8306) or **Sand Dollar Management** (800-845-6130). Other good rental companies on the island are **Maximum Resort Rentals** (800-231-6622), **Coastal Home and Villa** (800-334-8678) or **Shoreline Rental Co.** (800-334-5012).

HOTELS/MOTELS

Well located on South Forest Beach Drive, the **Comfort Inn** ($-$$) is only a few hundred yards from the beach and near Coligny Circle where you will find a variety of restaurants, shops and a grocery. (803-842-6662)

The **Fairfield Inn** ($-$$) at 9 Marinaside Drive is a nice place to stay and enjoy the varied continental breakfast offerings. The outdoor pool is well maintained. (800-228-2800)

The **Hampton Inn** ($-$$) at 1 Airport Road has a pool, exercise room and Jacuzzi. (800-426-7866)

The Island's original motel, **Sea Crest Motel** ($$-$$$), is right on the beach off North Forest Beach Drive. (803-785-2121)

CAMPING

You'll find RV camping off Arrow Road, off U.S. 278 for a $30 per night fee. (803-681-3256)

Dining _____

Like all areas, there are certain indigenous foods that you seldom find elsewhere. Frogmore Stew and oysters steamed in burlap are Hilton Head Island's entry. Frogmore Stew is a combination of hot sausage, potatoes, corn, green beans and shrimp. Oysters, steamed in burlap until they can be easily opened with a knife, are found at various island restaurants. Try them, they are delicious, but you could also say the same for the wide array of this tiny island's international offerings. Everything from continental to Asian and Mexican restaurants is here. And, yes, you're still in the South so you can also count on barbecue and fried chicken. Naturally, seafood dominates the list. Here is a mere sampling.

Market Street ($-$$) is the "don't dress" hangout where islanders go. You can dine inside or outside and Greek dishes are the specialty. Try the Greek inspired sauteed shrimp, the delicious Greek Spinach Pizza or an inventive combo of Greek-style potatoes, sausage and stir-fry veggies. Market Street is on Coligny Plaza.

Native dishes abound at **Abbe's Shrimp House** ($-$$), so try its shrimp and okra or smothered fish island-style. The restaurant is located off William Hilton Parkway near Palmetto Dunes.

For some of the best Italian food in town, **Antonio's** ($$-$$$) at the Village at Wexford is highly recommended. The combination platter featuring ravioli with marinara sauce, chicken parmagiana, spinach fettuccini alfredo is a sure winner.

A four-diamond restaurant, the **Barony Grill** ($$$$) offers a superb Petite Filet Mignon and Grilled Norwegian Salmon combination. You won't soon forget a bowl of the Barony Onion Soup or the Angel Hair Pasta with Clams, either. The Red Snapper in Parchment is done to perfection as are the rich and creamy desserts. The Grill provides heart-healthy selections, too. A winner! Barony Grill is located at the Westin Resort in Port Royal.

At **Betsy's Gourmet To Go** ($-$$) you'll find good sandwiches and great pastas—all perfect for a picnic. On Coligny Plaza, it's convenient to the beach, too.

Other than the view from the top of the Harbor Town lighthouse, the ocean view from **Cafe Europa** ($$$$) is one of the best on the island. The view of its pastry counter is equally enticing. For an entree, baked scallops with lime-ginger butter is a standout here, as are the varied pastas. (803-671-3399)

Hudson's ($$) has two family-oriented restaurants. The one on the docks at Skull Creek has been there for 25 years and specializes in seafood. The other location is on Coligny Plaza.

Skillets ($) is a terrific little brunch cafe on Coligny Plaza that features everything from eggs benedict to pancakes.

The Old Oyster Factory ($$), with waterfront dining, overlooks Broad Creek. It's located on Marshland Road, about a mile off Matthews Drive. You'll find a selection of surf and turf here.

The Spirit of Harbour Town ($$$) offers a two-hour, narrated dinner cruise through Calibogue Sound. The buffet includes prime rib, seafood, etc. The cruise departs from Harbour Town Marina. (803-842-7179)

Julep's Restaurant ($$$$), on Greenwood Drive near Sea Pines Circle, offers continental fare and is a favorite for those very special celebrations. The food is wonderful with a Southern attitude. Try the roast duck with ginger peach sauce and Julep's mud slide for dessert.

The Carolina Cafe ($$$$) has a buffet that breaks diets. Broiled grouper with escargot, garlic butter. Prime rib, etc. Located at the Westin Resort in Port Royal, it is open for breakfast, lunch and dinner.

Should you be too pooped to find your car keys, but still starving, consider Express Restaurant Delivery. In 45 minutes to an hour, you can get room service no matter whether you're staying at a camp site, villa or hotel. Over 20 restaurants ranging from American to Italian and from pastas to prime rib are available. Pick up a copy of the *Hilton Head Island Room Service and Home Dining Delivery Guide* at newsstands around the island and in many hotel magazine racks.

Side Trips

DAUFUSKIE ISLAND
The Vagabond (803-842-4410), located at Harbour Town, will take you on a cruise to Daufuskie Island. Part of the

island is still inhabited by native Gullah-speaking Afro-Americans. On Daufuskie you can see the winery ruins, a former school house and an old church. In the recent past, one side of the island has become the home of **Melrose Resort**, one of South Carolina's most exclusive recreational developments. The only transportation allowed in the resort is golf carts.

FORT PULASKI

You can cruise to Historic Fort Pulaski on **The Spirit of Harbour Town** (803-842-7179). This is about a 25-minute boat trip from Hilton Head to the mouth of the Savannah River. The fort is a good ex-

ample of pre-Civil War seacoast fortifications. Managed by the National Park Service, the fort displays restored preservations plus surrounding outworks, period furniture and weaponry. A narrated tour is provided by the park ranger.

For More Information:
Lowcountry and Resort Islands Tourism Commission
P.O. Box 366
Hampton, SC 29924
803-943-9180

Hilton Head Island Chamber of Commerce
P.O. Box 5647
Hilton Head Island, SC 29938,
803-785-3673

The Westin Resort is one of only two AAA Five-Diamond rated, oceanfront resorts on the East Coast.

BEAUFORT

To Get There:

From I-95, take exit 33 onto U.S. 21 or take U.S. 17 south to U.S. 21 at Gardens Corner.

Drive through Beaufort's historic district first, then rent a bicycle at **Lowcountry Bicycles** (803-524-9585), or take a walk beneath deep-shading live oak trees with dangling tendrils of Spanish moss. You'll find that magnificent Lowcountry homes once belonging to ship captains and wealthy merchants have mellowed but not melded into the 20th century here. They stand apart, making local malls and fast food places appear to be trespassing.

A coastal seaport sees a lot of activity, and none more so than Beaufort. Its natural deep harbor on the banks of the Beaufort River (and today's Intracoastal Waterway) made it a prize for explorers. Established in 1711, Beaufort is the second oldest town in South Carolina and all told, seven flags have been whipped about by ocean breezes from nation's bent on acquiring this tiny jewel. Spain, France, England, Scotland and the Confederacy staked a claim before the U.S. flag and the South Carolina Palmetto flag finally flew here in residence.

Things To See and Do _____

TOURS

For a self-guided walking tour that will highlight significant points of interest with a map, stop by the **Visitors Center** at 1006 Bay Street. **Historic Beaufort Tours** (803-524-3163) can book you for a 45- to 60-minute horse-driven carriage tour with an informed guide ($9.50) or can book you for a tour to see Beaufort by boat cruise. The boat cruise costs $10.00 for adults and $6.00 for children. Children under 4 are free.

For a very special tour of churches, historic homes and gardens on the Sea Islands, check in advance for the **St. Helena's Episcopal Spring Tour**, scheduled for the second weekend in March. (803-522-1712)

If you can get away for the third weekend in July, make plans to take in the **Beaufort County Water Festival**. This is a week-long event with a fascinating air and water show, the Blessing of the Fleet, and much merrymaking with music, arts, crafts and Lowcountry food. (803-524-2332)

On the third weekend of October, the **Historic Beaufort Home Tour** sponsors a candlelight tour on Friday, followed by another tour on Saturday featuring historic homes and plantations in and around Beaufort.

WATERFRONT PARK

The Henry C. Chambers Waterfront Park, on the Beaufort River off Bay Street, serves as a diverse gathering place for many activities. A marina is there, plus an amphitheater, pavilion and playground. You can get a takeout lunch from one of several nearby restaurants and picnic or cast-net for shrimp during the season.

BEAUFORT ARSENAL MUSEUM

Located at 713 Craven Street in downtown Beaufort, this 1795 building was rebuilt in 1852. The 5th oldest military unit in America, Beaufort Volunteer Artillery, was once housed here and you can see the collection of American and Civil War artifacts. There're also plantation handicrafts. Open Monday through Friday from 10:00 a.m. until 12:00 p.m. and 2:00 until 5:00 p.m. No admission is charged. (803-525-7471)

JOHN MARK VERDIER HOUSE

This remarkable 1790 Federal-style home of Verdier at 801 Bay Street in downtown Beaufort houses the Historic Beaufort Foundation. Built in the most fashionable style of the 1800s, wealthy merchant John Mark Verdier spared no money to install the handsome Adamsesque fireplaces and hand-carved moldings. It is a bit unusual for original furnishings to remain in a home of this age, but there are many here that belonged to the Verdier family. The original pieces have been supplemented with antiques of the period. The home is open Tuesday through Saturday from 10:00 a.m. until 4:00 p.m. If you choose to visit only the Verdier House, admission is $3; for $5 you can get a combination ticket that includes a tour of the George Parsons Elliott House. (803 524-3163)

GEORGE PARSONS ELLIOTT HOUSE

A couple of blocks away from the John Mark Verdier House at 1001 Bay Street is the 1844 home of George Parsons Elliott who was a wealthy planter of Sea Island cotton as well as a noted politician. This house reflects the Greek Revival period in its exterior and interior designs and furnishings. During the Civil War, the home was confiscated and used as a Union hospital. It is open Tuesday, Thursday and Saturday from 10:00 a.m. until 2:20 p.m. Admission is $3 or $5 in a combination ticket with the John Mark Verdier House. (803-524-8454)

FISHING AND BOATING

Due to Beaufort's clean, unpolluted estuaries, you can catch flounder, spot tail bass, croaker and trout from fishing piers or from the surf. You'll need a fishing license for freshwater fishing, but it isn't necessary for crabbing or shrimping. Licenses are $4.40 and available at tackle shops, hardware stores, etc. Tackle shops are another good bet for letting you know the best fishing places at the time of year you want to fish.

Some of the best fishing is from **Paradise Pier** at Fripp Inlet on Hunting Island. Noted as the state's longest pier (1120 feet), and one that never closes, day or night, it is an excellent place to land anything from spot to big-game fish from March through December. As in most of the Lowcountry, the best fishing is in the spring and fall, but don't rule out summer when more than one angler has reeled in a wahoo or drum. (803-838-5455)

If you've hitched a boat to your car, you may be interested in some good offshore reef fishing. The **General Gordon Wreck**, a 250-foot steel-hulled sailing vessel, lies in Port Royal Sound. Two other possibilities lie off Fripp Island (a private island adjacent to Beaufort). **Fripp Island Drydock** has a 120x80x20-foot structure around this wreck where sea bass, sheepshead and bluefish can be found in abundance. Great bottom-fishing for black sea bass, porgy and flounder is found at Fripp Island Reef.

Of course, you can charter a boat at a number of marinas. A few in the area include **Port Royal Landing Marina** (803-525-6664), **Battery Creek Marina** (803-521-1441) at Port Royal, **Beaufort Marina Center** (803-524-3949) at Lady's Island, or **Downtown Marina** at 1010 Bay Street (803-524-4422). Chartering a boat can be great fun, but be forewarned that the tab can run from $180 to $800.

If you want to schedule some diving or a trip out to the Gulf Stream for deep sea fishing, call **Capt. Wally's "Seawolf IV."** (803-525-6664) The same half- or full-day outings are offered by **Capt. Eddie Netherland** (803-838-5661), whose specialty is king mackerel. **Capt. Doug Gertis' Low Country Fishing** (803-522-8066) is geared toward light-tackle inshore fishing for tarpon, trout, etc.

GOLF

One of the most notable recreations on the Sea Islands is golf, so be sure to pack your clubs.

Cat Island Golf Club

Par 71   *$35*

This course is located on the island of the same name. It was designed by George Cobb and is popular with visitors. (803-524-0300)

Golf Professionals Club

Par 72   *$23 to$25*

This is an economical championship course on Lady's Island. (803-524-3635)

Country Club of Beaufort

Par 71   *$24 to $36*

Also on Lady's Island, this course was designed by Russell Breedon. (803-522-1605)

HORSEBACK RIDING

For a romantic adventure that you've sometimes seen in the movies, think about horseback riding along the Intracoastal Waterway. This could be an excursion that you'll reminisce about on cold, wintry nights. **Waterside Rides** at Lowcountry Farms offers guided trail rides for $20 per hour. (803-689-3423)

Accommodations___

BED AND BREAKFAST INNS

Bay Street Inn Bed and Breakfast, located at 601 Bay Street, is the exact puzzle piece that completes the perfect picture of the antebellum South. Before you open the gate leading up to the Lewis Reeve Sams 1852 mansion overlooking the Beaufort River, the sight of the home has fulfilled your favorite Southern day dream, and you know why *The Prince of Tides* was filmed here.

Each guest room, where a fruit basket and decanter of sherry await you, has a private bath and is appointed with antiques. In South Carolina, this inn wins for the loveliest bridal suite. A full breakfast is served in the large dining room and you can sit out on the balcony reading the morning paper while you watch boats, bicyclers and joggers slip by. (803-522-0050)

Two Suns Inn is located at 1705 Bay Street. This is the kind of place that has made bed and breakfast inns so popular in America. Not only was it built in 1907, the attitude is also of the less hurried 1907 kind. It's casual and friendly, plus you have a wonderful view of the Beaufort River from the front porch where you'll want to spend some time just drinking in the atmosphere. The inn serves a wholesome, full breakfast, and you are encouraged to join the "Tea and Toddy Hour" in the afternoon. (800-532-4242)

HOTELS/MOTELS

You will find most of the chain motels in the area, but

Photo by Dawn O'Brien.

View from the balcony of the Bay Street Inn in Beaufort.

Howard Johnson Lodge ($$-$$$) on U.S. 21 is convenient to Parris Island and also serves a continental breakfast. (800-654-2000)

Battery Creek Inn ($$) on U.S. 802 is opposite the main gate for Parris Island. (803-521-1441)

CAMPING

If you want to mix in a bit of beach and camping time at one of South Carolina's most beautiful parks, take a short drive down U.S. 21, crossing over Harbor Island to **Hunting Island State Park** ($-$$). You can stay in a cabin or pitch your tent at one of the 200 sites. The campground provides showers, water and electrical hookups, a swimming pool, nature trails and three miles of uncluttered beach. (803-838-2011)

Dining _____

Harry's Restaurant ($-$$) is located at 812 Bay Street. This is a hangout with some of the locals for breakfast or lunch. Upstairs, dinner is served at the John Cross Tavern ($-$$). St. Helena's Seafood is the dish to order in this 1700s restaurant.

The Anchorage House ($-$$$) is located at 1103 Bay Street. This 1770s home is the epitome of gracious living. Overlooking the Beaufort River, it's a relaxing place for lunch or dinner. Check its daily seafood specials.

Plum's ($$) is located at 904 1/2 Bay Street. On the Waterfront Park, the restaurant overlooks the Beaufort River and is a great place for lunch or for those who want to stop in for their yummy homemade ice cream.

Emily's ($$) is located at 906 Port Republic Street. This is an upscale, intimate place where you can order continental cuisine from the *A la Carte* or Tapas menu. This restaurant and bar stays open later than most of Beaufort's restaurants.

Gullah House ($-$$) is located right on U.S. 21 about 7 miles south of Beaufort at 761 Sea Island Parkway. If you want typical Gullah fare, set your taste buds for shrimp, grits and cheese cassoulet with a side dish of tender fried okra and red rice with sausage. Weekend jazz sessions are well attended in this attractive restaurant with polished wood tables and benches. You can come here for breakfast, lunch or dinner and enjoy the best Lowcountry cooking on the island. The restaurant is closed on Monday.

Side Trips _____

FRIPP ISLAND
DATAW ISLAND

To Get There:

Fripp Island is 19 miles east of Beaufort on U.S. 21. Dataw Island is off U.S. 21, 6 miles east of Beaufort.

You'll find that these two privately owned sea islands have quite different personalities. Fripp Island has 3 1/2 miles of beach and an abundance of wildlife. You can play golf on the ocean, enjoy a number of boating activities at the marina and frequent several good restaurants and its club. Dataw Island, 6 miles east of Beaufort, is not available for vacation renters, but offers championship golf, tennis and wonderful fishing.

PARRIS ISLAND

To Get There:

Take U.S. 21 east from Beaufort and follow well-marked signs to Parris Island.

This island is where the Spaniards nosed out Native American Archaics during the 1500s in repeated efforts to form a colony on the Atlantic Coast. The town of St. Elena, established in 1566, became the Spanish capital of American colonies

for a short time. In 1883, after the Civil War, the island became a small naval station. Today, that modest station has grown to a Marine Corps Recruit Training Depot for nearly 20,000 marines.

You'll probably enjoy taking a trip to the **Parris Island Museum** housed in the War Memorial Building. This is not only a military museum. Over 4,000 years of history that stems from the Archaic Native Americans is displayed beside military uniforms, maps and material that show you the history of Marine Corps battles. You can also see evidence of the ongoing excavations at St. Elena. While on the island, stop by the Visitors Center for a map that will show points of interest on the base. The Visitors Center opens daily at 10:00 a.m. and closes at 5:30 p.m. each day except Thursday when it closes at 4:00 p.m. No admission is charged. (803-525-2951)

OLD SHELDON CHURCH RUINS

To Get There:

From Beaufort, take U.S. 21 northwest to Gardens Corner. Turn left onto S.R. 21 and go 1.7 miles north of the junction.

Prince William's Parish church, known as "Old Sheldon Church" was built between 1745 and 1755. Driving down this avenue of live oaks moves you back into an earlier time, and seeing the sunlight play through the church's brick arched windows is nothing less than a photographer's dream.

Although the church was built on land donated by Edmund Bellinger, the name Sheldon was used to honor the Bull family whose nearby plantation and ancestral home in Warwickshire, England, were both called Sheldon Hall. Patriot's arms were hidden in the Bull family's vault during the Revolution and the conti entals were allowed to drill - on the church grounds (activities that did not sit well with the British).

Still, looking at the row of Tuscan columns and imagining what it must have looked like in 1755, you can't help but wonder how British General Augustine Prevost could burn this temple-like church in 1799, and how General Sherman's Union soldiers could repeat the deed in 1865. For your convenience, a couple of picnic tables are near the road. There's no need to worry about packing drinks, the church's old fountain still pumps the tastiest water you'll find in the area.

SHERMAN'S MARCH THROUGH SOUTH CAROLINA

General Sherman began his tour of South Carolina by crossing over the Savannah River from Georgia at Two Sisters Ferry, and you can follow his trail during the winter of

The Old Sheldon Church Ruins

1865 on a 3-day tour that begins in Beaufort. Your initiation leg begins with a dinner cruise that explains the role of the Blockade Runners, who became the lifeline of the Confederacy. Following the cruise, you'll have dessert and coffee in Beaufort at the 1778 Anchorage House that overlooks the Beaufort River. During the War Between the States this beautifully restored home, built by a wealthy Port Royal Plantation owner, was turned into a Union hospital.

The first day of the tour will take you up the old Orangeburg Road a few miles from Two Sisters Ferry to the former **Gayfield Plantation**. Here, Lawton O'Cain will entertain and educate you with stories passed down through her family of the hardships and terror experienced during America's most turbulent period. From this plantation you'll move on to **Broxton Bridge Plantation** where 9th generation owners, Jerry and Gwen Varn, will feed you a sumptuous Lowcountry lunch. Afterward, Jerry Varn will take you to the very spot where the Union forces were held back from crossing the Salkehatchie River for several days. The view of the black-looking river, which General Oliver Howard said was, "indescribably ugly" is not ugly at all, but has a mystical quality of its own. Proceeding north toward Denmark, storyteller Don Eubanks will entertain you at the only plantation home that was not burned. You'll "make camp" the first night at the **Governors House Hotel** in downtown Columbia.

After a breakfast that includes special musical entertainment called *Songs of the Confederacy*, day two begins with a visit to the **State House Grounds** where bronze stars mark Union cannon fire that pockmarked, but did not destroy, the State House. Near Winnsboro, you'll see the 1788 **Old Brick Church**. Here you'll see a remarkably personal statement of apology written on the church's inside wall by a Union soldier. His troop was ordered to tear up church pews for lumber to rebuild a bridge that Confederate soldiers had burned to thwart Union advancement.

The **Winnsboro Town Hall**, once the O'Bear home, marks the place where defiant Southerner, Lila Carroll sang, "Oh Yes, I'm a Southern Girl, I Glory in the Name," while she paced the balcony's home as she watched Columbia burn in the distance. After lunch and a short walking tour through this historic town, it's on to historic Camden.

On the town's outskirts at **Boykin Mill Pond** you'll be at the site of the last skirmish fought in South Carolina between local forces and Union troops. As day two ends, you will enjoy one of the best meals in South Carolina at the **Mill Pond Restaurant**, and spend the night at the **Greenleaf Bed and Breakfast**.

At breakfast on the tour's last day, you'll be entertained by Louise Burns, author of *A Diary from Dixie*, who will point out the reconstruction experiences and take you through this lovely horse country town where the Camden Cup is raced twice each year. You'll hear more heroic tales as you go north through the nearby town of Liberty Hill to Stoneboro and past **Hanging Rock Battle Ground**.

After lunch, it's on to Cheraw. Called "The Prettiest Town in Dixie," Cheraw fortunately remained almost intact throughout the war. The visit includes **Sherman's Headquarters** and the 1770 **St. David's Church** and the **Lyceum**. As a remark found in a soldier's diary says, "This town has been a pleasant one, and has the Southern aristocratic bearing."

A rousing finale of "Huckleberry," a bluegrass band with samplings of 19th century music, will entertain you at a delicious dinner, followed by a recitation of General Robert E. Lee's farewell address.

To sign up for the 3-day $450 tour, call **Westbrook Tours.** (800-671-2866)

BROXTON BRIDGE PLANTATION & HUNTING PRESERVE

To Get There:
From I-95 take exit 57 at Walterboro and take S.C. 64 east to S.C. 641 to S.C. 601 south.

You can fly your plane onto the air strip at Broxton Bridge Plantation Hunting Preserve, home of 9th generation owners, Jerry and Gwen Varn. This encroachment of modern civilization is, however, in stark contrast to the rich history of the Plantation. Civil War buffs can visit the Plantation's fortifications where, in 1865, Confederate troops staged a fierce battle to prevent the Yankees from getting to the Capitol in Columbia, South Carolina. A reenactment of the battle was staged at the Plantation in February, 1994, by the Palmetto Battalion, which brought horses and replicated weapons to portray this piece of South Carolina history.

The Plantation's Hunting Preserve offers guaranteed hunting opportunities for quail, deer, and turkey. If you want to sharpen your skills, try the Sporting Clays Course, a combination of trap and skeet in a natural game habitat. If you have never hunted before, Broxton Bridge provides a hunting clinic on the last Saturday of each Month. It is taught by Dan Carlisle, a member of the U.S. Olympic Team for Skeet and Trap who has also won the National Championship for Sporting Clays. Carlisle teaches both beginning and advanced shooting techniques.

The hunting season in this county is a bit longer than in most areas. Deer hunting season runs from August 15 through January 1, and bird hunting from October 1 through April 1. (800-347-HUNT)

The Plantation's two-story **Kite Kinard Bed and Breakfast** ($$-$$$) has a warm, welcoming living room decorated with a hunting theme. Each bedroom in this restored 1850 home has a private bath. Next door is the 1880 **Howard Folk House** hunting lodge. All the rooms here have a private bath also, but since bathrooms weren't standard in houses of this age, some are accessed at close-by locations. Breakfast is continental. (803-866-2218)

ST. HELENA'S ISLAND

> **To Get There:**
> **Take U.S. 21 southeast**
> **from Beaufort**

Gullah-n-Geechie Tour

The highly recommended Gullah-n-Geechie Tour of St. Helena's Island is a wonderful teaching tool because it's different and so much fun. You can sign up for the tour behind the Gullah House restaurant on U.S. 21.

Photo by Dawn O'Brien.

The Chapel of Ease on St. Helena's Island.

You might easily pass by the freshly painted, one-room **Praise Houses** on St Helena's Island without even noticing. But the houses, built by plantation owners for their slaves, hold hundreds of years of West African traditions. Like and yet unlike a church, the Praise Houses were led by an elder who initiated the service combining singing and dancing.

Unable to bring with them the drums that were used in West Africa to relay messages to neighboring tribes, the slaves learned to send messages in the Praise Houses through song and the tapping of their feet. This is where slaves vented their sorrow and frustrations and worked with each other to keep their West Aftrican language alive. Known as Gullah, the language is a combination of English and West African words with a unique syntax. Lively, true Gullah-style meetings are still held on St. Helena Island at the Croft Praise House, usually on Tuesday and Thursday nights.

Later churches, like the 1855 **Brick Church,** had balcony galleries built by slaves for slave use. Plantation owners patted themselves on the back believing they'd done a good thing by including slaves in their worship services. When your tour stops here, a Gullah native will guide you through the church with a story told in Gullah.

Now on the National Register of Historic Places, you'll find that the still-operating Brick Church is simple in decor and the oldest church on the island constructed of brick. The Brick Church's minister, Ervin Green, is translating the Bible into Gullah.

The Brick Church was the first site of the famous Quaker-run **Penn School** from 1862-1865. The school was founded by two Pennsylvania Quaker women to teach black children the basics of education. The school moved across the road to its present site in 1865 and remained a vital institution for many years, gradually changing its basic curriculum to become a trade school. Today, **Penn Center** functions as a community center to promote the preservation of Gullah heritage and self-sufficiency among sea islanders. The Center's **York W. Bailey Museum** contains many African artifacts and paintings.

A trip down the **Avenue of Oaks** to the **Coffee Plantation** makes you think of the old wagons and buggies that traveled through here a hundred and fifty years ago. Wander through the Episcopal **Chapel of Ease**, an 1861 antebellum ruin built of unbroken shells (original tabby construction).

Overhanging magnolia leaves and Spanish moss now form the only roof, giving the Chapel a mystical feel. St. Helena's Mounted Volunteers met here for "The Big Shootout" in November of 1861.

If you stay overnight on the island, the **Royal Frogmore** ($$) is a convenient and comfortable place to stay. (803-838-5400)

For More Information:
Lowcountry and Resort Islands Tourism Commission
P.O. Box 366
Hampton, SC 29924
803-943-9180.

Greater Beaufort Chamber of Commerce
P.O. Box 910
Beaufort, SC 29901
803-524-3163

EDISTO ISLAND

To Get There:
Take U.S. 17 southwest from Charleston to S.C. 174 south.

When you cross over the Dawhoo drawbridge and drive down scenic U.S. 174, often bordered with ancient live oaks, the effect of wispy Spanish moss dangling from occasional over-reaching branches is old South to the core. And as the beach on Edisto becomes closer, you wonder what magical trinkets the

Earl of Shaftsbury dangled before the Native American Edistows to persuade them to sell this island in 1674.

The Edistows were originally attracted to the island for the same reasons vacationers are attracted today—the area's abundant wild life and rich o ean harvest. Three miles of near-faultless beach (with good beach access) still yield the best shelling prospects on the East coast. A giant pyramid of oyster shells, known as Indian Mound or Spanish Mount, was built by the first Edistows on the banks of Bay Creek in Edisto Beach State Park as a monument to these offerings of the sea. Time, weather and dredging operations in nearby Scott Creek, have eroded the original 15-foot-high mound, but bits of pottery and other artifacts continue to be found each year among the shells.

Early English planters found the land good for growing indigo, but they soon discovered that the climate and soil on Edisto combined to make this the best place in South Carolina to grow the famous longtime staple, Sea Island cotton. This golden crop produced near-instant millionaires who built lavish Lowcountry plantation homes and fine churches—some of which have survived both the Revolutionary and Civil Wars as well as a number of ferocious hurricanes.

Photo by Dawn O'Brien.

A country road on Edisto Island.

There are no neon-like glitzy recreations on the island—one of the major reasons that people come here to relax. Another attraction that has been drawing visitors to the area since the 1920s, is the landscape, which is quite a bit different from most beach areas. Just behind the 3-mile beach lies a long, thin lagoon, and beyond the lagoon is the area natives call the "jungle." It's a dense bramble of tropical vines, live oak, pine, palmetto and cedars where deer, raccoon, squirrel and a few snakes reside. Ibis can still be seen in the lagoon, and during the season "turtle watchers" often see the huge loggerhead turtles crawling out of the surf to lay their eggs on the beach. Environmentalists often place the turtle egg nests in safer spots until the little silver-dollar size hatchlings find their way to the sand's surface and can navigate a path to the ocean.

This quiet, family-type area is an annual source for "fossil hunting" for the bones of prehistoric creatures, believed to have been buried in ancient bogs that lie offshore. Teeth of numerous species of sharks can easily be found in a short stroll along the strand. Its many tidal creek beds still yield plenty of excitement for the young and young at heart who go crabbing for the tasty blue claw crabs, or cast their nets for shrimp.

Things To See and Do _____

EDISTO ISLAND HISTORIC MUSEUM

The Edisto Island Historic Museum is located in an old house on U.S. 174, approximately 7 miles from the bridge. This expanding museum holds quite a collection of historical artifacts from Native American inhabitants through the reigns of British, Spanish and French. Remnants of the Civil War and its effect on Edisto Island complete an interesting historical exhibit. In the Nature Room, you'll see samples of sea life, mounted animals and reptiles indigenous to this sea island.

TOURS

You can sign up at the Museum for tickets to the annual tour sponsored by the **Historic Preservation Society** the second Saturday in October. This self-driven tour leads you through several plantation homes and three pre-Revolutionary War Edisto Island churches: The Presbyterian Church, the old First Baptist Church, and the Trinity Episcopalian Church. Museum hours are Tuesday, Thursday and Saturday from 1:00 until 4:00 p.m. No admission is charged, but donations are welcomed. (803-869-1954)

There are two year-round tours of the Island that may interest you. On the **Island Tour**, guide Marie Elliott takes visitors on a 2 1/2-hour drive-by tour that includes many of Edisto's plantation homes and churches, with the background history of each place. At some locations, you can walk on the plantation grounds or go inside one of the historic churches. This tour also provides an opportunity for visitors to see the many beautiful creeks that intertwine with marshlands throughout Edisto. The Island Tour cost is $12. (803-869-1937)

The second tour, the **Shell Gathering Tour**, is hosted by guide Ron Elliott. You are taken through Frampton Inlet to an island that is accessible only by boat for a couple of hours of prime shell gathering. Botany Bay is a barrier island juxtaposed between Edisto Beach to the south and Seabrook and Kiawah islands to the north, with marsh stretching behind it. Elliott confides, "This is the most powerful place on earth— it's like one of those medicine places—like a church. I get my power, my reason for being, right here." You can find good shells on Edisto Beach throughout the year, but large conch shells and other collector's delights are found more intact at these tiny islands a few minutes away from Edisto. Ron Elliott also serves as a fishing guide for small groups. The cost for the Shell Tour is $7. (803-869-1937)

FISHING AND BOAT TOURS

You can fish from the pier or charter a boat to go out to the Gulf Stream at the **Edisto Marina.** (803-869-3504) You'll need a boat to experience the **Edisto Offshore Reef** located 23.5 miles from Stono Inlet. This one-mile-square reef originated as a mid-water trolling alley in 1980 and is the farthest offshore reef in the South Carolina system where amberjack, dolphin (fish), barracuda and Spanish mackerel can be caught.

EDISTO BEACH STATE PARK

Located off U.S. 174 on Edisto Island is one of South Carolina's most popular parks. Edisto Beach State Park has three distinctive landscapes, yielding a number of recreational options.

Like a magnet, the ocean front park's 1 1/2 miles of sandy beach draws sun lovers and anglers. Vacationers can fish in the surf, swim in the ocean and comb the beach for shells and fossils.

The park's four-mile nature trail weaves through the jungle-like maritime forest, that contains some of the state's tallest palmetto trees, and ventures out upon the aforementioned shell mound built by the early

Edistows. The forest area may also provide a quick glimpse of a native bob cat or white tail deer.

The trail then winds out along boardwalks to the park's third option—the salt marsh. A good nesting place, lucky hikers can observe life in the salt marsh, including terns, ducks and other indigenous species.

The park has 75 family camp sites and 5 cabins for rent, and if you call early enough, you can reserve a beach-front camp site. There is no restaurant in the park, but there is a gift shop. The park has playground equipment for children and a nature center that sponsors field trips and interpretative programs during the summer. There are several other good hiking and nature trails for nature study. Fees for camping and rustic cabins are moderate. (803-869-2756)

Accommodations___

Thankfully, no hotels or motels exist on Edisto Island, and the natives prefer to keep it that way. You will find vacation cottages, bed and breakfast rooms and camp sites.

BED AND BREAKFAST INNS

For the feel of Southern aristocracy of the 1800s, make reservations at **Cassina Point Plantation** ($$$-$$$$), the former 1847 plantation home of

Carolina Lafayette Seabrook Hopkinson. (The baby girl was named by General Lafayette when the honored guest stayed at Seabrook Plantation.) The third of the William Seabrook Plantation lands, the land was a wedding gift from Seabrook to his daughter.

You can reach Cassina Point by car, or wind your boat up the creek where, a mere 100 yards away, you'll see the four-story home. Fringed with 200-year-old-oaks, this stalwart Lowcountry-style home has withstood wars and hurricanes.

You may find guests engaged in a game of croquet or the English bowls game on the expansive lawn. Some may be sipping a cool drink on the screened piazza where a sumptuous breakfast of French toast, sausage stuffed mushrooms and fresh strawberries is often served. Some may be pretending to read in hammocks. This is the kind of place where you need never feel ashamed of doing absolutely nothing.

The house itself is a historical treasure. As you enter through either of the two front doors, your first view will be a graceful, curving mahogany staircase. The Gentlemen's Parlor is secreted behind pocket doors. And in the downstairs basement you'll find graffiti writings of Union soldiers who seized the house during the Civil

War. There are also drawings of gunboats and weapons that were left behind.

Owners Bruce and Tecla Earnshaw's, thoughtful, two-year renovation has added concealed air conditioning and heating to the home. High ceilings are part of gracious upstairs bedrooms that have floral comforters and balloon-curtained windows. Each room has retained its own marble or slate fireplace, but private half and full baths have been added.

The home is decorated with antiques ranging from American Revolution to Victorian English periods, which include 2 original family pieces. One is a handsome collapsible-type wardrobe that the Hopkinsons took with them before Union occupation. The other piece stays in the Earnshaw's private quarters.

Once a plantation that grew Sea Island cotton, today it yields asparagus used in scrambled eggs or shrimp and crab from the creek for afternoon appetizers. (803-869-2535)

CONDOMINIUMS/COTTAGES

Weekly villa rentals with 1, 2, and 3 bedrooms are available at **Fairfield Ocean Ridge** ($$$-$$$$), located at 1 King Cotton Road. (803-869-2561)

For weekly cottage rentals, call **Lyons Company**. (803-869-2516)

Photo by Dawn O'Brien.

Cassina Point Plantation was siezed by Union soldiers during the Civil War.

CAMPING

Camping information is provided above, under **Edisto State Park**.

Dining _____

For breakfast, lunch or dinner, the **Pavilion Restaurant** ($), located at 102 Palmetto Boulevard, is one of the island's more economical bets.

If you want to enjoy every moment of your getaway vacation by the water, then **Salty Mike's Restaurant** ($$), at 3702 Docksite Road, will let you enjoy the island's freshest seafood as you overlook Big Bay Creek.

For Calabash-style seafood lovers, the **Edisto Restaurant**, on U.S. 17 in Jacksonboro won't be too far to travel.

For not only the best dining on the Island, but one of the very best dining experiences on the East Coast, visit the **Old Post Office Restaurant** ($$$). Fabulous Lowcountry dinners, that may include quail, veal and broiled or sautéed fish, are almost always accompanied by Chef Philip Bardin's phenomenal stone ground grits. If you haven't developed a taste for grits, you will here. Reservations are needed. (803-869-2535)

For More Information:

Lowcountry and Resort Islands Tourism Commission
P.O. Box 366
Hampton, SC 29924
803-943-9180.

Edisto Chamber of Commerce
P.O. Box 206
Edisto Beach, SC 29438
803-869-3867

South Carolina
Bed & Breakfast
Association

278-K Harbison Blvd., Suite 120
Columbia, South Carolina 29212

(803) 734-1449

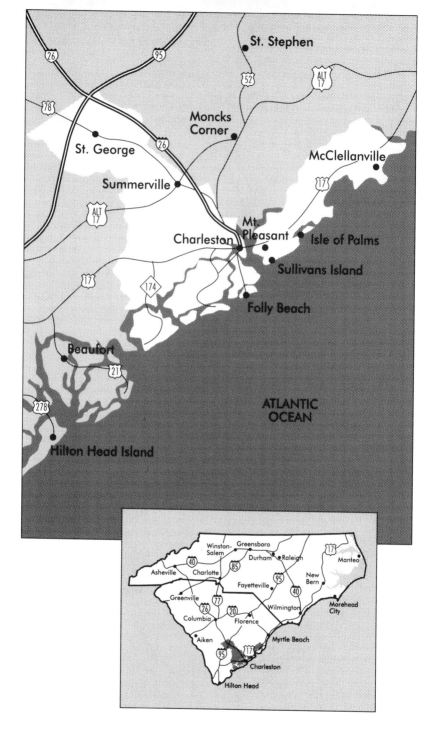

St. Stephen

Moncks Corner

St. George

Summerville

McClellanville

Mt. Pleasant

Charleston

Isle of Palms

Sullivans Island

Folly Beach

Beaufort

Hilton Head Island

ATLANTIC OCEAN

Winston-Salem
Greensboro
Durham
Raleigh
Manteo
Asheville
Charlotte
Fayetteville
New Bern
Greenville
Columbia
Florence
Wilmington
Morehead City
Aiken
Myrtle Beach
Charleston
Hilton Head

CHARLESTON

To Get There:
Take I-26 east or U.S. 17 north or south, and exit onto I-526.

"Charleston," said the French exchange student, "is a European city that moves to a Southern beat." The clip-clop of your horse-drawn carriage accentuates how it feels to ride through a living museum. You'll see over-300-hundred-year-old cobblestone streets, the result of ballasts thrown overboard from trading vessels during the period when this seaport rivaled Boston and threw a tea party of its own.

The pace of the ride gives you time to glance beyond ornate wrought iron gates at intriguing gardens of camellias and ancient magnolias. The homes behind these gardens represent architectural influences from Federal to Victorian designs. Yet, double-porch piazzas borrowed from Barbados are hallmark Charleston.

The choice of pastel colored houses was West Indies in origin to reflect the heat, but the "haint" blue color painted around doorways and windows was said to prevent evil spirits from entering. It must be working as Charleston has survived Native American attacks, pirates, devastating fires, hurricanes and earthquakes.

Come to Charleston on a day trip and you'll wish for a weekend. Come for a weekend and you'll make even longer "next time" plans.

GETTING AROUND
Parking isn't always easy to find in Charleston so once you find a spot, leave your car

there or use a parking garage. You may opt for a horse-drawn carriage ride at **Old South Carriage Company** (803-723-9712), at the corner of Anson and North Market streets, or for $1, you can buy an all-day ticket for the **DASH** (a trolley-like car) that can drop you off at all downtown points of interest. You may want to rent a bicycle at **Charleston Bicycle Rental** (803-722-7433) at 28 Cumberland Street, take a walking tour, or try a combination of the above.

Whatever your plans, the **Charleston Visitors Center** at 375 Meeting Street is a good place to begin. Here you can get an overview of what is available, find maps and purchase tour and museum tickets.

Things To See and Do

BEACHES

Since some family members may want only sprinklings of history at one time, consider dividing your time between historic house, museum and plantation tours and area beaches.

There are a number of beaches easily accesible from Charleston. Take S.C. 171 to **Folly Island** and spend the day "laying out" on the beach, or set off for a half or full day of deep sea fishing on a charter boat. Check out **Sullivans Island** where you can spend a leisurely

day swimming, surf fishing or perfecting your tan. You can play golf, ride bicycles on the beach at **Kiawah**, or rent jet skis or charter a deep-sea fishing boat on the **Isle of Palms** at Wild Dunes. Golf and horseback riding on the beach are available at **Seabrook Island**.

CITY MARKET

Don't miss the unusual downtown City Market where artisans weave sweet grass baskets as they talk to you. Here you will find antique and modern jewelry, Lowcountry rice and bean combinations, jellies, books, watercolor prints and T-shirts, plus an ever-changing array of other unique items. You'll find some antiques here, but serious antique collectors need to head for King Street. A variety of antique shops can be found on this street, many graced by elegant filigree-like cast-iron railings.

HISTORIC HOME TOURS

How would you like to stand where Confederate General P.G.T. Beauregard stood when the first shot of the Civil War was heard? The General stood on the upstairs piazza of the **Edmondston-Alston House** at 21 East Battery, looking through a telescope at the firing on Fort Sumter, three miles away. Today, admission is charged to this 1838 historic home as well as to the **Nathaniel Russell House, Heyward-Washington House** and the **Joseph Manigault House**. Unless you were in the Charleston social registry, or a visiting dignitary such as George Washington, or conducting business with the owners of these homes, it's unlikely that you would be able to tour these homes as you can today.

EDMONDSTON-ALSTON HOUSE

The Edmonston-Alston House at 21 East Battery is a modified single house built by wealthy merchant, Charles Edmondston and later transformed into Greek Revival style by rice planter, Colonel Charles Alston. The bright green Bavarian glass chandelier is an import as was the room's 1811 harp and 1820 piano. You can walk through the door-height windows onto the piazza for prevailing breezes. Admission for this home is $6; $10 when combined with the Nathaniel Russell House. It is open daily and is handicap accessible. (803-722-7171)

NATHANIEL RUSSELL HOUSE

Built in 1808 by another wealthy merchant, the Nathaniel Russell House at 51 Meeting Street is a neoclassical design with rooms in perfect symmetry. Still, its most breath-catching asset is the "flying staircase" that spirals from floor to floor. Baby cradles, mirror desk vanities and fine china imply that these owners weren't so dissimilar from us today, but accessories such as ornate window and mantel moldings and silk chaise lounges in parlor or game rooms spell the difference. You can see an orientation film at the Edmunds Preservation Center at 108 Meeting Street. To purchase a reproduction piece of Charleston furniture, check the showrooms at 105 Broad Street. Admission is $6; $10 with combination tours. The home is open daily. (803-724-8481)

HEYWARD-WASHINGTON HOUSE

This house, built by Daniel Heywood in 1772, has two distinctions: Heywood's son, Thomas, was a signer of the Declaration of Independence and George Washington did actually sleep here in 1791. You can visit the original kitchen (built away from the house), carriage house and gardens. You will also see samples of the expert craftsmanship of 18th century Charleston artisans through the furnishings in this Adams-period mansion. The home, located at 87 Church, Street is open daily and handicap accessible. Admission is $6 for adults and $4 for children. (803-722-0354)

Photo courtesy Charleston Trident CVB.

Overlooking the historic Battery in Charleston.

JOSEPH MANIGAULT HOUSE

One of the more remarkable things about this handsomely constructed 1803 Federal-style home is that amateur architect, Gabriel Manigault, designed it for his brother, Joseph. Although the Manigaults were French Huguenot descendants, both brothers were educated in England and the influence of Scottish architect Robert Adam is seen in this excellent classical example at 350 Meeting Street.

The domed street entrance, several yards from the brick-walled home, signals more elegant times. The cantilevered, curving staircase with its beautiful crystal chandelier hung from the foyer's center, provides a commanding view. On the second floor you'll see the combination ballroom/drawing room. Soothing ocean breezes made this the coolest room in the house.

Admission is $6 for adults, $4 for children, and $4 in combination with other Charleston Museum tours. The home is open daily and is handicap accessible. (803-723-2926)

BATTERY PARK

Fit in time to walk at Battery Park, also known as White Point Gardens, with its commanding view of the harbor and other activities.

ST. PHILIP'S EPISCOPAL CHURCH

This church, at 146 Church St., is known as the lighthouse church because a light was placed in its steeple to help guide ships to port. During the Civil War, the church bells were converted into cannon, but were replaced on July 4, 1976.

DOCK STREET THEATRE

This is the place where Lincoln's assassin, John Wilkes Booth, and others have performed. Open year-round, you might want to take in a play at the site of one of the first American theaters. Handicap accessible. 803-723-5648

ST. MICHAEL'S EPISCOPAL CHURCH

Significant churches abound in Charleston, but St. Michael's Episcopal Church at the corner of Broad and Meeting Streets, completed in 1761, is not only the oldest but has been singular in maintaining its original architectural design. And while on his 1791 Southern visit, George Washington slept at the Heywood-Washington house and worshipped at St. Michael's. The church's original eight bells still call parishioners to worship, although as prize booty, they were taken to England during the Revolution and sent back for recasting after they were burned in the Civil War.

MUSEUMS

Both the **Gibbes Museum of Art** (803-722-2706) at 51 Meeting Street and **The Charleston Museum** (803-722-2996) at 360 Meeting Street help you to identify and place Charleston from an artistic and historical perspective. Although you'll see family portraits in some historic houses, the Gibbes has a more extensive collection, plus scenic views of Charleston. At the Charleston Museum, you'll find the city's roots, dating from the culture of its Native American inhabitants with photos of mysterious ceremonial shell rings, arrows, pottery and plant life in one extensive wing that moves through colonial days into its famed rice planting period and past the Civil War.

A Decorative Arts wing displays silver produced by Charleston artisans as well as clothing, furniture and other artifacts. Admission is charged for both museums. For the Gibbes, adult admission is $5, $4 for seniors and $4 for students. The Charleston Museum admits adults for $5, children for $3. Both are open daily and are handicap accessible.

CHARLES TOWNE LANDING

While sorting through Charleston's historical roots, a trip to Charles Towne Landing is a good place to start as this is the site of the original settlement. This state park features bike trails, picnic areas, an animal forest featuring animals indigenous to South Carolina, a full-scale replica of a 17th century trading vessel and other attractions.

EXCHANGE BUILDING AND PROVOST DUNGEON

And there's also probably no better place to conclude your diggings than at the **Exchange Building and Provost Dungeon**. If you want to see where pirates, Native Americans and signers of the Declaration of Independence were imprisoned during the Colonial era, take a tour through the dungeon. 'Tis a far cry from prison standards today. The building, originally used as a town meeting house, was also Charleston's first customs house as well as the meeting ground for the convention that ratified the United States Constitution. Admission for adults is $3 and for children $1.50. It is open daily and is handicap accessible. (803-792-5020)

MAGNOLIA PLANTATION AND GARDENS

Nothing can give a better sense of "breathing the politest air in the South" than a visit to Magnolia Plantation and Gardens. Bright colored peacocks, a mere preview of color to come, strut beside a fenced off meadow where miniature ponies cause frequent double-takes.

They don't upstage the gardens, however, because few things achieve that at any time of the year. In the Spring, trying to describe the way paths wind past 250 varieties of azaleas and beneath a natural arbor of 900 different camellias tends to provoke adjective deficiency in most folks. Through time, Magnolia's early formal garden design gave way to the informal English garden where wisteria-cloaked lattice-rail bridges remain the Gardens' signature to this day.

When there's a cool breeze off the Ashley River, you can see Spanish moss stir from live oak trees that were already centuries old when Barbadan planters, Thomas and Ann Drayton, built their first home here in the 1670s. Murals grace the entrance of the just-opened indoor tropical Barbados Garden, and mirrored walls enhance the space lending a jungle-like atmosphere of tropical plants.

After General Sherman burned the second plantation house in 1873, the family floated their Summerville home down the river on a barge. A tour through this home provides you with a good example of how simply early planters lived after the Civil War.

Rent a canoe and paddle through the 125-acre Waterfowl Refuge or use boardwalks built out over the swamp to get a better view of the wildlife. Admission for the house tour is $4. For the garden tour, adult admission is $9 ($3 extra for Audubon Swamp) teens, $7, children 4-12, $4. The plantation and gardens are open daily and are handicap accessible. (803-571-1266)

MIDDLETON PLACE

The focal point at Middleton is the famous butterfly-shaped lakes. Best appreciated from an aerial view, most folks find up-close viewing to be pretty astounding as well. The truly astonishing fact is that it took over a 100 slaves a period of 10 years to dig these symmetrically balanced lakes. Begun in 1741 when Henry Middleton inherited the plantation and designed the land as formal gardens, they remained untouched through "our late unpleasantness" or "the war of Northern aggression" commonly known as the Civil War.

The Union army burned the Middleton's home, but you can see the mansion's one remaining wing along with the stable and outbuildings. Wander among the azalea-covered hillsides and beside the picturesque lakes. This garden has a number of beautiful statues and a gigantic, over 1000-year-old live oak tree where visitors like to have their pictures taken.

This tree has survived 11 hurricanes and 2 earthquakes.

Admission during the peak season—March through June—is $10 for adults and $5 for children. It's about $1 less July through February and there is an additional $6 charge for the house tour. Open daily, the house and gardens are handicap accessible. (803-556-6020)

DRAYTON HALL

Take a close look at the front hall mantel where one of Montgomery's Confederate soldiers carved his initials and the date—July 1864. And in one of the main floor's front rooms you'll see a special place where parents marked their children's heights. The last owner, having no children, recorded the growth of her dogs.

Photo by Dawn O'Brien.

Magnolia Plantation's country-English garden.

Unlike other plantation and historic house tours, Drayton Hall is unfurnished, but its rich hand-crafted details and moldings make it worth a visit. Following John Drayton's death, the 1742 home's original furniture moved to the city with his 20-year-old widowed wife and young children. Drayton's older sons maintained the pre-Revolutionary War home passing it down through seven generations. Today it is considered the oldest and best surviving example of Georgian Paladian architecture in the South.

Many historic homes are wreathed with trees, but this Greek temple-like home stands apart from shrubbery and flowers. Built with Carolina brick and constructed in Flemish Bond, the house's interior is as symmetrically balanced as its exterior, with the front entrance facing the Ashley River.

Admission for adults is $7, for children, $4. The house is open daily and is handicap accessible. (803-766-0188)

BOONE HALL PLANTATION

If there's a feeling of _deja vu_ as you drive up the avenue of Spanish oaks, don't worry, you have been here before—at the movies; both _North and South_ and _Queen_ were filmed here. In 1935 Boone Hall, the antebellum Georgian mansion, was rebuilt from handmade bricks produced on the plantation. A half-hour, guided tour of the manor house depicts the life of plantation owner, Major John Boone.

Adult admission is $7.50, children ages 6 to 12, $3; open daily; the home is handicap accessible. (803-884-4371)

Patriots Point

You may think that watching war movies has clearly defined how the Navy operates, but you'll find there's no substitute for seeing, touching and "walking their walk"—even on a self-guided tour.

Wear good walking shoes and choose a cool day or early morning as work and living quarters aboard the World War II submarine, **Clamagore,** destroyer, **Laffey**, Coast Guard Cutter, **Ingham**, and World War II aircraft carrier, **Yorktown** can become congested and cramped.

On board the carrier, you'll see over 20 vintage planes, ranging from a WWII basic trainer to jets that flew in Korea, Vietnam and the Persian Gulf. The hangar and flight deck house prop-driven fighters, bombers, and torpedo planes whose heroes fought throughout the Pacific during WWII. You will also see the B-25 bomber, similar to the ones of Doolittle's famed "60 Seconds Over Tokyo" raid, fighters that provided air support during the

Korean War and other famed jets from Desert Storm.

You'll be proud to walk aboard a destroyer that participated in the D-Day landings. Transferred to the Pacific, Laffey's heroic crew kept her afloat after being hit by 5 Japanese Kamikaze suicide planes and 3 bombs. And your chest will swell a bit more when you board the cutter Ingham that sank a German U-boat, took part in 31 WWII convoys, 6 Pacific patrols and 3 Vietnam tours.

You'll learn what close really means when you descend to the Clamagore's living quarters. This WWII sub patrolled the Atlantic, Mediterranean and tense Cuban waters in 1962.

Admission to Patriots Point is $8.00 for adults and $4.00 for children. It is open daily from 9 a.m. and is handicap accessible. (803-884-2727)

Don't miss the **Vietnam Museum**. Daily boat tours for **Fort Sumter National Monument** (where the Civil War began), as well as boat tours of Charleston Harbor are available from **Patriots Point** in Mt. Pleasant and from **City Marina** on Lockwood Drive with **Fort Sumpter Tours**. (803-722-1691)

GOLF

Few people are aware that in addition to a historical heritage of 300 years, Charleston was also the site of **America's first golf course**. This shouldn't be too much of a surprise when considering that the

Both **North and South** and **Queen** were filmed at
Boone Hall Plantation's antebellum Georgian Mansion.

Lowcountry offers golf architects some of nature's most scenic material. You can play on an oceanfront course or thread your way though forests of live oak and pine. The Charleston area has over 20 courses and most are located no farther than 30 to 40 minutes away. And since Charleston is not promoted as a "golf only" visit, its courses offer good starting times coupled with a leisurely atmosphere.

It was at the Ocean Course at **Kiawah Island Resort** that the Ryder Cup was recaptured by the United States in 1991. This challenging course, designed by Pete Dye, opened in 1991, and was named "America's Best New Resort Course" by *Golf Digest*. Ten of the holes lie along the beachfront, and the alligators have the right of way! (803-768-2121)

Designed by Tom Fazio who considered the site "an architect's dream," **The Links Course** at **Wild Dunes Resort** on the Isle of Palms has been described by one national publication as "the ultimate in seaside golf in America." Perhaps its most famous hole is the 18th that stretches out beside the Atlantic Ocean. (803-886-6000)

Architect, Jack Nicklaus, blends ocean and heavy vegetation into this championship course. **Turtle Point**, which opened in 1981 at **Kiawah Island Resort**, is a long, challenging course (6,396 yards from the blues). (803-768-2121)

Patriots Point Links, conveniently located on U.S. 17 in **Mount Pleasant**, is close to the city's historical district. Designed by Jack Spence, the course features lots of water and large greens. (803-881-0042)

Charleston National Country Club, designed by Rees Jones, this course in **Mount Pleasant** has recovered well from the ravages of Hurricane Hugo. The natural setting features marshland and lots of wildlife. (803-884-7799)

Ron Garl designed the **Links at Stono Ferry**, a public course off S.C. 162 in **Hollywood**. It's located about 20 minutes from downtown Charleston and, if you're lucky, you may run into its owner, Senior Tour player Jim Colbert. (803-763-1817)

FISHING

There is surf fishing and fishing from the pier, but the best is deep sea fishing in the Gulf Stream. Don't worry about equipment or bait, **Island Charters'** 30-foot, 21-passenger Island Hopper has everything you need—plus a catered lunch.

Captain Ivan Schultz, an outstanding tournament fisherman, takes you out to the Gulf Stream where even beginners reel in some big ones. Call to find out about specialty trips such as fishing for sharks. Half-day price range is up to $300 for 4, and $65 for each additional person. (803-588-6060)

Right behind the Trawler Restaurant at the north side of Shem Creek Bridge in Mount Pleasant, you can find the **Carolina Clipper**. This deep sea fishing boat leaves at 7:00 a.m. daily (weather permitting). Tackle, bait and ice are supplied and electric reels are furnished at no additional charge. A snack bar has lunch-type foods and soft drinks. (803-884-2992 or 881-0132)

Accommodations

Two Meeting Street Inn ($$$$), located at 2 Meeting Street, is signature Victorian with Tiffany windows. Wouldn't it be tough to start marriage with a 2-year European honeymoon and return to find that your inlaws had built a magnificent Victorian mansion for you across from Battery Park and the waterfront? You can stay in this honeymoon mansion that serves a continental breakfast by calling. (803-723-7322)

If you want to stay in a renovated slave bedroom with a newly added bath above a carriage house, choose the **Battery Carriage House** ($$$$), located at 10 South Battery. If weather permits you can have a continental breakfast in its enclosed garden or you can breakfast in bed. (800-775-5575)

For a more economical Bed and Breakfast only 1 block from the Battery, consider **The Hayne House** ($-$$$) located at 30 King Street. The home, listed on the National Historic Register, is furnished with antiques, good books and some fine art work. Private or shared baths are available. (803-577-2633)

If you're interested in a hotel-type stay, think about **Vendu Inn** ($$$-$$$$), located at 19 Vendu Range. Not only does this quaint inn offer lovely rooms and elegant suites, but it also has the superb **Library Restaurant** ($$$), which is filled with great books for guests to enjoy. (800-845-7900 outside South Carolina or 800-922-7900 inside South Carolina)

Another elegant hotel-like establishment is **Lodge Alley Inn** ($$$$), located at 195 East Bay Street. Even its least expensive rooms have a living room with fireplace, wet bar and refrigerator. Its penthouse suite has a living room with fireplace, dining room, 2 bedrooms with 2 1/2 baths and an outdoor patio. The accommodations are furnished with reproduction an-

Charleston Harbor from an East Battery Piazza.

tiques, and it also has one of Charleston's best restaurants—**The French Quarter** ($$$). (800-821-2791 or 803-845-1004)

The **Mills House** ($$$$), located at 115 Meeting Street, is a venerable old reliable where Paul Newman likes to stay. On weekends, the hotel includes chilled champagne and breakfast in bed. The hotel is on the corner of Queen and Meeting streets, close to terrific restaurants. (800-847-9600)

The **Omni** ($$$$) at Charleston Place between King and Meeting streets is adjacent to the City Market. This is a big city-type hotel with all the privacy of a big hotel and all the amenities of a good B & B. The rooms and baths are spacious and luxurious without going overboard. It too, has a great restaurant—**Louis's Charleston Grill** ($$$). (800-THE OMNI)

Hampton Inn Historic District ($$-$$$) is located at 345 Meeting Street. The Hampton chain has taken advantage of this building's historic location and has restored its beautiful wood floors and scattered oriental rugs amidst reproduction furnishings. Conveniently located across from the Visitors Center, this comfortable inn with attractive courtyard serves a superb continental breakfast.

Dining

Like New Orleans, some people go to Charleston just to eat. Almost any cuisine is available and most of it is the best of its kind. In truth, not the best of its kind, but a fast and economical lunch with everything from Lowcountry to pizza to Chinese, is available at the **Food Court** opposite the City Market.

Charleston has really great bars in historic settings where regulars and tourists stop by from noon on. A favorite is **Tommy Condon's** ($-$$), located at 160 Church Street. This is a combination Irish pub and restaurant. You can cool your sightseeing feet here, have a drink or dinner. The thing to order is Shepherd's pie.

Another economical restaurant that is terrific for breakfast is the **Baker's Cafe** ($-$$), located at 219 King Street. Its pastries are memorable, and you can take some back home or to your room. (The restaurant is also a good bet for dinner.)

Probably it's the setting that does it, but one of the most Charleston-looking restaurants is **82 Queen** ($$-$$$), located at 82 Queen Street. You can dine outside in the courtyard. Order the Lowcountry She Crab Soup first, and follow with Shrimp and Scallops in creamed spinach and tomato sauce.

The two hottest restaurants in Charleston are **Magnolias** ($$$), located at 185 East Bay Street, and **Carolinas** ($$-$$$), located at 10 Exchange Street. They are hot because they've learned the secret—cooking indigenous foods such as shrimp and collards and blackeyed peas in gourmet-healthy fashion. Order the blackeyed pea cakes at Carolinas or smoked quail stuffed with collards. At Magnolias, order anything accented with grits.

A very unusual Charleston restaurant is **Noelle's** ($-$$$), located at 83 Cumberland Street in a 1719 brick home. It serves authentic Caribbean food with all the good spices that make this cuisine special. Order the West Indian chicken curry and pumpkin fritters.

For More Information:

Charleston Trident Convention & Visitors Bureau 81 Mary Street, P.O. Box 975 Charleston, SC 29402 803-853-8000

AAA-Ashley Crossing Shopping Center 1975-K Magwood Rd. Charleston, SC 29414 803-766-2394

Photo courtesy Charleston Trident CVB.

Historic Charleston homes reflect architectural inflluences from Federal to Victorian styles.

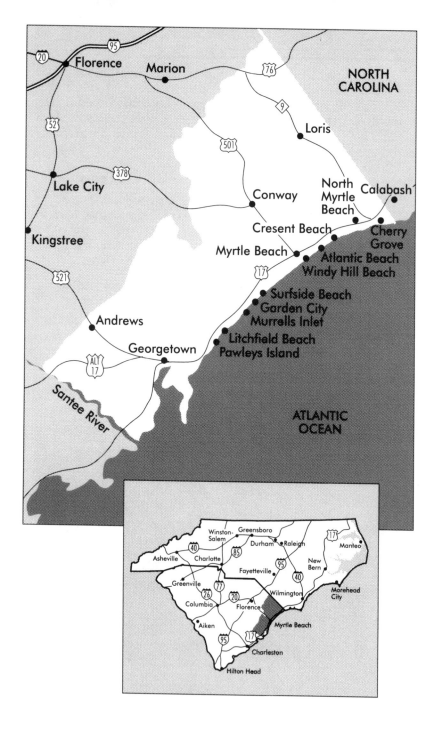

SOUTH CAROLINA'S
Upper Coast

GRAND STRAND

From northern to southern tips, South Carolina runs about 200 miles along the Atlantic Ocean, but has more than 3,000 miles of land adjacent to bays, sounds, rivers, and other waterways—much of this on the coastal plain. For 60 of those miles, the Grand Strand yawns and stretches, wriggling its way from Little River, right below the North Carolina state line, to Georgetown and Winyah Bay.

Native American Waccamaws and Winyahs fished from the ocean and paddled their dugout canoes up rivers to hunt wild boar, deer and duck in those palm and hardwood forests. Vacationers still come here to fish and hunt, but most come to play on the Strand's wide, cream-colored beaches. Some drop anchor at the smaller, family-style beaches, many are drawn to the glitzier, something-always-happening Myrtle Beach and some prefer the funky, "arrogantly shabby" Pawleys Island. But whatever your style, you're sure to find the perfect place for that weekend (or longer) getaway.

GEORGETOWN

To Get There:

From I-95, take U.S. 521 east to Georgetown, or take U.S. 17 north from Charleston or south from Myrtle Beach.

In 1729, when colonists surveyed and settled Georgetown, everyone knew each other's name. The story is the same today. This could be why a visitor was overheard to remark, "I think I've found the perfect place to retire."

Georgetown's main street, Front Street, sits beside the port on Winyah (pronounced win-yaw) Bay. Five rivers and creeks feed into Winyah Bay, all with Indian names such as the Pee Dee, which means "coming and going." In plantation days, indigo, rice and lumber were shipped out of Georgetown's harbor, making it the country's largest exporter of "Gold Rice."

Today, Georgetown bills itself as "the real South," and despite the recent renovation of the downtown area, history and tradition still play a major role in the life of the city. There are over 40 sites you can visit in the historic district.

Things To See And Do

THE RICE MUSEUM

You can't miss seeing The Rice Museum at the corners of Front and Screven streets. Individual clocks in its bell tower face all four sides of the steepled structure. Here, the rice story is told through dioramas, artifacts and a short audio-visual show. The museum is open from 9:30 a.m. until 4:30 p.m., Monday through Saturday. Admission is

The Georgetown waterfront with famed 4-sided clock.

$2 for adults and students are admitted free of charge.

PRINCE GEORGE WINYAH EPISCOPAL CHURCH

Prince George Winyah Episcopal Church on the corners of Broad and Highmarket streets was erected in 1747. The church still has its original enclosed box pews, some that face each other instead of the pulpit. The church is open to tour Monday through Friday from March through October.

HAROLD KAMINSKI HOUSE

At 103 Front Street, next to Joseph Hayne Rainey Park (named for Georgetown's first African American elected to the U.S. House of Representatives), stands the Harold Kaminski House. With a view of the Sampit River, this stunningly restored home displays antiques spanning 300 years. A favorite is the 1810 letter cabinet with pigeonholes for all alphabet letters except J and Y (the letter "I" replaced those letters). The home, built in 1769, is open to tour Monday through Saturday from 10 a.m. to 4 p.m. Adult admission is $4 and $2 for children 6 to 12 years of age.

CAPTAIN SANDY'S TOURS

Natives ask who died when they see Captain Sandy in socks, shoes and long pants, because attending funerals is about the only time the Captain goes formal. His commentary travels the same route, but with a lot more knowledge of the plantations, wild life, and flora and fauna that you'll be seeing from his pontoon boat.

He'll stop here and there on the three-hour cruise to gather wild persimmons to make jelly or to point out a red tailed hawk or blue heron. You'll go down narrow Kerr Creek where wild azaleas bloom and see duck blinds in green bearded fields which have replaced the rice paddies of the past.

Captain Sandy offers four different riverboat excursions. The old plantation and ghost telling tour is always a favorite, but children enjoy the hands-on barrier island nature tour. Call for tour schedules and fees. (803-527-4106)

HUNTING AND FISHING

The Native American tribes who lived along the coast knew the rich bounty of its hunting and fishing opportunities. Those same opportunities still exist today using some of the same methods.

Near McClellanville, the **Santee Coastal Reserve**, a tract of 24,000 acres donated by the Nature Conservancy, provides an abundant source of waterfowl and a wide variety of game and fish. A Wildlife Management Area permit is required for all hunting on the reserve.

Archery hunts for whitetail deer are allowed from Monday through Saturday during the first and last weeks in October. And archers can camp at the reserve during those times. Hunters are advised to keep a sharp look-out for poisonous snakes and are reminded that it is illegal to feed or harass the alligators. It's best to stay on the dikes as water levels near the dike roads are often quite deep.

You can fish from the Santee River dock and Hogpen impoundment from February through October. Fishing is also permitted on Murphy and Ce-dar Island beaches at any time of the year and the river is accessible by a public boat landing on U.S. 17.

The Reserve is open February through October for hiking, biking and canoeing, although due to water levels, the canoe trails may not always be accessible. Camping is also available to other visitors from February through October through prior arrangement. Additional primitive camping is available at Cedar and Murphy Islands. For more information contact Santee Coastal Reserve at P.O. Box 37, McClellanville, SC 29458. (803-546-8665)

Photo by Dawn O'Brien.

Georgetown plantation as seen from Captain Sandy's Riverboat Tour.

Accommodations____

BED AND BREAKFAST INNS

Staying at a beautifully restored bed and breakfast inn will make you feel more a part of this throw-back-to-another-time town.

For an all-round ideal B & B experience, **1790 House** ($$-$$$) at 630 Highmarket Street near downtown is the place to stay. Meticulously restored, with newly added large baths, this beautifully appointed home also offers bicycles for guests in a perfect biking town. For a full breakfast, like your mamma never made, the attentive innkeepers introduce different menus daily. They offer such gastronomic pleasures as bananas Hawaiian, fresh squeezed juices, eggs with 3 cheeses, cinnamon pancakes, from-scratch muffins made from a variety of fruits, etc. (803-546-4821)

Five Thirty ($-$$) on Prince Street near downtown has cleverly splashed rich color throughout its antique filled rooms. (803-527-1114)

Mansfield Plantation ($$$$) located on the Black River off Route 8 is one of Georgetown's newest B & Bs. Several guest houses have been converted into charming and private bedrooms with bath. This antebellum plantation dates back 150 years and you can stroll by the river where English ships boarded the plantation's valuable rice cargo. The staff serves a wonderful breakfast, and the plantation has been designated as the luncheon stop for special group tours from the Myrtle Beach area. (803-546-6961)

Dining _____

The River Room ($-$$) on Front Street, built as a dry goods and grocery store in 1802, also offers outdoor harbor-view dining. Its shrimp Creole is a standout, and don't pass up the slips-down-like-silk peanut butter pie.

Thomas Cafe ($) at 703 Front Street is the place the locals go for breakfast. If you want to soak up the local flavor, stop by here and engage in conversation.

For lunch you won't find a better spot than the attractive **The Pink Magnolia** ($) on Front Street. Don't turn up your nose at the Southern specialty, Hoppin' John Soup—it's one of the most nourishing and delicious foods you'll eat anywhere.

Land's End ($-$$$) on the water at 1 Marina Drive has a nice setting and good food, but it can be a bit pricey for what you get.

Greene's Ice Cream ($) on U.S. 17 south is where the

locals pick up a basket of red beans, rice, collards and cornbread (ask for a corner piece) for about $4.

Side Trips

HOPSEWEE PLANTATION

To Get There:

From Georgetown, travel 12 miles south on U.S. 17.

This home on the lovely North Santee River is the birth place of Thomas Lynch, Jr., one of the signers of the Declaration of Independence. Built before 1740, the handsome but sturdy plantation home, beautifully decorated with antique furnishings from the 1740s to the 1780s, is now the private residence of James and Helen Maynard.

Modeled after architecture of the West Indies, you'll see craftsmanship unique to the area. Built to keep wind-driven rain out, the outside window sills and porches are slanted at a downward angle. Even the black cypress siding is curved downward. The 1 1/2-inch-thick long leaf pine interior floors are more indestructible than loblolly pine and the doors are so perfectly engineered and hung that they've never sagged nor needed repair in over 250 years. The handmade candle-light-design molding throughout the house would be cost pro-hibitive today, but chair-railing that doubles as an interior window sill could provide a lesson in economy to builders of today.

You can visit all the rooms (something rare in a private home tour), including the attic and the furnished brick basement with a model of the rice plantation's irrigation gate. You can also visit two out-buildings that were used as kitchens. Best of all, however, the drive through century old live oaks with lacy moss tendrils, stamps the scene into a post card of the past.

The house and grounds are open from March through October from 10 a.m. until 4 p.m., Tuesday through Friday. The plantation is open by appointment the remainder of the year. Admission is $5 for adults and $2 for children. (803-546-7891)

HAMPTON PLANTATION STATE PARK

To Get There:

From Georgetown, take U.S. 17 south about 15 miles.

Located on U.S. 17 north of McClellanville and 15 miles south of Georgetown, General George Washington stopped by Hampton for breakfast in 1791, some 40 to 60 years after the plantation home was built by the Horrys, a French Huguenot family. Additions changed the house from a Georgian farmhouse to a Federal mansion. The evolving architectural styles are clearly shown in the purposely exposed walls and ceilings of the mansion's unfurnished rooms.

As interesting as the architecture and history of the plantation may be, the many stories and legends surrounding it are equally so. For example, during the Revolutionary War, Francis Marion is said to have escaped the British through an underground tunnel from the house to the river. The tunnel has not been sought since ecologically sensitive historians and naturalists fear that excavation could cause erosion.

Another legend involves 21-year-old John Henry Rutledge who had the misfortune of falling in love with a Georgetown pharmacist's daughter, a woman not of his class. The class system was nearly impenetrable during the 1900s and his family forbade the marriage. The love-stricken Rutledge committed suicide and to this day, as the story goes, John Henry's ghost continues to rattle the nerves of park rangers in the upstairs bedroom where he died. You'll find his grave in the back of the plantation, apart from the Rutledge family's burial plot.

This former rice plantation was last inhabited by state poet laureate, Archibald Rutledge, who left an indelible mark on Lowcountry beauty through his writings.

Hampton Plantation State Park offers varied programs for school children, including nature walks on Wambaw Creek. The park, near McClellanville, is open year-round Thursday through Monday, from 9 a.m. until 6 p.m. and the Plantation house Thursday through Monday from April through Labor Day. It is open Saturday and Sunday the remainder of the year. Admission for adults is $2 and for children $1.

HOBCAW BARONY

To Get There:

From Georgetown, take U.S. 17 north for about 1 1/2 miles.

In 1907, famed financier Bernard Baruch purchased ten former rice plantations (at $4 per acre) and turned them into a winter hunting ground for his family and friends. Baruch even constructed his own private airfield on the property to provide easy access for such distinguished guests as Winston Churchill and President Franklin D. Roosevelt. Gifts from notable guests can be seen throughout the brick and steel constructed house (the property's third mansion) on Winyah Bay.

Of Baruch's three children, only his daughter Belle found the activities and beauty of Hobcaw to her liking. Belle became such a Hobcaw enthusiast that, bit by bit, she bought the entire estate from her father and later turned it into a wildlife sanctuary.

Today, due to provisions in her will, all indigenous wildlife species roam the cypress tree swamps, salt and fresh water marshes and rivers in safety. The Belle W. Baruch Foundation has preserved the estate's stable that displays Belle's many medals, and the original slave village, once called Friendship Village. A small church, a medical dispensary and several one- and two-room slave cabins still stand, surrounded by tall gate-minder plants originally planted to keep evil spirits away.

This superstition is no doubt scoffed at by the serious research programs now carried on by both Clemson and the

Photo by Dawn O'Brien.

Bernard Baruch's home, Hobcaw Barony.

University of South Carolina to study the wildlife and ecology of the barony. You can get a good overview by watching the short film at Bellefield Nature Center, located at the entrance to the 17,500-acre estate.

A scheduled mini-van ride down one-lane dirt paths takes you past 90-year-old decaying pine trees, purposely left for endangered red-cockaded woodpeckers that will only nest in this type environment. Bring insect repellent and coat yourself liberally for the 3 1/2-hour tour. Reservations for tours must be made in advance.

Admission to the plantation is $10 for adults; tour reservations must be made 30 days in advance. (803-546-4623)

For More Information:

Georgetown County Chamber of Commerce & Information Center
P.O. Box 1776
Georgetown, SC 29442
800-777-7705

THE SOUTHERN BEACHES

To Get There:

Just south of Myrtle Beach on U.S. 17, lie Surfside Beach, Garden City, Murrells Inlet, Litchfield Beach, Pawleys Island and Debidue Beach.

Like the beaches to the north of Myrtle Beach, these beaches tend to be more family oriented, but with distinct personalities. Folks who vacation on the Grand Strand every year, find the beach that suits their interests and life style and seldom switch or try out another.

Litchfield Beach

This beach derives its name from Litchfield, England, the ancestral home of Litchfield Plantation rice growers. Today, this beautiful beach is a sprawling growth of upscale condos and the *piece de resistance* of the Grand Strand—**Litchfield By The Sea Hotel & Resort** ($$$-$$$$, 803-237-3000 or 800-845-1897). The resort claims three exceptional golf courses, plus a terrific restaurant, **Webster's** ($$-$$$), whose chef is a genius. If visiting in season, order the blue crab fritters or Louisiana style crawfish ravioli.

Behind the golf courses, you'll find **Litchfield Plantation Manor House** ($$$$), at the end of an avenue of oaks. Now operating as a bed and breakfast inn, this beautifully restored (with Jacuzzis) antebellum mansion does not admit visitors without prior reservations. (800-869-1410)

Pawleys Island

Pawleys Island looks like, and is, a throw back to another

time—the 1930s and 40s—with a few plantation-owner summer homes from the 1800s thrown in for luck. You'll find little-to-no air conditioning and that unpainted or peeling wood cottages, mostly behind brambles of trees and shrubs, comprise the landscape.

Bumper stickers describe Pawleys as "arrogantly shabby," but vacationers at other beaches say the Pawleys Island crowd has an attitude. The attitude stems mostly from a desire for privacy and preserving the beach's natural setting. This is the only beach on the Grand Strand that does not have a public beach access, a condition that is against South Carolina state law, yet remains unchallenged.

In the past, Pawleys Pavilion was the place to go to dance. Legendary bands like The Tams, The Travelers, James Brown and the Famous Flames swung this island into high gear. The Shag may have originated in North Myrtle Beach, but don't try to tell that to those who remember shagging here in the 50s. The Pavilion burned in the early 70s, and sadly, no one has been able to replace it.

Before turning off U.S. 17, stop by the **Pawleys Island Hammock Shop** at the causeway. It's a tough customer who doesn't leave here with a rope hammock.

Several good restaurants are located in this Lowcountry-designed shopping complex. **The Community House** ($$-$$$), once an old church, is located directly across the highway from the shopping complex. It serves excellent Northern Italian dishes, and is open for lunch and dinner. **Out Back At Frank's** ($-$$$) is an excellent place for lunch or dinner.

Murrells Inlet

The folks in this little fishing village saw more than their share of pirates in the 1700s. One native told me that it was originally named Murray's, but research records indicate that its name comes from John Morrall, who bought 610 acres here in 1731.

It's a great place for shrimping and crabbing, but an even better place to dine on such. Its restaurants are renowned. **Oliver's Lodge**, one of the oldest, is where resident and author Mickey Spillane was married and is a frequent guest. Oysters and the Lodge's fabulous corndodgers is a favorite order. Neither the exterior or interior look like much, and the owners joke, "It's the only place I know of that a coat of paint would ruin."

The marina at Murrells Inlet is one of the best places to sign up for deep sea fishing and an intriguing place to watch lo-

Photo by Dawn O'Brien.

The beach's natural setting has been preserved at Pawleys Island.

cal commercial fishermen bring in their catch of the day.

Garden City

Enthusiasts continue to arrive here because the beach is "family," but it has just enough of the Mrytle Beach glitz in a 2-to 3-block area to entice children to fork over their hard earned quarters for video games and the like. The wide fishing pier is not only a great place to cast your fishing line, but a terrific place to wind down at sunset when, on lazy summer days, live music is played at the pier's end.

The non-denominational **Garden City Chapel**, known as God's Little Fortress By the Sea is located 1 block north from the first stop light off the causeway and has been bringing the faithful from several beaches to its doors since 1952. Sunday School is at 9:45 a.m.; Worship is at 11:00 a.m. each Sunday.

Surfside

With the closing of the Myrtle Beach Air Force Base, the personality of Surfside is in transition. The base is being turned into a theme park that is expected to attract visitors of all ages and interests.

MYRTLE BEACH

To Get There:
From I-95, take U.S. 378 east to Conway and U.S. 501 south to Myrtle Beach. From I-20, take U.S. 501 south. From Georgetown, take U.S. 17 north.

Before the turn of the century, nothing inhabited this area except farms and timber operations. When railroad tracks were built from Conway to the beach area, vacationers began to come, stores began to open, hotels and small cottages were built and Myrtle Beach, originally called New Town, was born.

In the mid-40s when the word spread about Myrtle Beach's beautiful wide beaches, the area began to thrive and soon there weren't sufficient rental cottages and hotels to accommodate the visitors. This signaled the beginning of the building boom.

"Myrtle" is now an action-oriented beach, with a variety of night life, and sun worshipers who come to work on their tan for the season's various bikini contests. Still, many visitors come here year after year seeking no more stimulating exercise than unfolding a beach chair or watching commercial fishermen haul great nets of menhaden fish up onto the beach during a fall catch.

Young people who see the area's beautiful golf courses, towering condos and hotels have a hard time fathoming the important part that Myrtle Beach played during World War II. German submarines patrolled this coast, and the U.S. Government had a prisoner-of-war camp here, between 71st Avenue on Ocean Boulevard and U.S. 17. Prisoners worked at local lumber companies, cutting the area's abundance of yellow pine. Unfortunately, not a remnant remains of the prison camp. Two hurricanes, Hazel in 1954 and Hugo in 1989, destroyed the buildings. Enterprising entrepreneurs have built up every patch of land not occupied with private residences.

Things To See and Do

MYRTLE BEACH PAVILION AND AMUSEMENT PARK

Children won't let you get out of Myrtle Beach without taking them to the Myrtle Beach Pavilion and Amusement Park where they can twirl and swirl through thrilling, nail-biting rides. Try your luck on the Carolinas' biggest plume or take a turn at video games. Teenagers like to drop in at the teen night spot and grown-ups will appreciate the antique cars and sidewalk cafes. The park is located at 9th Avenue and North Ocean Boulevard. No admission is charged to enter the park, but tickets for individual rides cost $.50. Wrist bands, that allow unlimited access to all rides, cost $17.25 for adults and $11.00 for children under 42" in height. (803-448-6456)

GUINNESS WORLD RECORD MUSEUM

In the same area, don't miss the Guinness World Record Museum. Here, you can watch events and people beyond your wildest imagination presented on video tape, in replica, or in other interesting displays. The museum is located at 911 North Ocean Boulevard. Admission for adults is $3.95 and $2.95 for children from 7 to 12. The museum is open daily from 10:00 a.m. until midnight, mid-March through mid-October.

RIPLEY'S BELIEVE IT OR NOT MUSEUM

A few doors away from the Guinness World Record Museum, you can visit Ripley's Believe It or Not Museum. There are over 750 exhibits at the museum, including a wax replica of the world's tallest man who measures 8 feet, 11 inches. The museum is located at 901 North Ocean Boulevard and it, too, is open from mid-March through mid-October. Admission for adults is $4.95 and $2.95 for children 6 to 12. The museum is open daily from 10:00 a.m. until 10:00 p.m.

MYRTLE BEACH WAX MUSEUM

Many adults have been entertained by the life-like figures from history, religion and the entertainment world found in this museum. Stories are made more vivid through drama and sound accompaniment. The museum is located at 1000 North Ocean Boulevard and charges $4.50 for adults and $2 for children 6 to 12 years of age. It is open daily from 9:00 a.m. until 9:00 p.m., February through mid-October.

MYRTLE WAVES

Children will also enjoy this water park located on 10th Avenue at the U.S. 17 Bypass. **Myrtle Waves** is open from 10 a.m. until 7 p.m. daily, and admission is $13.95 for adults. Children measuring under 46" are charged $6.95.

MYRTLE BEACH STATE PARK

Located 2 miles south of the city on U.S. 17, this ocean front park has been popular since it was built in the early 1930s by the CCC (Civilian Conservation Corps). The park has over 100 acres of maritime forest with nature trails filled with live oaks, pines, magnolias and dogwoods that lead up to the beach.

There are seven boardwalks, complete with information boards, adjacent to the parking area making beach access easy. The info boards explain important environmental points, reminding visitors and campers to behave as good custodians of the earth, particularly in regard to staying off the dunes and being watchful of the loggerhead turtles that nest here.

Since Hurricane Hugo, a new pier has been built that divides the area for surf-casting anglers and swimmers. And for those leery of ocean swimming, there is a swimming pool that is open through the summer months.

There are 5 rental cabins, 2 apartments and 350 available campsites with laundry facilities, electrical and water hookups. The Fishing Pier is open from March 1 through November 30 and you can fish all day for $4. There are two camp stores, one for bait, etc., the other for groceries and such. Campsites rent for $15 per night and you can make reservations by writing to Myrtle Beach State Park, U.S. 17 South, Myrtle Beach, SC 29577. (803-238-5325)

OPRY

Myrtle Beach, already known as the Capital of Golf and Shag Dancing, now seems destined to rival Nashville and Branson as the Capital of Country Music. Five state-of-the-art

MERCEDES PROPERTIES, INC.

1501 SOUTH OCEAN BOULEVARD
NORTH MYRTLE BEACH, SC 29582

Say Yes!… to breathtaking views and casual,
carefree living at North Myrtle Beach.
All ocean ont condos with private balconies.
Pool • Jacuzzi
Ocean Front Rentals: Daily or Weekly

1-800-633-9679

opry theaters play nightly to packed houses. Their repertoire scats from jazzed-up Beethoven to country and western splashed over with corny jokes, beautiful women in sequined, figure-hugging-gowns and lots of family fun. Regardless of your musical preference, before you know it you're toe-tapping to the beat.

Calvin Gilmore brought the business to his **The Carolina Opry,** located at the junction of U.S. Business 17 and Bypass 17. (803-238-8888) **Alabama Theatre** is located at Barefoot Landing. (803-272-1111 or 800-342-2262) Gilmore says, "Beach is the King, Golf the Queen and I'd be happy if Country was the Prince of Tides."

S.O.S. WEEKEND

In the '50s the northern end of Myrtle Beach became the centerpiece of the Grand Strand when dance crazy teenagers gave birth to the "Shag." As those youngsters grew up, the dance scene dwindled until a few years back when some nostalgic souls sent the word out that a shag reunion would be held at the beach. The expected crowd of 400 to 500 turned into thousands, and folks of all ages have been shagging up and down the Strand ever since. The third weekend after Labor Day is officially known as S.O.S. weekend. If you're in the shagging

mood (or just want to observe), check out **Fat Harold's Beach Club** at 210 Main Street, or **Duck's** at 229 Main Street in North Myrtle Beach. Last fall the crowd had multiplied to the point that shaggers were dancing in the surf beside the **Spanish Galleon** at the end of Ocean Drive.

GOLF

Although the late fall and winter may attract fewer "laying on the beach" types, Myrtle Beach with 90 plus golf courses, has become an affordable golfer's paradise for those seasons. Drawn by the area's mild winters and special hotel and golf packages, vacationers now flock to the beach year-round. Restaurants and night clubs that once closed during the off-season now remain open, making Myrtle Beach one of the liveliest places on the East Coast.

Here are some player picks for favorite golf courses (listed alphabetically) to get you started. For more information or to make reservations or tee times in advance, call **Golf Holiday.** (800-845-4643)

Azalea Sands
Par 72   *Inexpensive*
With lots of trees and bunkers, Azalea Sands on U.S. 17 in North Myrtle Beach is "a honey to play on" according to one golfer. "Not super hard, so

you don't get frustrated." (803-272-6191)

Blackmoor
Par 72   *Expensive*

Laid out by Gary Player, Blackmoor is known for its narrow fairways. It is located in Longwood Plantation on S.C. 7070, along the Waccamaw River. (803-650-5555)

Dunes Golf & Beach Club
Par 72   *Very Expensive*

Designed by Robert Trent Jones, the 13th hole of this course has been ranked as one of the world's top Par 5's. The Dunes has been selected as host site for the 1996 U.S. Senior PGA tournament. It is located at 9000 North Ocean Boulevard in Myrtle Beach. (803-449-5914)

Heather Glen
Par 72   *Expensive*

Another course featuring great scenic beauty, Heather Glen was chosen by *Golf Digest* as the "Best New Public Course in America" in 1987. It's in Little River on U.S. 17 north. (800-868-4536)

Heritage Golf Club
Par 72   *Expensive*

Ranked among the top 50 resort courses in America, even non-golfers would enjoy the scenery. As one golfer described, "It's like walking through a southern plantation with its

massive oaks and magnolias." The course is located in Pawleys Island on U.S. 17. (803-626-3887)

The Legends
Par 72   *Expensive*

This complex on U.S. 501 in Myrtle Beach offers three distinctive courses and a beautiful St. Andrews-style clubhouse. The Parkland Course offers tree-lined fairways along massive undulating greens. The Heathland Course is a Scottish Link Course and noted for wide fairways and large greens and was rated as one of the top 10 new courses by *Golf Digest*. Designed by Pete Dye, the Moorland Course with its deep bunkers is perhaps the most challenging of the three courses. (800-552-2660)

Litchfield Golf Club
Par 72   *Moderate*

Litchfield Golf Club on U.S. 17 in Pawleys Island offers three beautiful and varied courses. Once an old rice plantation, the scenery, with Spanish moss draped trees, is another standout. (803-448-3331)

Long Bay
Par 72   *Very Expensive*

Originally private, this Jack Nicklaus-designed course provides an excellent challenge for golfers of all skill levels. It's ranked as one of the top 10 courses in the state by *Golf Digest*. Long Bay is located at Murrells Inlet on S.C. 9. (803-249-5510)

Marsh Harbor Golf Links
Par 71   *Expensive*
Designed by Dan Maples, Marsh Harbour is ranked among the top 25 public courses in the U.S. If you like water holes, you'll find some of the area's most challenging created by the low-lying marsh that surrounds the course. Marsh Harbor is located in Calabash (North Myrtle Beach) at 201 Marsh Harbour Road. (803-249-3449)

Pine Lakes International
Par 71   *Very Expensive*
Pine Lakes is known as the "Granddaddy" of Myrtle Beach golf courses. Located on Woodside Drive off U.S. 17 in Myrtle Beach, this venerable old course, designed by Robert White, is beautifully kept and steeped in tradition. In deference to its Scottish origins, Lowcountry clam chowder is served by kilt-dressed gentlemen right on the golf course. (803-449-6459)

Possum Trot Golf Club
Par 72   *Moderate*
Voted "most friendly," Possum Trot has wide fairways and nice greens. This older course on U.S. 17 in North Myrtle Beach is kept in excellent shape. (803-272-5341)

The Witch
Par 72   *Expensive*
Unlike any of the other beach courses, The Witch winds through wooded hills and wetlands. It is a Maples-designed course, located at 1900 S.C. 544 in Conway. (803-347-2706)

FISHING
Fishing is the reason a lot of people go to the beach. Hurricane Hugo wreaked havoc when it sailed in destroying or severely damaging most of the piers that fishermen had fished from for years. After repeated delays and four years of reconstruction, most of the piers are now back and doing a thriving business. Here is a list of some of the most popular fishing piers. Most have season passes available, and all rent rods and other fishing gear. If you plan to bait a hook, about all you need to do is bring a bucket for your catch, that can range from whiting to king mackerel.

Cherry Grove Beach Pier
960 feet long and 16 feet wide
Admission: $4-$10

Second Avenue Pier
905 feet long and 20 feet wide
Admission: $4-$6.50

Springmaid Pier
1,060 feet long and 36 feet wide
Admission: $4.50

**Myrtle Beach
State Park Pier**
700 feet long and 12-45 feet wide
Admission: $4 (Discount with parking fee ticket.)

Surfside Pier
720 feet long and 16 feet wide
Admission: $5-$10

Garden City King Fisher Pier
Admission: $5-$10 for rods and bait. Extra for pier fishing.

At any of the marinas you can charter a boat or book 1/2-, 3/4- or full-day deep sea fishing packages on head boats. The 2 1/2-hour trip out to the Gulf Steam is worth it as this is where the great game fish frolic.

If you're not into fishing, you can just stroll along the piers. Most piers are free while others charge $.25, and it's hard to find a recreation cheaper than that, especially when you consider the exceptional views.

HUNTING

It surprises some to learn that not everyone comes to Myrtle Beach to play golf, fish or eat. During the hunting season, excellent game is found a few miles inland at the **Lewis Ocean Bay Wildlife Manage-ment Area**, which natives call the Biust. This is an area rich in wild turkey, bear, deer and quail. From Little River, take S.C. 90 that curves westward into flat, forested countryside for many miles. The main gate is at Kingston Road.

At the end of Kingston Road lies the **Peter Horry Wildlife Refuge**. Currently in stages of development, board-walks lead out across marsh areas in this immense forest.

SHOPPING

If you hit a rainy day, there's more shopping at the famous **Waccamaw Pottery and Outlet Park** than you could pick your way through in a monsoon season. This sprawl-ing maze on U.S. 501 contains 50 outlet stores with more across the highway.

There are many shopping centers and malls, but the two most popular are **Myrtle Square Mall** and **Briarcliffe Mall** with its 100 specialty shops and department stores. And, of course, there are countless sou-venir stores and specialty shops scattered throughout the area.

For a unique shopping experience, take a look at **Bare-foot Landing** on U.S. 17 in North Myrtle Beach. You'll find a mixture of retail and outlet stores, a dozen restaurants and a 40-foot carousel, all built in a waterfront setting.

Oceanfront — Flagship — **Open Year-Round**

Myrtle Beach

1800 S. Ocean Blvd.
Myrtle Beach,
South Carolina 29577

(In SC and
Canada)
803-626-3505

Call Toll Free
1-800-321-7556

*I*f your family is looking for a quiet well maintained oceanfront motel nearby many of the Myrtle Beach attractions, the Flagship Motor Inn is for you!

Every effort is made by our resident owners to provide our guests comfort and privacy surrounded by a relaxed family atmosphere. We know how important your vacation is and we'll do our best to make this special time together one to always remember.

We feature clean, well equipped and modern accommodations and facilities designed for your family's enjoyment.
• Heated Oceanfront Pool
• Kiddie Pool
• Sundecks
• Parking on Premises
• Private Oceanfront Balconies
• Great Location Near Tennis, Theatres, Shopping, Restaurants and Amusements
• Catering to Families, Senior Citizens & Vacationing Couples

Set Sail for Quiet Family Vacations

Accommodations

Staying at the beach is affordable, but the rates will reflect the seasons. As you travel up and down the Strand, you will be amazed at the range of accommodations—from modest cottages to lavish, ocean front resorts. At last count, over 50,000 rooms were available. Believe it or not, on many occasions you'll be hard pressed to find a bed between Little River and Georgetown, so reservations are always suggested.

RESORTS

Myrtle Beach Resort ($-$$$), located between Myrtle and Surfside, this is an all ocean front, family resort with 6 swimming pools, tennis courts and a pool bar. (800-845-0629)

Litchfield By The Sea ($$$) is a lovely, full resort offering 3 golf courses, 26 tennis courts, 10 pools, a spa, sauna, 3 restaurants and 7 miles of beach. (800-845-1895)

HOTEL/MOTELS

When asked where to stay at Myrtle Beach, without hesitation a friend answered, "**The Mariner**. Our family discovered it 21 years ago. It's casual—just the way the beach should be—and it won't cost you an arm and a leg." It's not the fanciest motel on the beach, but Innkeepers Stoke Cromley and Gale Kennedy are there to help you have a good time, much like what you might find at a good B & B. (803-449-5281)

Carolina Reef ($$), at 1501 South Ocean Boulevard in North Myrtle Beach, is a condo-type operation with attractive rooms and a slower pace. (800-633-9679)

At 1800 South Ocean Boulevard in Myrtle Beach, **Flagship Motor Inn** ($-$$) is such a "pleaser" that a repeat guest brought the owners a gift for their exceptional service and caring attitude. (800-321-7556)

The **Inn at Myrtle Beach** ($-$$$$) is on the ocean and has an olympic-size swimming pool, hot tub and "kiddy" pool. Its restaurant, **Martin's At The Inn**, serves breakfast and dinner. A shuffleboard court and a putting green are also on the grounds. (800-845-0664)

CONDOMINIUMS AND COTTAGE RENTALS

If interested in renting a condominium or a beach cottage, call **Beach Rental**. (800-255-5997)

CAMPING

Many of the camp grounds have been replaced by high-rise condos or hotels, but there are still some excellent camping facilities available. Two favorites are **Myrtle Beach** (803-238-5325) and **Huntington Beach State Park** (803-237-4440).

Dining _____

Between **The Carolina Opry** and **The Dixie Jubilee**, off U.S. 17, lies an area known as Restaurant Row. You'll find more beautiful restaurants with diverse cuisines in this area than in any other area of the beach, although Murrells Inlet has become famous for its good restaurants as well. Here's a sampling.

To start off your day with a bang, try breakfast at **Dino's House of Pancakes** ($-$$) at 2120 U.S. 17 south—just across from the entrance to Azalea Sands Golf Course. It has everything from croissants to corn beef hash.

The Driftwood ($-$$), 3500 N. Ocean Drive in Cherry Grove, is at the pier and has Eggbeaters for breakfast. It serves breakfast, lunch and dinner and is a great place to enjoy a cool drink as you watch children play in the ocean.

The **Flamingo Restaurant** ($$) on the corner of 71st Street North on U.S. Business 17, is a sohpisticated, contemporary restaurant that serves excellent trigger fish.

Inlet Crab House ($) at 3572 Business 17 in Murrells Inlet isn't fancy, but has the best Oysters Rockefeller found on the Strand.

Latif's ($$) at 506 61st. Avenue North, off U.S. 17 in Myrtle Beach, is the classy place to go for Sunday Brunch. It features live classical music with wonderful pastries and coffees. It serves lunch and dinner.

Lee's Inlet Kitchen ($) serves good dishes made from family recipes. Its located 1/2 mile south of **Captain Dick's Marina** on Business 17 in Murrells Inlet.

Oliver's Lodge ($-$$) has been a favorite of generations of beach-goers for good seafood. It's off U.S. 17 in Murrells Inlet.

Outback at Frank's ($-$$$) at the stoplight in downtown Pawleys Island combines unusual food bedfellows to produce tasty results.

The **Parson's Table** ($$-$$$) in Little River is in an old church that has been converted into a gourmet restaurant. Stain glass windows decorate the premises, including one entire ceiling. The food is as lavish as the decor.

Planters Back Porch ($$-$$$) offers an upscale menu in a country-comfortable setting. It's located on the corner of U.S. 17 south and Wachesaw Road in Murrells Inlet.

In North Myrtle Beach, **Preston's** ($) at 4530 U.S. 17, has the **best** country-style cooking buffet on the beach. It has a fun atmosphere and is a great place for family dining. Well-known local Chef Prince Bowens

has been profiled in at least two New York magazines. This place is a real favorite of the beach-going crowd.

Rice Planter's ($$-$$$) at 6707 Kings Highway (U.S. 17) in Myrtle Beach is constructed from materials assembled from historic structures and displays a variety of antique farming tools. The food is exceptional.

Sea Captain's House ($), one of few restaurants on the ocean, is open for breakfast, lunch or dinner at 3000 North Ocean Boulevard in Myrtle Beach. It is casual, but elegant.

Skeeter's ($) on U.S.17 at 70th Avenue was voted the best breakfast on the beach.

Side Trips

BROOKGREEN GARDENS

To Get There:

Brookgreen Gardens is on U.S. 17 south of Myrtle Beach and north of Georgetown, 3 miles from Murrells Inlet.

Filling your lungs with fresh, salt air while baking in the sun is the undisputed lure of the beach, but a visit to Brookgreen Gardens can open a new world to you. The natural beauty of the original indigo-turned-rice plantation, inspired Archer Milton Huntington and his wife, Anna Hyatt Huntington, a famous sculptor, to re-serve this pocket of beauty for an outdoor sculpture garden. Sometime between 1930 and 1933, the Huntingtons built their winter home, Atalaya, on the ocean directly across from the gardens.

Brookgreen's traditional figurative sculpture garden was created to enhance the magnolias, camellias, boxwoods, azaleas and 2,000 other plants, plus animals indigenous to the region. The garden's center yields a live oak avenue of trees reminiscent of Twelve Oaks in *Gone With The Wind*.

Today, this garden has the largest permanent American figurative sculpture collection in the world, displaying the works of Remington, French, Milles, Lachaise, Borglum and many of Mrs. Huntington's remarkable works. The power of the 500-piece collection of fine sculpture is stunning.

This is a great place to take children as well. What child doesn't like to watch wild animals in their natural habitat? And most are flabbergasted by the startling sculptures. As one local resident remarked, "Every child in Horry County learned anatomy at Brookgreen Gardens."

Brookgreen is an unmatched experience that also offers tours and many free programs with the price of admission: $6 for adults, $3 for children 6-12.

Photo by Dawn O'Brien.

Brookgreen Gardens has the largest permanent American figurative sculpture collection in the world.

HUNTINGTON BEACH STATE PARK

To Get There:

The Park is across U.S. 17 from Brookgreen Gardens, 3 miles from Murrells Inlet.

Huntington Beach State Park was the winter home of the Huntingtons until 1960 when it became a state park. The park has the widest beach on the Grand Strand and offers camping facilities. Also, be sure and tour the Huntington home, **Atalaya**, a sand castle-like structure based on Moorish architecture, which is part of the Park.

INTRACOASTAL WATERWAY

To Get There:

To reach the Wacca Wache Marina from Myrtle Beach, take U.S. 17 south to S.C. 62 (about midway between Garden City Beach and Murrells Inlet). Travel west on S.C. 62 to the marina.

A trip down the wide Intracoastal Waterway can provide a relaxing and interesting glimpse into a lesser known side of life along the Grand Strand. Even folks who've been coming to the beach for years aren't aware of the area's diversity. They often find that a relaxing day on the river is a pleasant respite from traffic and blink-ing neon signs. Rent a john-boat and buy a map at the marina if you don't have a river guide with you.

The Intracoastal Waterway is comprised of three rivers: the Waccamaw, the Pee Dee and the Black. For a great starting point from Myrtle Beach, put into the Waccamaw River at the **Wacca Wache Marina** and head south. As you float or motor down this peaceful river you begin to see what the Spanish saw when they traveled through these waters in the 1500s. Little has changed. The wood duck houses and duck blinds are new, as are the markers jutting out of the river to guide you along the way, but nature remains remarkably loyal in this area.

At marker # 67, behind the saw grass, is Sandy Island. Today, about 300 slave descendants still live on this soft, sandy spit of land that measures about 40 square miles. This island property was deeded to the forefathers of the present residents nearly a hundred and fifty years ago. On the back side of Sandy Island, the water begins to become rather bumpy and, despite water moccasins and alligators, it has become a favored place for water skiing.

If you spend a day or morning exploring the Intracoastal Waterway and its tributaries, you'll pass a number of former indigo and rice plantations where old water control gates stand like reminders of the past. You'll see Arundel, Hassell Hill, Exchange and Hasty Point. Hasty Point gained its name from a "hasty" retreat made by the Swamp Fox, Colonel Francis Marion, during the Revolutionary War. This wily little Colonel, one of the first guerrilla fighters, functioned best by hassling the British and leading them astray.

After a morning on the river, stop by the **Conch Cafe** ($) for a delicious conch salad. Its located on Waccamaw Drive between Surside Beach and Garden City Beach. For dinner, you might head over to the **Charleston Cafe** ($$$$) on 1st Avenue at Surfside Beach.

ALL SAINTS WACCAMAW EPISCOPAL CHURCH

To Get There:
To reach the the church from Myrtle Beach, take U.S. 17 south to S.C. 255 to All Saints Waccamaw Episcopal Church.

This historic church closely resembles the one first built in the 1700s. But perhaps the most interesting aspect of the church is its cemetery. The who's who of Lowcountry planters are buried in this beautiful old cemetery where you will also find the grave of Alice Flagg. Legend has it that Alice's aris-

tocratic family forbade her marriage to a local tradesman, and in an effort to make her forget him, packed her off to boarding school in Charleston. But, Alice did not forget, and withered to the point that her brother, Dr. Allard Flagg, brought her back to Murrells Inlet. Here she died in his plantation home, the Hermitage. Her grave is marked only by the name Alice and there is a faint circular path around her head stone. As legend has it, if you walk backward 7 times around Alice's grave, you'll see her apparition in the distance. (Good luck!)

NORTHERN BEACHES

To Get There:
Take U.S. 17 north to Windy Hill, Atlantic Beach, Crescent Beach, Ocean Drive, Cherry Grove and Little River.

Windy Hill

Areas often derive their names from chance remarks; such was the case for Windy Hill. It seems that on George Washington's trip through this area in 1791, he made reference to the area as a "windy hill." The name stuck.

Washington would be amazed, as would anyone who hasn't visited in the last 40 years, to cross over White Point

Swash and see the montage of shops and motels that have overtaken the beach dunes. The swash is still an ideal place for crabbing and shrimping, or for a walk on the beach. Almost anytime you look up in the sky you'll see—coastal birds? No. Overhead, during the height of the season, you'll see a veritable traffic jam of airplanes trailing their advertisements behind them.

Atlantic Beach

Atlantic Beach has set itself apart from the Northern Grand Strand on purpose. In earlier days when beach property was segregated, a portion of this ocean front property was set aside for African Americans to enjoy. After the Civil Rights movement, Black citizens were welcome at all beaches. But a few years later, when the Northern Grand Strand was being formed, the Board of the incorporated area of Atlantic Beach refused all efforts to become part of the alliance. Maintaining its independence has hurt the area financially, but the beach has nonetheless remained a great source of pride for its citizens and visitors.

Crescent Beach

You could swim or sail from Atlantic Beach to Cres-

Photo by Dawn O'Brien.

The Northern Beaches are relaxed and family-oriented.

cent Beach, but to drive there you've got to go back to to U.S. 17, turn north for less than a half mile and turn east back toward the ocean. This is not as confusing as it sounds.

Shaped quarter-moon like a crescent, this family-oriented, lovely beach is where you're more likely to see children building sand castles than surfers catching a wave. However, just about all water activities, including parasailing and jet skiing, can be seen along this less crowded beach.

Ocean Drive

During the '50s the northern end beaches became the centerpiece of the Grand Strand when dance-crazy teenagers gave birth to the "Shag" —on Main Street in Ocean Drive. The scene has changed some since those early days, but Ocean Drive remains popular with the younger crowd, especially during "Spring Break" and Easter vacation. **Fat Harold's Beach Club** and **Crazy Zack's** are landmarks. Ask anybody, the real action in North Myrtle Beach is—Ocean Drive.

Ocean Drive is also a great spot for family fun and it is not unusual to find vacationers whose families have been coming to this beach for generations. Here, perhaps more than at any of the other beaches, you will find parents vicariously re-

living their early beach days by watching their children.

Cherry Grove

Named for a prosperous orchard located here before the Civil War, Cherry Grove extends south to an area called, "The Point." For many years, this beach had little more than scattered beach cottages. Today, condos and restaurants line every available inch of the still quiet beach. Like the hard-packed beaches at Hilton Head Island, Cherry Grove's beach is sufficiently packed to encourage bicycle riders and joggers who love feeling that cool ocean breeze whip through their hair.

Little River

There are few tangible reminders of George Washington's visit to **Little River** on his 1791 tour down along King's Highway (U.S. 17) except that our first president kept an excellent diary. In *The Diaries of George Washington,* Washington notes that before continuing down the coast, he had lunch at the home of Revolutionary War hero James Cochran (near what is now the intersection of U.S. 17 and Mineola Avenue).

Little River, the first stop across the North Carolina border, remains a quiet little fishing village except for two days in the fall when the **Arthur**

Smith King Mackerel Tournament is held. A triangle of reefs (excellent for fishing) lies between Little River and Myrtle Beach and there's never a shortage of commercial fishing captains eager to take you for a half- or whole-day of good fishing.

You can buy space on one of their "party" boats that will take you out 10 to 15 miles to fish for black sea bass, snapper and porgy, or you can opt for a charter out to the Gulf Stream for some deep-sea game fishing.

The area is also well known to visiting gourmets who reserve at least one night of their beach vacation for dining at the **Parson's Table**, just off U.S. 17. Housed in a little clapboard church with an amazing assemblege of stained-glass decorating its interior dining rooms, this restaurant remains one of the coast's best.

For More Information:

Myrtle Beach Area Chamber of Commerce and Info Center
1301 N. Kings Highway
P.O. Box 2115
Myrtle Beach, S.C. 29578-2115
800-356-3016

Myrtle Beach Hospitality Association Reservation Service
P.O.Box 1303
Myrtle Beach, S.C. 29578-1303
800-866-9785

AAA Carolinas
845 Briarwood Drive
Myrtle Beach, S.C. 29572
803-272-1141

Photo by Daintry O'Brien.

The beaches north of Myrtle Beach are popular family destinations.

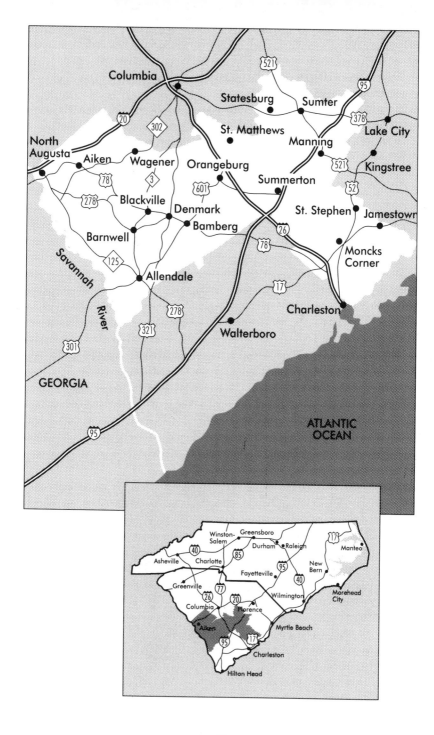

Lower Midlands

AIKEN

To Get There:
From I-20, take S.C. 19 south to Aiken.

Aiken is known as Thoroughbred Country, a term generally used to distinguish pure blood lines in horses; yet the purity of Aiken's Southern hospitality continues as thoroughbred today as it was in its antebellum days. Hard-packed dirt roads are easier on horses' hoofs than asphalt, which is why many roads remain unpaved. You'll even see stoplights for horse traffic, which implies that life here often moves with a steady plod on four iron-shod feet.

Rising some 500 feet above sea level, Aiken became a favorite second home for Charlestonians trying to escape the dread malaria in the 1800s. This practice continued until the Civil War. Like most Southern towns, Aiken suffered during the war. Few accomplishments are more remembered than the Battle of Aiken when Confederate soldiers defeated a division of General Sherman's, thus delaying the march to Columbia.

Following the war, some of the North's wealthiest and most sports-minded people discovered Aiken's favorable climate and excellent horse and hunting country terrain. Names like Hitchcock, Astor, Vanderbilt, and many other wealthy families came down for the winter and liked what they found in the rolling countryside. As early as 1882, these first northern families began building Aiken's first Polo field. This dates the area's equine history and marks the first of what would become 16 Polo fields in the Aiken area. In 1889, the Aiken Polo Club joined the U.S. Polo Association and, for many years, Aiken was known as the

Polo Center of the World. (For a mere $2, you can go to one of these polo games, played with a mallet and ball, on Sunday at 3:00 p.m. from March through July and September through November at Whitney Field. (803-648-7874)

Things To See and Do _____

TOURS

Fashionable winter residences, many with stables, were built for the "Winter Colony" people and can be seen today on the **Aiken Tour** that operates every Saturday morning at 10:00 a.m. The tour includes the **Thoroughbred Racing** **Hall of Fame** that gives you background on harness (sulky) racing, steeplechase and fox hunting. All of these equine interests brought by the "winter people" continue in the area throughout the seasons.

On the Aiken Tour you'll see the restorations of homes and churches along shaded double avenues. These double avenues are especially beautiful with large azalea and flowering-tree-planted medians running between one-way streets that were laid out by two railroad engineers in 1832. Colleton Avenue, Hayne Avenue, South Boundary, and Whiskey Road (with its own stoplight that can be activated for horses), reveal a collection of Historic Register

Photo courtesy Greater Aiken Chamber of Commerce.

Harness racing in Aiken.

homes, each noted for its architectural integrity by a bronze Historic Aiken plaque. (803-641-1111)

TRIPLE CROWN

A few years ago, a group of Aiken business men wanted to expand the social aspects of horse training, and the popular result is the Triple Crown. Coming at the beginning of Spring, the Triple Crown is held for three successive racing weekends in March, starting on the second or third weekend and sometimes going into April, depending on the schedule of the National Steeplechase committee. Call the **Greater Aiken Chamber of Commerce** for precise dates. (803-641-1111)

March, a month not overly filled with activities elsewhere, makes Aiken an ideal time for you to visit. First, the **Aiken Trials** begin the festivities held at the **Aiken Training Track**. After finishing a long winter training season, this important preview offers you a chance of seeing up and coming racing thoroughbreds that could make racing history. This flat racing event gives many young horses their first racing experience under full grandstand conditions. Post time is at 2 o'clock, but the gates open at 10:30 a.m. to give tailgaters time to set up their festive lunches and see what's going on at the race.

The following weekend is the **Aiken Hunt Club Meet**

For many years Aiken was known as the Polo Center of the World.

Photo courtesy Greater Aiken Chamber of Commerce.

held at Clark Field. This is the first of 42 steeplechases on the circuit. The Hunt races are held over a set of 7 jumps set up on the oval track, with most races scheduled for 2 circuits around the track. Post time is at 1 p.m., but gates open at 10:00 a.m. for another party event. Folks don campy-to-elegant attire and consume equally elaborate fare, always attempting to outdo the previous year.

Winding up the Triple Crown is one of America's oldest sports—harness or sulky racing for pacers and trotters, held at the **Aiken Mile Track**. Again, post time is at 1 o'clock, with gates opening at 10:00 a.m. for a more family-oriented gathering. Tickets for the Triple Crown are relatively inexpensive, ranging from $2 for children to $10 for adults, with an additional $5 for parking. If this is your first Triple Crown time and you're spending the weekend in town, it's only a little over a mile from downtown to the training track, the steeplechase or polo fields.

GOLF

Although horse racing and hunting came first, golf didn't lag far behind. Today, Aiken has five private and semi-private golf courses, with an additional 16 within a short drive. Check out **Cedar Creek Golf Club**, a public 18-hole 72-

par course with putting green and moderate fees. (803-648-4206) **Highland Park Golf Club** is another public 18-hole 70-par course with a putting green. The fees here are inexpensive. (803-649-6029)

FISHING AND HUNTING

Fields and woods and rivers near Aiken are widely known for their excellent fishing and hunting. Quail, dove, wild turkey, wild hog and dear attract many hunters from all over the country. **Crackerneck Wildlife Management Area** (803-725-2441) contains 4,780 acres of U.S. Government land where you can hunt and fish. Crackerneck WMA is about 20 miles south of Aiken off S.C. 19. Fishing licenses and WMA permits, as well as a special DOE permit, must be in possession before entering the area. But you can get a free permit by writing: U.S. Forest Service, Savannah River Forest Station, P.O. Box 710, New Ellenton, SC, 29809-0710. Be sure to give your full name, address, social security number, and country of citzenship. Deer hunting is allowed on a controlled basis.

With Aiken within a few miles of both the Savannah and Edisto Rivers, there's as much good fishing as there is wilderness scenery to bring you back often. **Edisto River's North Fork**, east of Aiken, can be described as like paddling through a tunnel of ancient cypress and hardwoods where alligators may glide along beside you. Other than the sound of calling birds, you may hear little more than the snap of your line when you've hooked a bass or bream. It's that quiet.

To the west of Aiken, try your luck at **Silver Bluff Landing** on the **Savannah River**, or **Jackson Landing** which has a hard surface ramp. It's located off S.C. 125 on S.R. 432, near Jackson, South Carolina.

AIKEN COUNTY HISTORICAL MUSEUM

The Aiken County Historical Museum does an excellent job of displaying Aiken's history in upclose, walk-through exhibits from Native Americans to the Savannah River Plant. The museum is housed in **Banksia**, a grand "Winter Colony" mansion built in 1931. Also on the grounds you'll find **Ergle Log House**, a completely furnished 1808 log cabin that is thought to be the oldest standing building in Aiken County. Inside, there's an interesting display of household furniture, kitchen utensils and farm tools. The **China Spring School** is an 1890 one-room little red school house that has also been moved to the museum property with its modest furnishings and school supplies.

In the main house museum, you'll see material from **Fort Moore**, the fort built by the British in 1716 that functioned as a trading center for back country settlers. (Back country refers to the interior lands back from the coast.) There are displays chronicling the **Graniteville Mill** that was built in 1847 by William Gregg. You'll learn that this textile mill, saved during the Civil War in the **Battle of Aiken**, was the first of its production capacity in the South. And though the "winter people" put Aiken on the national map in the late 1900s, its unlikely they would have come in such volume had it not been for the railroad. When the 136-mile-long track was completed into this little cross roads hamlet in 1833, it connected Aiken with Charleston and Hamburg, making it the longest track in the world at that time. The local citizens were so proud that they named their new town Aiken after railroad President, William Aiken.

If you are in town from Tuesday through Friday or on the first Sunday of the month, make your first stop the Aiken County Historical Museum. Located at 433 Newberry SW, the museum is open from 9:30 a.m. until 4:30 p.m., Tuesday through Friday; from 2:00 p.m. until 5:00 p.m. on the first Sunday of the month. No admission is charged, but donations are welcomed. (803-642-2015)

HOPELAND GARDENS

Located at the corner of Whiskey Road and Dupree Place, Hopeland Gardens stands at the intersection of time. Winding, sandy paths, more beautiful than nature ever intended, swarm with deodara cedars, magnolias, dogwoods, azaleas and radiating fountains that spray into reflecting pools. Over 100-year-old live oaks spread their limbs out across the quiet landscape. Imagine what it must be like not to have sight, yet wander along the Touch and Scent Trail during the spring or autumn. Braille plaques identify luxurious herbal fragrances, and handicapped visitors are encouraged to rub wax myrtle leaves and smell this gift of nature, or compare it to the texture of fuzzy loquat leaves or those of the heady, tea olive. Linked by a cape of rope, slate plaques are distinguished along the path by brick pads. This lovely path leads to a performing arts stage where free outdoor concerts are performed every Monday evening during the summer.

This 14-acre estate, once the home of Mrs. C. Oliver Iselin, is now the home of the **Thoroughbred Racing Hall of Fame**. Located in a renovated carriage house, the hall displays

Braile plaques line Hopeland Gardens' Touch and Scent Trail.

Photo courtesy The Greater Aiken Chamber of Commerce.

many of Aiken's trained thoroughbred national champion horses. You'll see 1981 Kentucky Derby winner, Pleasant Colony, and Kelso, named Horse of the Year for five consecutive years in the 1960s. There's also a reference library and 84 Engelhard trophies and other changing exhibits of equine art. Next door at **Rye Patch**, you can see a collection of carriages dating to the 1900s inside a converted stable.

Hopeland Gardens is open daily from 10:00 a.m. until sunset. The Thoroughbred Racing Hall of Fame is open Tuesday through Sunday from 2:00 p.m. until 5:00 p.m. No admission is charged. (803-648-5461)

Accommodations____

For a more pampered hunting and fishing adventure **The Plantation** ($$-$$$$), located about 20 miles south of Aiken off U.S. 278 between Windsor and New Ellenton at 548 Cooks Pond Road is a good choice. You can overnight at the luxurious lodge, which provides a Jacuzzi, swimming pool and three ample Southern cooked meals a day. This is also an opportunity to do some horseback riding and fishing in the Plantation's motor boats. During season you can hunt for turkey, quail and deer with experienced guides and trained dogs.

Be assured that the Plantation works closely with South Carolina Wildlife Department in order to maintain the record population of trophy-sized whitetail deer, wild turkey and Russian boar. (800-643-HUNT)

The Willcox Inn, ($$$-$$$$), located at 100 Colleton Avenue and the corner of Whiskey Road, has been Aiken's premiere country inn since English owner, Frederick Willcox, opened the doors of his Georgian mansion to guests in 1898. The Duke of Windsor, Winston Churchill, Franklin D. Roosevelt are a few of its famous guests. Restored in 1984, the luxurious lobby is graced by open-hearth, granite fireplaces, original pine paneling and beams, plus comfortable sofas and a grand piano for evening entertainment. The lobby, dining room and bedrooms have been redecorated with an accent on English country, which looks well in the horse country, and many bedrooms come with a fireplace or tiny refrigerator. (803-649-1377)

The **Holly Inn** ($$$-$$$$) is located at 235 Richland Avenue. The town of Aiken was still celebrating its heyday in 1929 when B.F. Holly built his state-of-the-art hotel around a courtyard with a lovely pool as its centerpiece. Right at the heart beat of the historic district, the inn with individually designed high-ceiling bedrooms, remains one of Aiken's most sought after accommodations. Its restaurant lounge serves excellent food. (803-648-4265)

For bed and breakfast lovers, **Constantine House** ($$-$$$), located at 3406 Richland Avenue, is like staying with the "Winter Colony" people. Built in 1935 on a hilltop that overlooks the countryside, this Georgian mansion is no place like home. Bedrooms and baths are richly appointed with antiques, and a gourmet breakfast will hold you until time for the nearby Sunday afternoon polo games. (803-642-8911)

Now if you'd prefer to sleep under an antique quilt in an antebellum home that has been placed on the National Register of Historic Places, then the 1854 **Chancellor Carroll House** ($) is for you. Breakfast comes with this charming home that has two bedrooms with a shared bath. (803-649-5396)

CAMPING

Just 16 miles east of Aiken, you can camp at one of **Aiken State Park's** ($) 25 campsites. Millions of years ago the Atlantic Ocean swept over these lands, and the springs left behind created four lakes. This makes the park an ideal landscape for camping. No need to bring a boat as you can rent one here and fish or spend a leisurely day on the South Edisto River. There are nature trails, playground equipment and an interpretive center with scheduled programs throughout the summer. (803-649-2857)

Dining

If March isn't a convenient time for your visit, you can still go and watch tomorrow's champions workout at the training track from September mornings on until the **Aiken Trial.** A native confides that a good place to find out what's going on in the equine world is the **Track Kitchen** ($), down Mead Avenue in the middle of the stables near the training track. Locals joke about the cement block building, saying there's nothing that would induce you to stop at this restaurant if someone hadn't told you that it is the hangout for such horse people as jockeys, trainers and owners. The Track Kitchen, a casual place where you get your own coffee and juice while waiting for your breakfast, promises to be where it's happening.

A popular restaurant is **Olive Oil's Italian Restaurant** ($-$$) located at 232 Chesterfield Street. The restaurant is housed in a 1920's cottage that keeps expanding to serve its guests. At both lunch and dinner you can get anything from pizza to Cioppino, a classic Mediterranean dish of steamed seafood in a saffron-seasoned tomato sauce.

Natives flock to **Up Your Alley** ($-$$) located at 222 "The Alley," downtown in the historic district. This is a casual, eclectic place with church pews, stained-glass and photos of opera stars. For lunch try fried tempura seasoned haddock or Mexican burritos; for dinner— scallops or steak are good.

The Willcox Inn ($-$$$), located at 100 Colleton Avenue, remains this writer's preference. Breakfast, lunch and dinner are more than reasonable. Large, country-type breakfasts that are reminiscent of London's B & Bs. The luncheon and continental dinner menu offer such quality dishes as Farmhouse Pepper Duckling in a brandy-based peppercorn and mustard sauce.

Side Trips

MONTMORENCI VINEYARDS

Wineries have not made significant inroads in the South, which makes Aiken's **Montmorenci Vineyards**, located 2 1/2 miles east of Aiken on U.S. 78 of special interest. If you've never seen a wine operation that uses the grapes it grows, this is an opportunity to watch how wine is processed commercially and sip a few of the offerings. Tours from January through March are $5. Free wine tastings are held throughout the year, but dates vary. (803-649-4870)

REDCLIFFE PLANTATION STATE PARK

From Aiken, an interesting side trip is to Redcliffe Plantation State Park. Here, you can tour the grounds and former 1850s plantation home of Governor James Henry Hammond, one of South Carolina's most controversial and colorful historical figures. The gigantic mansion last served as the home of his great-grandson, John S. Billings, former editor of *Time-Life*. Especially interesting are the many original family pieces and artifacts displayed.

Redcliffe Plantation is located at 181 Redcliffe Road in Beech Island, off U.S. 278 about 7 miles southeast of North Augusta. Free grounds tours are held Thursday through Monday. House tours are held Saturday from 10:00 a.m. until 3:00 p.m. and Sunday from 12:00 p.m. until 3:00 p.m. Admission is $2 for adults over 19; $1 for guests from 6 to 18. (803-827-1473)

For More Information:
The Greater Aiken
Chamber of Commerce
P.O. Box 892
Aiken, SC 29802
803-641-1111

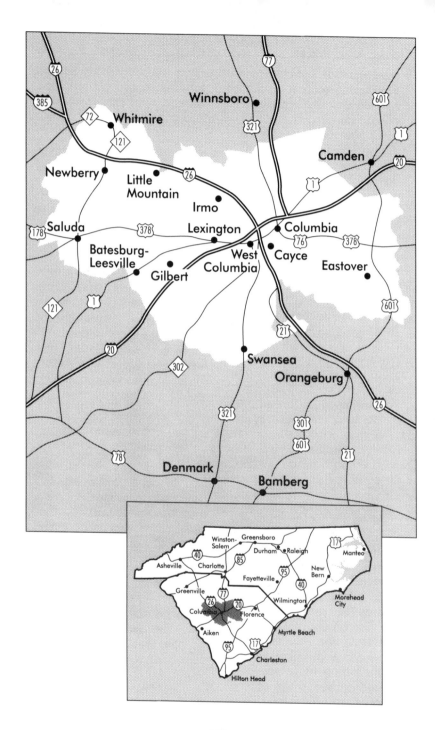

Capital
City

COLUMBIA

To Get There:
Columbia can be accessed from I-77, I-20 and I-26.

From the dynamically open-landscaped downtown **Findley Park**, the copper-domed State House beams in the sun. Looking out at this city radiating in all directions from the Capitol, it's hard to imagine that Sherman torched it. But, like other cities whose citizens refused defeat, Columbia rebuilt and repaired. The State House, the University of South Carolina, the South Carolina State Museum, the Columbia Museum of Art, Gibbes Planetarium and Riverbanks Zoo are a testament to the industrious spirit and personality of New Columbia—a city of the New South.

Things To See and Do

SOUTH CAROLINA STATE HOUSE

In 1790 state legislators chose to move the Capitol from Charleston to the state's geographic center that, after much squabbling, they named Columbia. When General Sherman burned Columbia 1865, the then new, $3.5 million fireproof Capitol Building escaped, but now wears 6 brass stars to commemorate the punctures of Sherman's cannon shells. His army did destroy most of the city and intended to burn the First Baptist Church on Hampton Street, the site where the Ordinance for Secession was written. Legend claims that Sherman's sister played the piano at First Baptist Church on Hampton Street and successfully interceded on the church's behalf. Another legend claims the church's sexton directed the Union soldiers to the Methodist Church, which they mistakenly burned instead.

The Italian Renaissance-style Capitol is an engineering marvel. It's domed ceiling, rose mosaic stained-glass windows above the Legislative Library and live palmetto palm trees (preserved) bank the main lobby dome's interior. The building is worth a visit.

The State Capitol is located on Main at Gervais Streets. Free guided tours are given Monday through Friday from 9 a.m. until 4 p.m., and parking is available one block over in the AT&T garage on Gervais and Lady Streets.

UNIVERSITY OF SOUTH CAROLINA

Just behind the Capitol, center stage of the University of South Carolina, stands the Horseshoe. This beautiful drive, no longer open to the public, made an exception when Pope Paul came to visit. The school's oldest buildings stand amidst the quadrangle. These include the imposing **McKissick Museum** with its art exhibits, geology and gem stone exhibits and the handsome collection of silver donated by Bernard Baruch, and the **South Caroliniana Library** that was the first separate college library building in America.

Don't miss another 1865 survivor, the **Robert Mills Historic House**, named for the designer who became the state's most renowned architect.

SOUTH CAROLINA STATE MUSEUM

The museum makes its home in a textile mill that, in 1894, was the first operated completely by electric power. Today, its 3-foot thick walls house four floors of fascinating explanations and exhibits of South Carolina artifacts, history, crafts and natural resources. You'll see a gigantic map that shows Columbia as part of the Atlantic Ocean 100 million years ago. You'll hear gurgling streams in mountain habitat vignettes that show black bears climbing trees. And sounds of breaking waves are heard as you see pelicans in beach vignettes and learn why sea oats are vital to dune preservation.

Another floor displays a mountain cabin so complete that you feel like walking inside. And, of course, South Carolina's participation in both the Revolutionary War and Civil War are interestingly documented. Yes, this is an educational museum, but not a stuffy one. It has one of the best museum gift shops around, and it is well worth the price of admission.

Future plans for the museum are to incorporate a total spectrum access system. If accomplished, this museum would be the first in the world to mainstream blind, hearing-impaired, deaf and mobility-impaired visitors with coincidental spill over for the learning disabled.

The State Museum is located at 301 Gervais Street. Open Monday through Saturday from 10 a.m. until 5 p.m.; Sunday and New Year's from 1 p.m. until 5 p.m. Admission is $4 for adults, $3 for seniors and military personnel and $1.50 for children from 6 to 17. Children under 6 are free. (803-737-4921)

HISTORIC HOMES TOUR

You can visit four of Columbia's beautiful historic homes on a guided tour spon-sored by the Richland County Historic Properties Commission. The homes included in the tour are: the **Hampton-Preston Mansion** at 1615 Blanding Street, the **Mann-Simmons Cottage: Museum of African-American Culture** at 1403 Blanding, the **Robert Mills Historic House and Park** at 1616 Blanding and **Woodrow Wilson's Boyhood Home** at 1705 Hampton Street.

The tours begin at the gift shop in the Robert Mills House. There is a tour each hour beginning at 10:15 a.m. until 3:15 p.m. Tuesday through Saturday, and from 1:15 until 4:15 p.m. on Sunday. You can buy a ticket to see a single home for $3

Photo by Joanne Barham.

This life size 43-foot model of the prehistoric giant white shark "swims" above the natural history floor of the South Carolina State Museum.

or a combination pass that is good for all four homes for $10.

CONGAREE VISTA DISTRICT

The State Museum is part of an area known as the **Congaree Vista District**. This group of brick warehouses, formerly an industrial park, have been readapted to house upscale antique shops, art galleries and casual restaurants operated by local Columbia families. A row of restaurants and shops border the former railroad tracks, which are now underground.

COLUMBIA MUSEUM OF ART AND GIBBES PLANETARIUM

Art galleries, once the province of the intellectual-only group, have changed course both in presentation and in their displays to the public. Not that they don't still aspire to fine art, they do. Today they simply make their displays and programs more inviting. At the Columbia Museum you'll see the works of masters of the Baroque and Renaissance areas in eclectic galleries, along with contemporary art. It's interesting and fun to see how tastes have evolved, and how often we borrow from former periods.

The museum also has a children's gallery, an unheard of innovation a few years ago. There's always something new to see with its traveling exhibits, and everyone enjoys the varied planetarium shows at the Gibbes.

The Columbia Museum of Art is open Tuesday through Friday from 10:00 a.m. until 5:00 p.m.; Saturday and Sunday from 12:30 until 5:00 p.m. Admission is free for the museum. Admission for the Gibbes Planetarium is $2.50 for adults and $1.50 for students. Shows are held at 2:00, 3:00, and 4:00 p.m. on Saturday and Sunday. (803-254-7827)

RIVERBANKS ZOO & GARDEN

Some habitats in this zoo make you feel as if you are on the African Serengeti, in a tropical rain forest or peering out of a mountain cave. Many of the habitats are not segregated to one species. You can watch the antics of baboons commingling with Nubian ibex, much as they might in their native environments.

You may wonder what keeps lions, tigers and monkeys from bounding over the rocks and across their open, bar-less habitats to land in your lap. Over 2,500 animals are housed in these natural exhibits that use psychological barriers such as moats, water and light to create a cage-less environment.

You can't and won't be tempted to pet these animals, but at the zoo's Farm you can touch farm animals, and at 10 a.m. you can see how milking is done.

Photo courtesy of Riverbanks Zoo & Garden.

*Over 2,500 animals are housed in natural exhibits at
the Riverbanks Zoo & Garden.*

Look at the park schedule you receive with your admission ticket and go to the feeding areas at the designated feeding times. That's when animals are more likely to prance and play. The sea lions clap their flippers and bark for food. And if this makes you hungry, stop at any of the in or outdoor snack bars scattered throughout the beautifully landscaped park.

Prior to the tropical rain forest demonstration, you'll smell what you'd vow is the way air smells just before it rains. Then cracks the sound of thunder, and zigzags of lightening cross the forest. Birds sqawk. Rain falls gently until it builds to a shower. A gush of water rushes down a natural rock formation.

You know it's curtaintime when someone behind you says, "Let's go see the penguins, again." Their glass enclosed 40-degree air and water tank is adjacent to the rain forest. These little waddling penguins may look equally stunned to see you peering through their glass.

And there are few sights more visually stunning than the flamingo habitat that looks like a picture out of Dr. Doolittle's book of animals.

The **Aquarium Reptile Complex** (ARC) is the zoo's new centerpiece. Floor to ceiling tanks teem with a Technicolor show of tropical and East Coast fish that appear to be larger, smaller and funnier-shaped than the imagination can comprehend. Due to many myths, misconceptions and mysteries about reptiles and amphibians, the zoo's educational center has ongoing special programs to educate the public in a variety of hands-on classes. These help all of us to better understand our relationship with the animal world.

Riverbanks Zoo is located at 500 Wildlife Parkway—just off I-126 at Greystone Boulevard. It is open daily except Christmas and Thanksgiving from 9 a.m. until 4 p.m. weekdays; and until 5 p.m. summer weekends. Admission is $4.75 for adults, $2.25 for children 3 to 12, and admission is reduced for seniors and students. (803-779-8717)

LAKE MURRAY

Lake Murray comprises 50,000 acres of outdoor water fun and is only a short drive from Columbia. In fact, as you cross what was formerly the world's largest earthen dam, you can see Columbia in the distance. This is where Columbians go to play. The fishing is excellent and the area offers a variety of camping opportunities.

Accommodations___

BED & BREAKFAST INNS
Claussen's Inn at Five Points ($$-$$$), located at 1003

Greene Street, is a convenient location for shoppers who enjoy the unique shops and great atmosphere of the Five Points section. This once historic bakery, carefully restored to a quaint inn, is not your average B & B. It caters to business people who can take advantage of the conference and board rooms. All bedrooms have private baths and a light continental breakfast is served. (803-765-0440)

Chestnut Cottage Bed and Breakfast ($$-$$$$), located in Columbia's Historical District at 1718 Hampton Street, delivers the most for your money. This circa 1850 Federal-style house, the former home of Mary Boykin Chestnut who wrote about life during the Civil War in *Diary From Dixie,* gives you a feel for the era. You can stand on the same porch where Confederate President Jefferson Davis delivered a speech. And you're certain to enjoy a full Southern breakfast. Each antique bedroom has a modern bath. (803-256-1718)

Comfort Inn ($$) in Lexington is not at all your usual chain motel. Management has combined a B & B with a former motel to produce a lovely hybrid at affordable rates. (803-359-3099)

CAMPING

Sesquicentennial State Park ($) is on U.S. 1, 13 miles west of Lexington. At this park you can swim, fish take a pedal boat ride, and/or tour a 1756 log cabin. (803-788-2706) **Cedar Pond Campground** ($) in Leesville is 1 1/2 miles south of I-20 on U.S. 178. (803-657-5993)

Dreher Island State Park ($), located in Prosperity, is six miles southwest of Chapin. There's a host of water-related activities on this island park with 112 campsites, a park store and tackle shop. You can swim, fish go boating or hike along its nature and hiking trails. (803-364-3530) **Holland's Marina and Campground** ($) in Prosperity on Lake Murray, is six miles south of Prosperity. (803-364-CAMP or 800-597-4342)

Dining

Villa Tronco Restorante ($$) located downtown at 1213 Blanding Street is one of the most intimate, romantic and reasonably priced restaurants in Columbia. Its Italian dishes are authentic, and the homemade amaretto cheesecake is to die for. Both lunch and dinner are served. Go.

Richard's ($$-$$$) located at 936 Gervais Street (in the Congaree Vista area downtown) is another winner. Southern food is the staple, but a combination of tried and true with bold and new is found here for lunch and dinner.

California Dreaming ($-$$$) is located at 401 South Main Street in the former Union Station Depot that has been skillfully redesigned. It serves good lunches and dinners. Salads with the restaurant's own honey-mustard dressing is great, as are its desserts.

Cinnamon Hill ($$-$$$) is located in a Victorian home in Lexington. The owners were as careful with the restoration and decor as they were with the excellent food.

You can dine outdoors in seasonal weather at the casual **Dixie Seafood** ($-$$) restaurant in the Congaree Vista District, the former freight depot right beside the railroad tracks. In addition to seafood, it serves "beach-water" grits. The best. Or try the baked quail.

Side Trips

EDISTO MEMORIAL GARDENS

To Get There:
From Columbia, take I-26 south to U.S. 301 south at Orangeburg.

One reason that gardens are so popular in the South is due to the long blooming sea-son. With so much of the landscape staying green with magnolias, pines and live oaks, something is either blooming or in various shades of green throughout the year. This can make a visit in winter a pleasant outing, but it can't be compared with spring's audacious explosion of color. Located along the bank of the north fork of the Edisto River, Edisto Memorial Garden turns down the page on romantic beauty. If a "young man's fancy doesn't turn to love" after a stroll through the garden's dogwood, wisteria and azalea covered grounds, then he needs to be put out to pasture!

You may think "a rose is a rose is a rose," but after a late spring, summer or fall visit to this testing ground for the All-American Rose selection process, you may change your mind. This garden abounds with a stupendous 9,500 array of roses, which may not make it the last word on roses, but it comes close.

Bring a picnic lunch to the garden's picnic facilities for an inexpensive day trip. And, don't forget to take a stroll through the second floor of the adjacent Arts Center.

Edisto Memorial Gardens are open daily from 8:00 a.m. to dusk. No admission is charged. (803-533-6020) The Arts Center is open weekdays only, and it, too, is free. (803-536-4074)

CONGAREE SWAMP NATIONAL MONUMENT

To Get There:
The Monument is located 20 miles southeast of Columbia off U.S. 48.

Most of us envision a stone statue when thinking of a monument. So, it's a stretch of the imagination to call a swamp a monument until you read the dictionary's fourth interpretation of monument as "Any place or region officially designated as having special interest or significance, and maintained and preserved by a government."

To protect this 15,000-acre preserve that is geologically an alluvial flood plain, our government adopted the swamp. The age of size 20-foot radius tree trunks make this river-bottom forest one of the last remaining swamps in America. The swamp has a 3/4-mile boardwalk for the handicapped that overlooks Lake Weston, and another 18 miles of hiking trails that take you through a dark-water magical time. You can also canoe through self-guided trails or sign up for the guided nature walks each Saturday at 1:30 p.m.

The Monument is open daily, year-round. No admission is charged. (803-776-4396)

For More Information:
Columbia Metropolitan Convention and Visitors Bureau
P.O. Box 15
Columbia, SC 29202
800-264-4884

Lake Murray Tourism and Recreation Association
P.O. Box 1783
Irmo, SC 29063
800-951-4008

AAA Carolinas
810 Dutch Square Blvd.
Columbia, SC 29210
803-798-9205

The South Carolina State House.

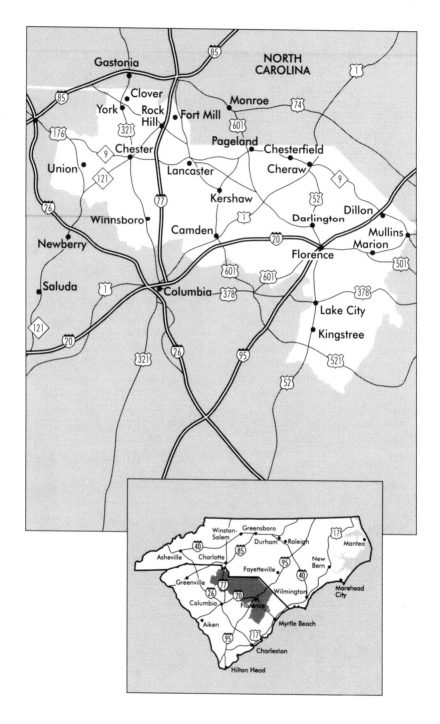

SOUTH CAROLINA'S
Upper Midlands

CAMDEN

To Get There:
From the north, take I-77 and exit onto S.C. 34 east through Ridgeway and Lugoff. From the south, take I-20 east or west and then take exit 98 onto U.S. 521.

When you read the street signs: "Horses forbidden on sidewalks," you know you're in horse country. Most folks associate Camden with horse racing—the **Carolina Cup** just before Easter, which draws 65,000, and the **Colonial Cup** in mid-November. (For specific dates, call 803-432-6513.) These famous races and the town's six equine training centers have made Camden into the Steeplechase Capital. Wherever you find horse racing, there are parties. And these lavish outdoor tailgate cup parties have folks donning their spiffiest. Some of it is

tongue in cheek, with tuxedo clad butlers and maids in fishnet stockings serving everything from locally hunted quail to collards and chocolate grits. Each season the **Fine Arts Center of Kershaw County** at 810 Lyttleton Street pulls out all the stops with new equine art exhibits to kick off the weekend.

Things To See and Do _____

HISTORIC CAMDEN

Horses, hunting and history may be recreational reasons for visiting Camden today, but Camden's Revolutionary War involvement is equally intriguing. You won't find many towns in America interested in preserving their Revolutionary War history to such a degree that they perform yearly reenactments of the battles fought there. Camden does. People come from all over the East Coast to perform in the reenactment the first weekend in November at Historic Camden.

Besides these **Revolutionary War Field Days**, Historic Camden, once a part of the British palisade wall that enclosed the original town, offers a great historical introduction. Here, you'll see the reconstruction of Joseph Kershaw's 1777 2-story Georgian home sitting in command position on a hill that once overlooked American Revolutionary War troops in training. This must also have appealed to General Cornwallis

who used it as his headquarters, making the house known thereafter as the Kershaw-Cornwallis home.

Today, the home's furnishings display antiques from the 18th century plus a few of Kershaw's original pieces. A fine portrait of President Andrew Jackson hangs above the fireplace. Jackson's face is turned aside to hide scars inflicted by Tory soldiers when he was 14 during his Camden imprisonment. Tour guides take you through the elegant home's lower floors and into the lovely back garden. Last year an actual 18th century-style wedding

Photo courtesy of Olde English District Tourism Commission.

Steeplechase has become synonymous with Camden.

was held here during the reenactment of the Revolutionary Battle of Camden.

A number of other 1800s buildings have been moved onto the Historic Camden site. You can visit several log cabins and also the 1796 one-room Craven home, completely restored down to its candle light molding mantel. Above the fireplace hangs a portrait of Baron Johann de Kalb (a German soldier), who fought with the Americans and is considered the hero of the Battle of Camden. Also, take a peek inside what historians believe was once Dr. McCaa's medical office, a current work in progress.

Historic Camden is located on South Broad Street on the town's outskirts. Its excellent gift shop, the 1840 Cunningham house, has many historic reproductions. Hours for tours are Tuesday through Saturday from 10:00 a.m. until 4:00 p.m.; Sunday from 1:00 p.m. until 4:00 p.m. Admission for adults is $4.50, for students, $1.50. (803-432-9841)

TOURS

Unless this is a spur of the moment day trip for you, call ahead (24 hours minimum) for the **HisToury Driving and House Tour**. The tour takes from 1 1/2 - 2 hours and is worth every moment. You'll learn that Camden is the oldest existing inland town in South Carolina.

In 1730, King George II sent instructions to set up a town "on the River Watery." The town, laid out in 1733-34, was called Pine Tree Hill. An 18th century costumed guide takes you inside one of Camden's many 1800s mansions where tea and refreshments are served on the front verandah Lowcountry porch. When you inhale fragrant tea olive blossoms while walking up the mansion's front porch steps, it's like opening a book and finding a pressed corsage. The memory that corsage evokes isn't unlike the memory and imagination that stirs when another costumed hostess opens the mansion's front door. Foyers that you could almost play basketball in lie at the bottom of double-sided "Good Morning" stairways.

You'll also drive past the home where the message, "Thou shalt be satisfied," was etched into the window pane with a diamond ring by Colonel's Shannon's widow. The disgusted widow had lost her husband in South Carolina's last duel. Equally disgusted, the state legislature passed a law against dueling.

Famed architect, Robert Mills, designed Bethesda Presbyterian Church in 1822. You can stand beneath the church's front columns, as Marquis de Lafayette did to deliver the eulogy for his friend, Baron de Kalb, who is buried beneath the obelisk monument on the front lawn.

HisToury Tours takes as few as four people and the price for tours ranges from $4 to $55. Call (803) 432-1723 for details.

ANTIQUING

If golf widows and others want to do some antiquing, they should head for the **Camden Antique Mall** at 830 South Broad Street and visit the **Granary Artisans' Guild and Gallery** for eclectic contemporary pieces. Don't even think of calling it a day without going out to the **Broom Store** (south of town) located in a restored slave cabin right beside the soon-to-be-operating **Boykin Mill**.

Plans are to again mill flour and grits there. Inside the Broom Store you can watch brooms, made from broom corn, being made by hand with the aid of 100-year-old tools.

Accommodations____

BED & BREAKFAST INNS

The **Greenleaf Inn Bed and Breakfast** ($$-$$$) is located at 1308-10 N. Broad St. Known as the Reynold's house, this former home is where Dr. George Todd (Mary Todd Lincoln's brother) treated Confederate wounded during the Civil War. (803-425-1806)

The Kershaw-Cornwallis House at Historic Camden.

Photo courtesy of Olde English District Tourism Commission.

Next door, the stately **McLean Home** built in 1810, and recently renovated, has lovely bedrooms as well as an elegant restaurant.

Dining

The **Mill Pond Restaurant** ($$-$$$), next door to Boykin Mill, is a former post office that has been cleverly recycled into an upscale rustic restaurant. It overlooks the idyllic pond that provides hydro power for the Boykin Mill. Oysters, grilled quail, filet mignon and duck, each done to perfection, will treat your palate to one of the best dinners you'll eat in South Carolina.

The **Paddock** restaurant ($-$$$) at 514 Rutledge Street is a good bet for lunch. You can order anything from burgers to crab meat salads or great big club sandwiches.

> **For More Information:**
> **Olde English District Tourism**
> **Commission**
> **P.O. Box 1440**
> **Chester, SC 29706**
> **800-968-5909**

UNION

> **To Get There:**
> **Union is located on S.C. 49**
> **about 23 miles east of I-26.**

Things To See and Do

ROSE HILL PLANTATION STATE PARK

The best time to visit the former 8,000-acre plantation home of Secessionist Governor William Henry Gist is in late May to June when the roses are at their peak but, whenever you come, you'll find it full of interesting history and antiques original to the family or of their period. Gist's ancestor's date back to the Revolutionary War when his grandfather fought at King's Mountain for the Loyalists.

The home sits on a hill and from the balcony you can look out through giant magnolia trees down at the rose and boxwood garden. Prior to the War Between the States, Gist's original hand-made brick home of Federal style architecture was redesigned, stuccoing and scoring over the brick exterior and adding two-story piazzas. In the foyer, you'll see rope molding, a design reserved only for wealthy citizens of the time.

Gist, with a strong belief in states' rights, entered politics in 1840 and became elected Governor in 1858. A uniformed portrait hangs in the downstairs dining room of the Governor's

Photo courtesy of Olde English District Tourism Commission.

*Rose Hill Plantation State Park in Union was the home
of Secessionist Governor William Henry Gist.*

first cousin—States Rights Gist. (Sentiments for states rights ran that long and that deep.) In the handsome antique decorated parlor stands a mannequin dressed in his second wife's dress. Mary Rice Gist wore this dress, with its 23-inch waist, after having borne 12 children! In a back downstairs bedroom, Gist's navy blue uniform lays atop his four poster bed. Although the Confederacy color was gray, many uniforms were homemade in varying shades of brown, blue and gray.

Upstairs, you'll see the ballroom with twin fireplaces containing wooden partitions that allowed the room to be divided into two bedrooms. When you think of how limited dressmaking tools were, the tiny hand-tucked doll's bodice and clothes in the upstairs bedrooms are a marvel.

Outside, there were many out buildings. Today, you'll see the restored, detached kitchen where holiday baking comes to life during the Christmas season when recipes of the period are prepared. Rose Hill became a state park in 1960.

To get to Rose Hill Plantation State Park from downtown Union, go 8 miles south down U.S.176 and turn onto a gravel road to the park. A nominal admission is charged for a guided tour through this restored 1828-1832 plantation home. The plantation is open for tours Saturday from 10 a.m. until 3 p.m.; Sunday from noon until 3 p.m. and Monday, Thursday and Friday from 1 until 4 p.m. There is no admission to the grounds. (803-427-5966)

BOATING, FISHING AND HUNTING

If the weather is warm enough, take a float trip down the nearby scenic Tyger River, or a canoe trip down the Enoree. In the fall, hunting is good in the **Sumpter National Forest**. Call the U.S. Forestry Service for information on hunting seasons for wild turkey and deer. (803-427-9878 or 800-968-5909) Locals fish at **John's Creek Lakes Complex**. From Union take S.C. 49 west, then left onto S.C. 98 to S.C. 18 and turn left. Take first left onto Forest Service Road, S.R. 347. Catfish, bass and bream are caught here.

Accommodations___

Spend at least one night at the antebellum **Inn at Merridun** ($$), a few blocks away from Union's downtown at 100 Merridun Place. Breakfast is served in the 14-foot-high dining room beneath fresco ceilings painted by Otto Hammer. William Keenan, who built the house in 1855, brought Hammer from Germany to paint the ceiling. Innkeeper Jim Waller says the home's 30 Doric columns were converted to Corinthian, but the handsome mosaic tile foyer and pink Venetian chandelier in the upstairs sitting room are original to the house.

As a descendant of the renowned Pickens family, Waller has framed his documented lineage in the room called Lucy's Garden Retreat. Waller laughs as he points to the framed $1 and $100 dollar Confederate bills bearing Lucy Pickens portrait on them. "She was known as the uncrowned queen of the Confederacy," he says, standing in her whimsically decorated room with a green picket fence headboard standing opposite a green tiled fireplace. The adjoining bath's claw-footed tub is filled with water from the tub's bottom, and Waller (if asked) will show photographs of a female spirit's face clearly recorded on film in the tiled bathroom. No, she's not Lucy Pickens, who was never a guest, but a Canadian clairvoyant has identified the female energy source along with 9 other spirits who, from time to time, hang around the library and kitchen.

You'll have a choice of 5 guest rooms, all with private baths. The Wallers are retired Navy personnel who've traveled and collected interesting pieces in their tours of duty. Expect to be impressed. (803-427-7052)

The Inn at Merridun was built by William Keenan in 1855.

For More Information:
Olde English District Tourism
Commission
P.O. Box 1440
Chester, SC 29706
800-968-5909

YORK,
HISTORIC
BRATTONSVILLE

To Get There:
To reach York from the
north, take U.S. 321 south
from I-85. From I-77, take
S.C. 5 northwest.

When driving through York, for a moment it may seem that you've happened into an early 1900's time warp. That should supply enough intrigue to do a little exploring. In the hardware store you overhear an elderly native talk about what his mama would do to him if she caught him talking to those circus people. Barnett Brothers Circus wintered here between 1929-1945 and though their elephant carried Santa Claus in the annual Christmas parade, townspeople weren't thrilled with roaring lions and trumpeting elephants exercised on the downtown streets. Folks remember those times when they pass the fading building on Trinity and East Jefferson Streets that reads: Barnett Brothers Circus Winter Home.

If you stand on the corners of Liberty and Congress Streets, you are at Fergus Crossroad, the exact spot where York began in stage route days. Known as the Charleston of the Upcountry, York has the second largest historical district in the state with 340 acres containing 180 structures and landmarks. Since York isn't very big, the Yorkville Historical Society has prepared a historic walking tour booklet. You can find copies at the Chamber of Commerce, located in a 1900 Railway Depot at 21 East Liberty Street, or at many of the unique gift and hardware stores on North Congress Street. There's also a factory outlet for golf clubs on this street.

The area was settled first by the Scotch-Irish around 1740, but the architecture you'll see ranges from Colonial to Victorian with plenty of Georgian antebellum and post-Civil War styles.

Things To
See and Do _____

McCELVEY CENTER

Visit the 1850's McCelvey Center at 212 East Jefferson Street, the historical center of York County. Once, the Female Academy of York, the old school now houses an art gallery, beautiful theater and a wing opened by a magnificent wrought iron gate adorned with a single white rose (York's emblem) at its center. This area is devoted to historical research.

MUSEUM OF YORK COUNTY

One of the best museums in South Carolina is the Museum of York County in Rock Hill. You'll find it off Celanese Road on Mt. Gilead Road.

Its phenomenal animal exhibits are reminiscent, although on a much smaller scale, of New York's Natural History Museum. The museum has several excellent art galleries and a fascinating space exhibit. A day trip to the museum is well worth the admission price—adults $3, children and seniors, $2. It is open from 10 a.m. until 5:00 p.m. Tuesday through Saturday, and from 1:00 p.m. until 5:00 p.m. on Saturday.

HISTORIC BRATTONSVILLE

When you get out of your car at the Visitors Center, listen for the bleating of sheep, the squealing of pigs or the cackle of chickens. What's odd about these animals is that they are not from the 20th century. The pigs look like wild boar, the chickens have more feathery legs and the sheep aren't what you'd expect either. All the farm animals, some you can wander amongst, are descendents from animals from the 18th and 19th centuries.

Authenticity is the key word here. You'll see and feel that in the home of Revolutionary War hero, Colonel William Bratton, who moved here from Virginia in 1780 and in his son, Dr. J.S. Bratton's home, built in 1823. The latter, Homestead House, is more luxurious with fine faux wainscoting, a library, harp and a huge, detached dining room built for the doctor's wife and 14 children. Kitchens were usually detached in those days, but rarely dining rooms.

Colonel Bratton fought and won the first Tory defeat on July 20, 1780, at Huck's Defeat, not far from his home. As a consequence, he became a leading economic and political figure. His son later embellished his father's holdings, branching out into banking, merchandising and establishing a Female Seminary in his father's former home.

Perhaps one of the more fascinating activities at Historic Brattonsville Educational Program is the Summer History Camp for 3rd to 8th grade youngsters. These kids get a real hands-on learning experience by picking cotton in a field planted with an 18th century plow and mules. They learn to spin yarn from cotton, use vegetable dyes, cook on a wood stove, tan leather, and care for the animals.

Long Hunters and Six North Carolina Reenactment Society live in some of the restored log cabins and brick slave houses at Brattonsville for a few days at a time, which gives tours a now-it's-happening approach to how life was lived in the past.

Historic Brattonsville is near McConnells, South Carolina, 9 miles south of York off S.C. 322 on S.R.165, Brattonsville Road. Signs mark the place to turn for this restored Revolutionary and Civil War settlement.

Historic Brattonsville is open March through November.

Tour hours are Tuesday and Thursday from 10 a.m. until 4:00 p.m., Saturday and Sunday from 2 p.m. until 5 p.m. Admission is $4 for adults, $2 for students. Call for dates of Christmas tour. (803-684-7262)

For More Information:
Olde English District Tourism
Commission
P.O. Box 1440
Chester, SC 29706
800-968-5909

Photo courtesy of Historic Brattonsville.

Historic Brattonsville, a step back in time.

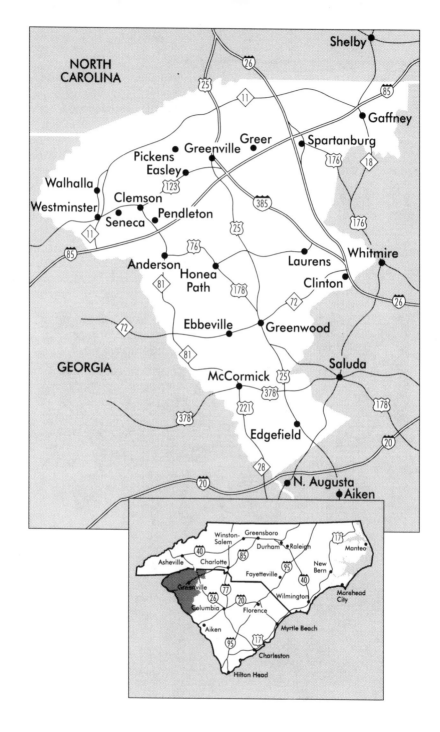

THE FOOTHILLS

From the Upcountry's agricultural, industrial and educational midsection, gently rolling hills begin to escalate as the land stretches northwest into the Blue Ridge Mountains. Gigantic 900- and 400-foot waterfalls tumble and trickle down these rugged mountain slopes.

JONES GAP STATE PARK

To Get There:

From I-85, take S.C.11 west to Cleveland to Jones Gap State Park marker.

The only way you can record the scent of a place is in your brain. Even more dramatic than the sight of the mountain rising above you or the sound of the rushing stream beneath the bridge at Jones Gap's entrance is the sweet, grape-like smell of—surprise—kudzu blossoms. Kudzu hadn't been brought here from Japan when Solomon Jones, known as the patriarch of the mountains, cut a trail through this patch of the Blue Ridge Mountains in the 1850s for a toll road. Legend has it that cutting through the lower section was not difficult. Jones' road followed the Saluda River Gorge as far as possible. But the route from the mountain top was tough. Old timers say that "Solomon Jones carted a couple of his pigs to the ridge top, turned them loose and followed them home, marking the way." Now, pigs, though smart, don't possess terrific cartographic skills, but they do have an eye for scenic beauty. Today, that same 5 1/2-mile trail, known as the "mountain bridge" connects backpackers and hikers to Caesars Head State Park. In late summer, you'll get an occasional whiff of blossoming kudzu along this easy trail that winds along the Middle Saluda River.

The park also offers many smallish waterfalls and a good many wading pools that children can explore. For the skilled hiker who has some experience with navigating down steep slopes with the assistance of ropes, Rainbow Falls is your destination. And after getting permission from a park ranger, you can take a rugged one-hour side trip from the trail to this full-blown waterfall. It cascades over 100 spectacular feet from the sheer cliff on Standingstone Mountain.

If primitive camping (with a hot shower comfort station) will be adequate, then sign up with the park ranger for one of the park's 17 sites. Drive your tent stakes into the loamy earth beside either the Middle Saluda or the Cold Spring Branch Rivers, where you can catch dinner. Twenty picnic tables and grills are available.

Trout swim in the restored pond next to the park's new log and stone environmental learning center. This represents an interpretative remnant of the old Cleveland Fish Hatchery, which remained in operation until 1963. With a state fishing license, you can register to fish for rainbow, brook and brown trout in the Middle Saluda River, one of the few

Photo by Dawn O'Brien

Jones Gap State Park

native streams that naturally renews itself. These clean rivers carry high levels of dissolved oxygen, so it's okay to wash your face, but wiser not to drink the stream water no matter how clear it looks.

This Upcountry wilderness is known for its undisturbed natural ecosystem that protects over 400 species of plants and 200 species of birds. Bring your camera and, if lucky, you may glimpse an occasional brown bear or bobcat, and at certain times you'll see deer and wild turkey. This makes Jones Gap an ideal and inexpensive way to get to know nature a little better.

Jones Gap State Park is open 7 days a week year-round

from 9 a.m. until 6 p.m. Register (first come, first serve) for designated tent sites at $1 per person, per night. (River sites go first.) Picnic tables are also available. (803-836-3647)

CAESARS HEAD STATE PARK

To Get There:
From I-85, take S.C. 11 west past Cleveland to marker for Caesars Head State Park.

If you could choose the perfect site for a summer home, a mountain top from which you could see as far away as Greenville and Paris Mountain to your left and Table Rock Mountain to your right, it could

Photo by Dawn O'Brien.

Caesars Head State Park

be Caesars Head that stands at 3,208 feet. Adjectives like majestic seem paltry when you stand on the summit of Caesars Head to watch the annual mid-September migration of 10,000 hawks. Members of the Hawk Watch program say the migration usually takes place in two to three days, but occasionally in just one.

At a back stairway corner of this panoramic mountain overlook, you can walk down through a narrow, stone crevice passageway, created through intense pressure and heat thousands of years ago, to Devil's Kitchen. From here you can see the profile of Caesars Head, which some think resemble the head of Julius Caesar.

Bird watch programs and hiking the 85-mile trail between Oconee State Park through to Jones Gap, known as the "foothills hiking trail," can take up to two weeks. Don't be misled by the name "foothills," this is steep, rugged mountain wilderness country. Of course, most hikers will take time out to fish in the trout-filled cold water streams and camp at the primitive camp sites along the trail. (Prior to your trek, write to the Foothills Trail Conference, P.O. Box 4031, Greenville, S.C. for a map and information.)

If you aren't up to 85 miles, hike 2 miles down to Raven Cliff Falls, a 420-foot mountain cascade that you'll hear and smell long before the falls come into view. This view, that sprawls across the mountain's summit, could easily tie with the "perfect site for a summer home." Both neighboring Jones Gap and Caesars Head offer designated primitive camping sites, picnic tables and comfort stations. Campers are asked to follow the ethics of "no trace" camping by treating this wilderness area with respect.

Caesars Head has re-opened its park store, which features mountain crafts and gifts. A variety of programs and workshops are offered by park naturalists for overnight backpacking trips, bird walks and exploration of indigenous plant life.

Caesars Head State Park is open year-round, 7 days a week, from 9 a.m. until 6 p.m. Camp sites are available for $1 per person, per night on first come, first serve basis. (803-836-6115) A state fishing license is $10 per year; $11 for 7-day out-of-staters.

TABLE ROCK STATE PARK

To Get There:

The park is located on S.C. 11 north of Pickens, South Carolina.

When you look out from the rounded dome of Table Rock

Mountain, you can see Caesars Head in the distance, and on a haze-free day, most of the South Carolina Upcountry. Like Pilot Mountain in North Carolina, Table Rock served as a landmark for Native American tribes and later settlers to the area. Because of its longevity and natural beauty, Table Rock is one of South Carolina's most popular state parks. There's plenty to do for the whole family. There are 100 tent sites and 14 cabins available for rental.

Children will enjoy programs at the nature center and trying their skills at carpet-golf, or taking in some splash time in the swimming area. And if an adult is handy to supervise, the children can rent a pedal boat or go out with the family in one of the park's fishing boats. Many folks like to fish from the pier, and you need not worry if bait runs scarce, there is a tackle shop at the park as well as a small convenience store. If you don't want to cook your own food, the park has a restaurant open from Tuesday through Sunday, year-round.

Many local people, when they have a couple of hours off, enjoy coming to the park to hike through the wooded nature trails or the more rigorous exercise trails. Table Rock, like all South Carolina parks, has handicap facilities.

For more information on park activities, call (803) 878-

9813. The park is free, but there is a fee ($) for camping and a slightly higher fee for cabin rental.

DEVIL'S FORK STATE PARK

To Get There:

Devils Fork State Park is located at 161 Holcombe Circle in Salem, South Carolina.

Going to Devil's Fork State Park is like going to a upscale rustic resort with a lake at your front door and the Blue Ridge Mountains at your back door. You won't see its equal, except for scenery, in any of the state parks in this region.

Most state parks have camp sites that will accommodate RVs and tent camping, as does Devil's Fork. Many have rustic cabins, but none have posh two- and three-bedroom villas on the scale represented at Devil's Fork. Roughing it in old cabins has its own kind of charm, but there's still a lot to be said for these new, beautifully decorated villas with carpeting, microwaves and color TVs. You may have sworn off amenities, but there are many of us spoiled to creature comforts. This is the kind of getaway you'd select if you are an outdoor kind of person who enjoys fishing and hiking and

wants to impress your boss or mother-in-law with your discriminating taste.

If camping is what you're after, there's no more ideal state park in the Carolinas. Each camp site has water and electrical hookups, a picnic table and grill. You'll find that rest rooms with hot showers and laundry facilities are conveniently located in the camping area. These camp sites are available on a first-come, first-serve basis. There are also 20 lakeside tent sites with elevated pads and access to comfort stations. Another good option available here is the two RV camp sites that have been set aside for the exclusive use of handicapped. These may be reserved in advance.

There are few experiences lovelier than hiking through Devil's Fork in the spring when Jack-in-the-Pulpits, rare Oconee Bells, bloodroot, trout lily and woods violets make the nature trail come alive with color. Spring is also a good opportunity to see wild turkeys, grey foxes, white-tail deer and the endangered specie—peregrine falcon—that has recently been introduced into this area.

Amateur nature photographers wanting to improve their skills may be interested in the park's fall nature photography weekend workshops. Taught by professional photographers, these workshops cost $35. Special techniques for creating moods while photographing waterfalls and rivers are emphasized.

Or you might want to sign up for the Fall Foothills Backpacking Weekend Trip that takes you along mountain ridges and across two of South Carolina's most beautiful rivers, the Thompson and Horsepasture. At a cost of $10, this is quite a deal.

The best time to fish in the park is from March through November. The park store has bait, tackle and other fishing supplies. If you have a boat, bring it. The park stretches around 75 miles of Lake Jocassee's shore line. There is a boat ramp and parking area for boat trailers, but the parking area is reserved for the exclusive use of visitors staying in the villas.

Lake Jocassee is the only lake park in South Carolina where trophy trout and smallmouth bass swim—two reasons that this lake is rapidly becoming a favorite fishing spot for anglers all over the Southeast. The deep, crystal-clear water provides an excellent habitat for many species of fish, including brown trout, rainbow trout, white bass, largemouth bass, bluegill, and black crappie.

You may enjoy one of the tour-and-fish trips scheduled through Lake Jocassee's custom guide service. **Fish Inc.** (803-878-9292) has a 32-foot pontoon boat and offers a variety of fishing and overnight trip tours that feature sightseeing at the area's famed waterfalls and other scenic places. The company also provides transportation for scuba divers and shuttle transportation from the Foothills Hiking Trail to any of the lake's three access points.

Three creeks converge into Lake Jocassee: Corbin, Howard and Limber Pole. And although no one really knows why, this area has been known as Devil's Fork since 1780.

Office hours for the park are Monday through Friday, from 9:00 a.m. until 5:00 p.m.; Saturday and Sunday from 11:00 a.m. until noon and from 4:00 p.m. until 5:00 p.m. The park offers villa rentals ($$$$) and camp sites ($). Call for villa rental information and reservations. (803-944-2639)

Side Trip

WHITE WATER RAFTING

If you've come for the weekend or longer, and you're interested in high adventure, it doesn't get much higher than a day of shooting white water rapids on the Chatooga River. About 50 minutes away near Long Creek, South Carolina, this wild, scenic river is considered one of America's top ten rivers. *Deliverance* was filmed here.

For a taste of these churning rapids you can make reservations by calling **Wildwater Ltd.** (800-451-9972) Prices range from $34.75 a person on weekdays, to $183.50 to raft the whole Chatooga for the weekend. If you want to sharpen your skills in canoeing or kayaking, Wildwater also holds special instructional clinics. For those who may not want to make that 50-minute jaunt, you can make arrangements to stay at the **Chauga River House**. Fully equipped cabin accommodations with kitchens are located on the banks of the scenic Chatooga River and begin at $39.

GREENVILLE

To Get There:
From I-85, take I-385 north.

Things to See and Do

GREENVILLE ZOO

Beautifully landscaped, the paths wind upward to the elephant habitat. A small waterfall and rock and grassy terrain won't make you think you're in Africa, but it presents a more humane setting than zoos have had in the past. Quite a good collection of reptiles can be seen

Photo courtesy Travel & Tourism.

For a day of high adventure, white water rafting can't be beat.

(behind glass) in the Reptile House. Varieties of monkeys are found in different continent areas, but few species are more amusing than the Colobus monkey with its shaggy, white-tipped tail when it leaps from one end of the cage to the other. If you hear a shrill, honking screech don't think ducks, it's the Siamang Gibbon monkeys (mother and child), either in an argument or demanding food. These black chimpanzee-looking animals seem to be in perpetual motion, which excited a toddler to say, "Ook, monkey. Take home."

If you didn't bring a picnic lunch to enjoy in the park's designated dining center, there is a snack bar with a nice adjacent gift shop. Around the circular, winding path lies the Asia/Australia habitat that houses tiny Muntjac deer and Wallabys (small kangaroos). Continue on the same path to the Africa habitats. You'll be astounded to see the biggest cat in these parts—a white Bengal Tiger. He fascinates older children as he licks his coat (cat like) with a large pink tongue. The lions look up, stare at you, decide it's not worth the effort of getting up and continue to nap. It's fun to watch the Aldabra Tortoise in action. His neck slowly juts out and is reminiscent of Stephen Spielberg's "E.T." Curl back down the path to the South American exhibit. You'll see

Toucans, little Squirrel Monkeys with intense eyes, a Pale-headed Saki that looks as if he's wearing a white headband, and the Golden Tamarin monkeys that shake their lion-looking beards at you.

Clever landscaping allows you to spend a lot of time here without walking yourself to death. A nice children's playground is set across from the parking lot.

The Greenville Zoo is conveniently located near downtown and is open daily, year-round from 10 a.m. until 4:30 p.m. Admission is $3 for adults, $1.25 for children 3-15.

NIPPON CENTER YAGOTO

In America only two authentic Japanese tea ceremonies exist: in Washington, D.C., and at the Nippon Center Yagoto in Greenville, S.C. You must make reservations at this beautiful new cultural center for a guided tour, tea, lunch or dinner. The center introduces us to Japanese culture, which has long been a mystery to many Americans.

The center's exterior is encompassed by a Japanese green garden with symbolic waterfall and wooden bridge, while a dramatic walled, dry rock garden, surrounds this handsome building modeled after Japanese military residential architecture between 1336 and 1573. Landscape architects patterned this garden after the Ruoan-ji garden in Kyoto, Japan.

When Americans think "garden," we think greenery and seldom challenge our imaginations to consider that a tree or rock could represent something entirely different. The Japanese garden is designed for peaceful contemplation, whether it's a garden of boulders and pattern-raked gravel or one of lush greenery with waterfalls. The walled Zen garden, seen only from the varied dining rooms inside the center, calls upon your imagination. Large boulder-like mountains set amidst swirling gravel designs represent ocean waves with small island outcroppings. Night time spotlights intensify the garden's drama.

Photo by Dawn O'Brien.

The Janpnese Garden at Nippon Center Yagoto.

An authentic Japanese lunch or dinner is served in its four varied dining rooms, and each dish is interpreted for you. Presentation is unequaled. And yes, you'll be asked to remove your shoes and place them, with heels touching the step entrance. The cuisine is 16th, 17th and 18th century, which is not quite as spicy as American versions unless you order tempura. Save room for green tea ice cream that tastes and looks a bit like pistachio. The restaurant has a beautiful sushi bar made from one solid piece of cypress tree where rice and fish dishes are offered. The center is a study in elegance through simplicity.

Nippon Center Yagoto is located at 500 Congaree Road. Take I-385 to the Haywood Mall exit. Circle around the back of the mall onto Congaree Road and look for Nippon Center on the right. The center is open Monday through Saturday. Call for advance reservations. The tour, including lunch costs $18.75. (803-288-8471)

BOB JONES UNIVERSITY MUSEUM OF SACRED ART

Prepare to be dazzled. Although the university is small, its religious art collection is not. In fact, the museum houses 30 galleries, making it the largest collection of religious art in America. You'll be astounded at the display of European sacred art spanning the 13th through the 19th centuries. And if you thought work of the great masters hung only in Europe, you are in for another surprise. You can find the work of Rembrandt, Rubens and Van Dyck along with many other artists. And when thinking of priceless antiques, consider the museum's collection of Renaissance furniture. The Biblical costumes give the museum a more three-dimensional expression, and its Russian icon collection is quite representative of this form of religious art. It will take some time to go through the entire museum, but you can absorb a lot in an hour or so and then return for a later visit.

This museum is found on the campus of Bob Jones University at 1700 Wade Hampton Boulevard in Greenville, S.C. The museum is open Tuesday through Sunday, from 2 p.m. until 5 p.m. Admission is free, but children under 6 are not admitted.

Accommodations___

BED AND BREAKFAST INNS
Pettigru Place Bed & Breakfast ($$-$$$$) is located at 302 Pettigru Street near downtown Greenville. This handsome brick, Georgian Federalist style home offers five differently decorated bedrooms, each with private bath. A full breakfast with juices, coffees, fresh baked breads and quiche-type entrees are served in its lovely dining room each morning. (803-288-4839)

Dining ___

Falls Cottage ($), located at 615 South Main Street, is a restored two-story 1894 house that has been converted into a restaurant of charm, panache and super food. In seasonal weather, a favorite dining spot is the upstairs outdoor patio that overlooks Reedy River Falls Park (a pastoral downtown park). Lunch, with homemade soups, pleases most tastes as does the hot chicken salad casserole. Falls Cottage serves lunch only.

Seven Oaks ($$$-$$$$), located at 104 Broadus Avenue in Greenville, serves dinner only. It took more than a million well-spent dollars to restore and decorate this 1895 mansion. Fortunately the continental cuisine stands up to the decor.

For More Information:

Discover Upcountry Carolina Association
P.O. Box 3116
Greenville, SC 29602
800-849-4766

AAA Carolinas
430 Haywood Rd., Suite 1
Greenville, SC 29607
803-297-9988

PENDLETON

To Get There:
From I-85 take 76 east into
Pendleton.

Pendleton's historic downtown square still looks as if it's part of the 18th century. Quaint shops line the square and grand plantations speak of the past.

Things To
See and Do _____

ASHTABULA PLANTATION

In the early 1700s nobody knew mosquitoes caused the "summer sickness"; they just knew that moving to the Upcountry from April through November protected families from contracting the dread disease. In 1725 Lewis Gibbes (from a prominent Charleston family) built a lovely two-story Charleston-designed home for his family outside Pendleton, South Carolina. You'll see a widow's walk atop the roof, a wide verandah, fresh cut flowers throughout, and rooms filled with antiques from 1725-1760. In the record's room a map drawn by a Gibbe's son in 1851 proved an expert guide to the California gold mines, discovered in 1849. A diary kept through the War Between the States describes a visit from a group of Union Cavalry who were a part of the "Stoneman Raiders."

Mrs. Gibbes (Mary Henrietta), a recognized botanist in her own right, cultivated a friendship with the Audubons. In the upstairs landing, be sure to note her Audubon prints. Children will love the dolls and teddy bear, considered to be older than the house, but may crinkle their noses at the white lacy clothes worn back then.

In an adjacent out building, thought to be older than the plantation home, is a restored kitchen. Check out the United States map above the fireplace mantel. It may be a surprise to learn that both North and South Carolina's boundaries originally extended all the way to the Mississippi River.

This house has been lovingly refurbished and maintained through the efforts of Mrs. Frances Schackelford, a lady now past her 93rd birthday. Each Sunday she comes to Ashtabula to answer questions and explain the plantation's extensive history.

Take I-85 to S.C. 76 west into Pendleton and take S.C. 88 3 miles to Ashtabula Plantation. It's open on Sunday from 2 p.m. until 6 p.m. from April through October. Admission is $3 for adults and $2 for children 6 to 14.

WOODBURN PLANTATION

The best time to visit Woodburn, the plantation summer home of the distinguished Charles Cotesworth Pinckney family, is the first weekend in April. You can have a made-from-scratch lunch in the home's downstairs kitchen or picnic on the beautiful grounds amidst ancient holly, cedar, fig and oak trees. This is another home with wide, Charleston-type piazzas designed to capture every available cool breeze for all four floors. Had not the mountains been Indian territory in the early 1700s, families would have built summer homes in those cooler climes.

The twin downstairs parlors are distinguished with black marble mantels, which are not original to the house. Summer homes were not appointed as formally or as expensively as the town houses of Charleston, Atlanta and other southern cities. Further evidence of this is in Woodburn's substantial but less than grandiose stairway. The dining room table in one of the home's prettiest rooms, is set with red fruit course napkins to keep stains from showing. Each dining room chair is covered in needlepoint that commemorates South Carolina birds. The upstairs bedrooms open to the second piazza balcony and are decorated with antique furniture and clothing.

Woodburn Plantation is off S.C. 76, across the highway from Tri County Tech. (It's tricky to find due to lack of marker signs). Woodburn Plantation is open from 2 p.m until 6 p.m, April through October. Admission is $3 for adults and $2 for children.

For More Information:
Pendelton District Historical, Recreational & Tourism Commission
P.O. Box 565
Pendleton, SC 29670
803-646-3782

CLEMSON

To Get There:
From I-85, take S.C. 76 east into Clemson.

When Hollywood movie scouts look for the ideal college town, they need go no further than Clemson, home of Clemson University. This normally quiet academic setting roars to life in the fall when thousands of Clemson Tiger fans descend into "Death Valley" for an afternoon of fun and football.

Things To See and Do _____

CLEMSON BOTANICAL GARDEN

You shouldn't go through

without visiting the 256-acre Clemson Botanical Garden. Tall pines, small footbridges over clear streams and winding paths are perfect for a bicycle ride in the early springtime or fall when the mums bloom in a variety of rich autumn colors. You can stop for a moment at the Garden of Meditation with its pagoda ensconced beside a reflecting pool. Then peddle on to the Pioneer Garden with its authentic log cabins, farm implements and grist mill that give you a view of the past. If hiking, you can spend more time identifying the over 1000 species of trees. Formerly, this was the University's Horticultural and Forestry Arboretum, and offers many trails containing thousands of ornamental plants that include both native varities and those that have adapted from other regions.

This Garden plays host to a Horticultural lecture series and the annual Daffodil Festival, among others. In the past few years low-chemical-input methods for producing vegetables have been tested in a 3-acre garden. Other methods for reducing pressure on landfills is under study and the wildflower meadow serves as a further research tool.

Springtime, with its sunshine-colored daffodil collection and paths of overflowing azaleas and camellias rival each other in color making this a show not to be missed. Fall, with its craft festival, games and country music is an ideal time to visit as well.

The Garden has miles of nature trails that are used every day of the year by joggers and bird-watchers. And if you're in town and can pry yourself out of bed on the first Friday of the month for the 7 a.m. nature walk, you'll discover more about the Garden's plants and birds than is possible on your own.

Clemson Botanical Garden is open from sunrise to sundown, and there is no admission charged. From I-85 take S.C. 76 east into Clemson. The Garden is on the eastern side of Clemson University, off Perimeter Road.

JOHN C. CALHOUN HOUSE MUSEUM

Located in the center of the Clemson campus is the final home of Clemson's most prominent son, John C. Calhoun. He lived in this stately Georgian mansion from 1825-1850 and it has now been designated a National Historic Landmark. Calhoun named his 1,100-acre plantation home "Fort Hill" for the fort built there in 1776.

The home has been so beautifully restored by the Daughters of the Confederacy that you would think the family had just stepped out for a Sunday stroll around the Botanical Garden. In fact, there are a good many of the Calhoun and Clemson furnishings in the house. Although this is clearly Calhoun country, Calhoun's son-in-law, Thomas Green Clemson, who later lived in the home, willed the plantation home, its acreage, and a cash endowment to form an agricultural college here in 1888. The town honored Clemson by naming not only the University but also the town after him.

The museum is open Monday through Saturday from 10 a.m. until 5 p.m., and Sunday from 2 p.m. until 5 p.m. Admission for adults: $3, students $2, children 6-12 $1.

Accommodations

BED AND BREAKFAST INNS

Liberty Hall Inn Bed and Breakfast ($$-$$$), located at 621 South Mechanic Street in Pendleton, is a great combination of continental restaurant with accommodations that look like a page out of an 1800s book. Private baths and air conditioning have been added, but this hasn't altered the inn's charm. Try the open-range veal or if you like crab cakes, these have more crab meat than you'll find anywhere. Save room for their Chocolate Sin dessert. There is an enticing buffet for breakfast. (803-646-7500)

Dining

Drop by for a drink in the pub area of **Pendleton House** ($$), located in a restored home at 203 East Main Street. Dinners that span the gap from Southern to continental cuisine are more than worth the price, especially the pan-broiled lamb tenderloin or "salmon" trout.

Farmers Hall Tea Room ($) is located on the square in downtown historic Pendleton inside the still active 1820s Farmers Hall. This print-and-pastel cubby hole of a restaurant is open for lunch only but delivers a variety of tasty dishes. Try the Chicken Reuben Casserole with sour cream biscuits and the Hummingbird Cake.

For More Information:

Clemson Chamber of Commerce
P.O. Box 202
Clemson, SC 29633
803-654-1200

ANDERSON

To Get There:
From I-85, take S.C. 76 west into Anderson.

As you drive down Main Street, don't be surprised if you see 1900s looking streetcars. Anderson, known as "The Electric City" since it became the first electric power operated cotton mill and cotton gin in the South, was also among the first to have street cars.

Things To See and Do _____

ANDERSON JOCKEY LOT AND FARMERS MARKET

People come to Anderson from all over the world to go to the Anderson Jockey Lot and Farmers Market. It's considered the South's biggest and the world's best flea market. Now covering 65 acres with 1,500 spaces, you can get everything from sweet potatoes to Persian carpets here. Wear good shoes and plan to walk a lot. No merchandise or days are alike, but the crowd averages between 30,000-60,000 a day. The Jockey Lot is located on U.S. 29, 10 miles north of Anderson.

ANDERSON COUNTY ARTS CENTER

The gallery is small but unique in its offerings. You need spend little more than a half hour if you're in a hurry, but you won't get worn out either. The center houses collections of both local, national and internationally recognized artists, and changes exhibits frequently.

Located at 405 N. Main Street in Anderson, the Center is open Monday through Friday from 9:30 a.m. until 5:30 p.m.,

and Sunday from 1:30 p.m. until 3:30 p.m. Admission is free, but donations are accepted.

Accommodations _____

BED AND BREAKFFAST INNS

River Inn Bed & Breakfast ($$), located at 612 East River Street in Anderson on the original busy trolley and carriage route to the capitol, still remains busy. In the entrance hall of this two-story home built by Dr. Archer Leroy Smethers in 1914, a collection of raccoons peak at you from the wall.

You'll also see them atop the dining room mantel where owner, Pat Clark, serves a huge breakfast. Her menu changes, but grits are served everyday "whether you eat them or not," she jokes. She also bakes her own English muffins and serves (from the garden) fresh sliced tomatoes along with eggs and bacon. This isn't like breakfast at home unless you always dine in a Victorian appointed dining room with antique china and silver.

All the bedrooms have fireplaces and private baths and the Roy Nance Smethers room (most requested room) has white stenciled floors and its own private side entrance off a screen-enclosed porch with an old-fashioned swing. This handily leads to the back yard's hot tub Jacuzzi, which is amply supplied with sheet-size towels. Doctors' incomes in 1914 were so insufficient that Mrs. Smethers took in "lady school teachers." The upstairs Alice Humphreys room is named for such an author-teacher.

Open year-round, this family-type B & B is a fun place to stay. (803-226-1431)

Dining _____

The Morris Street Tea Room, located at 220 E. Morris Street in Anderson, is not your typical tea room. It offers cozy alcoves and pretty dining rooms. It's famous for its delicious Quiche Angie, named for owner Angie Finazzo, and its Italian cream pie goes down real easy, too. This is also a nice place for dinner.

1109 South Main, located as you might expect, at 1109 South Main Street in Anderson, is the picture of old South romanticism. The 1860 Greek Revival mansion was built as a wedding present and converted into a fine continental restaurant. With southern as well as South Sea Island cuisine, this restaurant is an excellent choice.

For More Information:
Anderson Area Chamber of Commerce
P.O. Box 1568
Anderson, SC 29622
803-226-3454

COWPENS NATIONAL BATTLEFIELD

To Get There:
From I-85 near Gaffney, take S.C. 11 west. The battlefield is approximately 2 miles east of Chesnee.

Taking a youngster with you to this battle site and interpretive Visitors Center could increase your own enjoyment. (So, if you don't have one, borrow a kid.) There's a short film that will jog your memory of what happened on that cold January 17, 1881, morning when the know-it-all British General Banastre Tarleton met up with the savvy strategist American General Daniel Morgan. Portraits of Daniel Morgan, Andrew Pickens, William Washington (a cousin of General George Washington), John Eager Howard of Maryland, whose Continentals were the meat of Morgan's army, and others who played significant roles in the battle, plus a panoramic painting of the battle in full swing are displayed in the central exhibit room.

For guests to feel the battle action, the center devised a unique game table with sound. You activate its push button system and watch how the battle occurred in sequence. This is where you're apt to hear, "Neat,

Dad!" or "Look! the red lights! Those are the red coats. They are pushing right through the line!" But you soon learn that the brilliant field tactician, Morgan, buoyed with a little unforeseen luck (also known as divine providence), readied his troops with three lines of battle.

Tarleton, wanting to surprise Morgan, began marching his troops toward Cowpens at 3:00 a.m. Morgan, who had known for over 24 hours that Tarleton had been sent to finish off his army, had surveyed the meadow at Hannah's Cowpens and marked out the entire battle the previous day. So, when Morgan's men were alerted to imminent attack, they had sufficient time to finish their breakfast. The patriots drew Tarleton's troops towards the gently rolling field of the Cowpens where the terrain gave them the advantage of seeing Tarleton's horseback approach, while they themselves could not be seen.

After a hard-fought battle, the "bloody Tarleton" as he was called, turned tail and ran. Fleeing in defeat, the British had lost a staggering 120 men, over 200 wounded and 500 more captured. Morgan had lost only 12 men with 60 wounded. The actual battle lasted for one mere hour, but was another important link in the chain of British miscalculations in the South

that ultimately led to their final defeat in Yorktown.

There are a few uniforms and weapons in glass cases and other Revolutionary War items of interest. You can walk the well-marked battlefield with way-side exhibits through the heart of the action and see exactly where the positions of combat took place. There is a picnic area with a shelter at the rear of the battlefield.

Cowpens National Battlefield is open daily from 9:00 a.m. until 5:00 p.m., and from 1:00 p.m. until 5:00 p.m. on Sunday. No admission is charged.

CHEROKEE FOOTHILLS SCENIC HIGHWAY (S.C. 11)

One of the most beautiful rides that you can take in the fall or spring is along this ancient Cherokee path. It begins in Gaffney off I-85 and makes a 130-mile loop through peach orchards and tiny towns, ending at the Georgia line. You'll pass by Cowpens Battlefield and over I-26 and by several state and county parks that are perfect for a picnic.

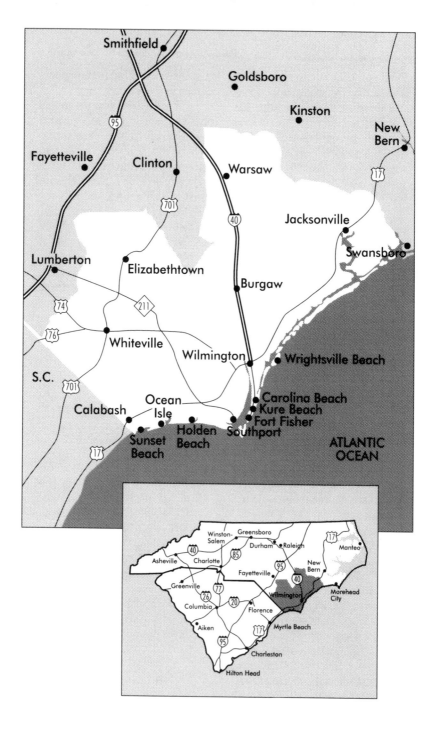

Southern Coast

THE BRUNSWICK ISLAND BEACHES

When the Intracoastal waterway was created in the 1930s, a string of islands, called barrier islands, was formed between it and the Atlantic Ocean. The winding, marshy waterways surrounding these islands provide ideal conditions for fishing and for some of North Carolinas most popular beaches at Sunset, Ocean Isle, Holden and Oak Island.

SUNSET BEACH

To Get There:

From N.C. 179 turn east onto the pontoon bridge (near the South Carolina border).

Working on the premise of "rest," this homey, family-type beach is a great place to relax and build a few sand castles on the clean, wide beach, play a little golf or do some fishing from the pier ($4.00 to fish, a quarter to stroll). Action here comes mostly from surfers and kite flyers. This beach is so laid-back that the heaviest action some folks exert is burrowing their bodies into the sand—sculpting it to the relaxed contours of their torsos.

Things To See and Do _____

BIRD WATCHING

Watching the 200 species of birds, including white ibis, osprey, egret and painted bunting, grows on you when you get into the wind-down mode. If you're looking for a place where you can really talk to nature, wait for low tide and head to the west end of Sunset Beach. A 30-minute walk across Mad Inlet will take you to Bird Island, one of the last undeveloped islands on the Carolina beaches. If it's very low tide you can ride a bicycle across the inlet. The base of the windswept dunes provides a good vantage point to watch pelicans and sea gulls, some of the species that give the island its name.

This secluded island holds another delightful surprise for those adventurous enough to get here. Sitting atop a weathered post is an ordinary looking mail box with the words "KINDRED SPIRIT" written across its side. Inside the mail box are several notebooks in which earlier visitors have written messages and recorded reflections of their experience for those who follow. It touches a deep chord to relax in the beauty and solitude of the island and read what others before you have written. You can sit on the only park bench on the island and add your thoughts before returning the notebooks to the mail box. You'll need to time your visit—if you lose track and stay too long you'll have to roll up your pants' legs to wade back!

A note: don't put off visiting the island too long. Its owner has development plans, although local citizens are working to persuade the government to buy and preserve the island.

FISHING

Contact **Captain Jim's Marina** in Calabash for deep

Photo by Dawn O'Brien.

A pristine refuge on the East Coast.

sea fishing. For night fishing, call 910-579-3660 and for trolling, 803-249-4575. If you want to watch the shrimp boats come in (a scene in itself), take N.C. 179, which becomes Beach Drive in Calabash, and turn south onto River Road.

GOLF

On N.C. 179 you'll find **Sea Trails Plantation & Golf Course**, a golf haven if there ever was one, with three different but challenging courses. Environmentally designed to preserve the marshes and wetlands, the courses here have elaborate mounds, sculptured in varied designs. (910-579-4350)

A favorite golf course in the area is **Oyster Bay Golf Links**. One visitor, while passing by and seeing the par-3 green set in the middle of a lake, remarked, "I don't care if it costs a $100 to play that course, I'm going to do it." (910-579-3528)

Pearl Golf Links is another favorite in the area. The two courses at The Pearl were designed by Dan Maples and built on a 900-acre marsh preserve, providing stunning natural beauty. (910-579-3528)

HORSEBACK RIDING

When you tire of the beach or of playing golf, you can go horseback riding at **Farwinds**

Stables in Longwood off N.C. 179 or U.S. 17 south—about 20 minutes from Sunset. (910-287-6315)

Accommodations

Sea Trail Plantation & Golf Course ($$$$) offers luxurious condos, many overlooking a golf course. This full 2,000-acre resort, located on N.C. 179 west, offers swimming, tennis and volleyball along with two clubhouses and restaurants. (800-624-6601)

Beach house rentals on Sunset Beach are mostly by the week, but there are a few condos and motels around for weekend-only guests. Try **Williamson Realty** (910-579-2373), **Carolina Beach & Golf Resort** (800-222-1524) or **Sunset Beach Motel** (910-579-7093).

Dining

If you didn't know about it, you'd probably never stop at **Big Nell's Pit Stop** ($). This race-car-oriented restaurant is **the** place for breakfast. Big Nell says, "This is the place to bring your joys and problems." Nell's Belgian Waffles, served with spiced hot apples, are bigger than normal and real good under strawberry whipped cream. Nell won't give away her grits recipe, but says the secret is left-handed stirring. Big Nell's is on N.C. 179 between Ocean Isle and Seaside.

For dinner, try **Crabby Oddwaters** ($$) at 310 Sunset Boulevard, thought by many to have the best and freshest seafood in the area—nothing is cooked before you arrive.

Many golfers and beach goers believe no trip is complete without a trek to the little fishing village of **Calabash**. Restaurants line up, one after the other through the town. Your best bet is to arrive before five to avoid standing in line. Fried fish, hushpuppies, cole slaw and French fries are the style here, and you'll have to pay about $1.50 or more extra if you prefer broiled.

Tip: While in Calabash, check out the Christmas Shop adjoined to **Calabash Nautical Gifts** on N.C. 179 for fun and fantasy.

> **For More Information:**
>
> **N.C. Brunswick Islands**
> **P.O. Box 11352**
> **Southport, NC 28461**
> **800-795-7263**

OCEAN ISLE

> **To Get There:**
>
> Travel east on N.C. 179
> and cross over the new
> high-rise bridge.

Ocean Isle stretches for 8 uncrowded miles of clean beach with good boat docks and marinas for those who arrive by water. You'll see shark-shaped kites flying overhead as you bird watch or "bait up" to surf fish.

Things To See and Do

MUSEUM OF COASTAL CAROLINA

The distinctive difference at this beach is the **Ocean Isle Museum of Coastal Carolina** on East 3rd Street. Take a left at the water slide to find the museum. Now, in its 4th year, this nonprofit museum displays a wealth of things to see and experience. You'll find artifacts of Tuscarora and Lumbee Indians as well as reproduced weapons and tools used before recorded time.

If you're curious about the shells you've found or the fish you've caught, you can identify your discoveries at the museum. You'll see native animals such as bobcats, red fox, black bear, etc., in the habitat diorama.

Maybe the best room in the museum is the under sea diorama. Displayed among the varied fish swimming above, below and beside you is the wreckage of a ship that blew ashore at Fort Fisher during Hurricane Hugo. There are also interesting Civil War memorabilia, salvaged from where they lay underwater for over a 100 years, and 24 rifles recovered from the wreckage of the blockade runner, Ranger, that sank off Holden Beach.

Admission for adults is $2, and $1 for children.

FISHING

Many go on a head boat or charter a boat—it's only 35 miles out to the warmer Gulf Stream where you can fight with sailfish and catch red snapper and grouper. Spring and summer are the months when blue fish, drum, summer and small flounder are biting and a good time to go shrimping or clamming. Fall and winter is the time to land large Spanish mackerel, spot, puppy drum, blue fish, gray and speckled trout or Virginia mullet and do some serious oyster harvesting. To find out what is biting, call the North Carolina Marine Fisheries in Wilmington (800-248-4536) or in Morehead City (800-682-2632).

Here, as at all of the South Brunswick beaches, you can scuba dive and deep sea fish or fish from refurbished piers. **Ocean Isle Marina** is a good place to rent boats or bikes—even jet skis. (910-579-0848)

For a lot of fun and a chance at a $50,000 cash prize, head for either the Little River or Southport Municipal Docks, the inlets of Shallotte, or Lockwood Folly for Labor Day weekend when the **King** (Mack-erel) **Classic** fishing tournament is held.

NORTH CAROLINA OYSTER FESTIVAL

In mid-October the annual North Carolina Oyster Festival is held between Sunset Beach and Ocean Isle with a road race at Holden Beach. Test your skills in the oyster shucking contest where you race the clock for time, neatness and precision. In addition to the oyster, flounder and shrimp roast, Country Western and Beach music groups entertain. The area's best storytellers pit their skills in the bull shooting contests, and you can take home a hand-crafted item from one of the festival's 100 exhibitors.

Accommodations and Dining ___

To rent a cottage or condo in Ocean Isle, call **Cooke Realty**. (910-579-3535) For a weekend, try the **Ocean Isle Motel** ($$-$$$, 800-352-5988) or **The Winds Clarion Inn** ($$$, 800-334-3581). For that Calabash taste, try **Riverside at Calabash** ($$) at 103 West Bay Street on Ocean Isle Beach.

For More Information:

N.C. Brunswick Islands
P.O. Box 11352
Southport, NC 28461
800-795-7263

HOLDEN BEACH

> **To Get There:**
> Take N.C. 179 to N.C. 130 south and cross over the high-rise bridge.

Holden is a wooded island beach framed by dogwood, palmetto and live oak trees. This 11-mile-long beach, located between Lockwood Folly and the Shallotte River, was purchased by Benjamin Holden in 1856 and claims a number of "firsts." In 1924, Holden's grandson, John, surveyed a section that he called "Holden Beach Resort," which became the first subdivision of beach property in Brunswick County. He later built the island's first bridge and first hotel.

Many folks come to Holden year after year because it falls into that "off the beaten path" category. Even in high season summer months, you can still find a patch of beach all to yourself.

Things To See and Do

NORTH CAROLINA FESTIVAL BY THE SEA

Each October, Holden Beach hosts the North Carolina Festival By the Sea. A Halloween-type carnival begins the festivities on Friday night of this three-day festival. On Saturday, an arts and crafts event takes place with lots of great seafood and entertainment. A parade, a road race and a street dance celebrate this event. And you can hear the area's best gospel singers on Sunday afternoon.

ESPECIALLY FOR KIDS

While 'tis true Holden has more condos than other barrier island beaches, this has also brought about more activities for youngsters. At the **Super Track Go-Cart Raceway** on Holden Causeway, a water slide and a miniature golf course offer fun alternatives. (910-842-5050) Or, you can combine swimming and horseback riding at **Sea Horse Riding Stables** on Boones Neck Road where you'll find 18 acres of shady riding trails. (910-842-8002)

FISHING AND BOAT TOURS

Several pleasure boats have scenic and ocean cruises available from the **Holden Beach Marina**, located at 3238 Pompano Street, S.W., near the high-rise bridge on N.C. 130. You can charter deep sea fishing boats here, too. (910-842-5447)

Accommodations

To find a rental, call **Craig Realty**. (910-842-2777) The only motel in Holden is the **Gray Gull Motel** ($). (910-842-6775)

OAK ISLAND

To Get There:
To get to Long Beach, Yaupon Beach and Caswell Beach, take N.C. 17 north to N.C. 211 east and N.C. 133 south.

The ambiance of the island is best explained by the bumper sticker that reads: "I wasn't born on Oak Island but I got here as quick as I could." Oak Island sits at the confluence of the Intracoastal Waterway, Atlantic Ocean and Cape Fear River. The island is linked to the mainland by a modern high-level bridge, and includes the communities of Long Beach, Yaupon Beach and Caswell Beach. Like Holden Beach, it also is swathed in live oaks. What you notice first is that nature has not been replaced with neon. This is one of the safe islands where the giant logger-head sea turtles choose to lay their eggs in the warm early summer sands, trusting that islanders will get their baby turtles back out to sea.

Things To See and Do _____

There are many things to do here besides eating, sleeping

Photo by Daintry O'Brien.

Some fun at the beach doesn't cost a dime.

and walking the beach. The obvious activities are soaking rays and fishing or playing golf at **The Oak Island Golf and Country Club** at 928 Caswell Beach Road. (910-278-5275) But Oak Island also offers some unique activities.

ULTRA LITE

At 380 Long Beach Road you'll find something a bit different—**Brunswick County Airport**. (910-457-6483) On the face of it that may not sound too exciting, but you'll change your mind when you find yourself soaring in an ultra lite aircraft. You can take an aerial view tour of the barrier islands or flight instruction.

ESPECIALLY FOR KIDS

On rainy days or at sunset, zip over to the corner of Ocean and Barbie Boulevards in Yaupon to **Flagship Amusement Park**. It's right across from the Yaupon Fishing Pier. Let the kids release some of their pent up energy in a bumper car while you take in an ocean sunset on a boardwalk bench beside the pier.

FISHING

Of course you could join those fishing on the pier ($5 adult, $2.50 children) who are reeling in flounder, Spanish mackerel, trout and blues. The other piers, Long Beach and Ocean Crest also charge $5 for fishing, with reduced children's rates. Of course plenty of folks find sport in raking in clams and oysters, or doing the crabbing and shrimping thing.

HORSE-A-THON

Each year during February or March (check with the Longbeach Volunteer Fire Department at 910-278-1000 for the exact date) you can bring your horse and ride up and down the Oak Island beaches in an all day Horse-a-thon.

FORT CASWELL

At the tip end of Caswell Beach, you'll find Fort Caswell Baptist Assembly Retreat. The fort was built between 1826 and 1836 and named after Richard Caswell, the first governor of North Carolina. The fort was sold to the Baptist Assembly after WWII. On Wednesday mornings at ten, you can go on a guided tour through the ruins of this pre-Civil War fort. The ruins are in quite good condition, and as in other undisturbed forts, you'll be able to see stalactites forming on the ceilings of the underground bunkers. (910-278-9501)

Accommodations ____

For rentals, contact **Scruggs and Morrison Realty** (910-278-5405) or **Shirly**

Fowler & Associates. (800-637-4383)

Dining _____

Jones' Seafood House, at 6404 Oak Island Drive, is not where the tourists usually go (probably because they don't know about it). Just ask any islander and they'll point you to "the best seafood in town."

Another favorite, because you can eat until you pop, is **Lucky Fisherman** at 4419 Long Beach Road, S.E. It has a great salad bar and good country cooking with country style steak and terrific shrimp Creole, too.

If you have a sweet tooth, stop by the **Fudge Factory** on East Oak Island Drive. Its Amaretto Fudge is popular, but other flavors are good, too.

For More Information:

Southport-Oak Island Chamber of Commerce
4841 Long Beach Road SE
Southport, NC 28461
910-457-6964

SOUTHPORT

To Get There:
From U.S. 17, take N.C. 211 southeast or N.C. 87 south to Southport.

Even though this isn't a beach area, Southport, originally called Smithville, is one of those little seaports that people make the mistake of overlooking. Natives describe the location as where, "The pine meets the palm, and the Cape Fear River meets the sea." But what will intrigue you more than pine and palm are the town's live oaks. With their silvery moss hanging low, the live oaks are everywhere, even in the middle of the street. It says something about a town's values when it won't hack down a tree just to make uniform streets.

Before Wilmington's harbor was dredged, Southport was the deepest sea water port in North Carolina. That dredging left Southport sort of frozen in the 18th century. One native says: "There's nothing to do or anything commercial here, but its charm is marketable." That was the reason the movie *Crimes of the Heart* was shot here.

Named as one of the 10 best places to retire in America, Southport has seen an influx of people in the past few years. There is definite appeal for a sleepy fishing village with narrow streets and quaint houses.

Things To See and Do _____

KEZIAH MEMORIAL PARK
Tiny Keziah Memorial

Park at the corner of Moore and Lord streets, is where Native Americans once bent the bark on the gnarled 800-year-old live oak tree to mark their way.

SOUTHPORT MARITIME MUSEUM

Southport's new Maritime Museum at 116 North Howe Street is also worth a quick visit. Open Tuesday through Saturday from 10 p.m. until 4 p.m., the museum features pirates, blockade runners, river pilots, shipwrecks and maritime education. (910-457-0003)

FRANKLIN SQUARE ART GALLERY

Don't miss Franklin Square Art Gallery at East West Street (no, this isn't a typo). This recycled building began life in 1904 as a Masonic Lodge but now houses the pottery and art work of notable artists, many of them natives who teach at the facility. The gallery is open from 10 a.m. until 5 p.m., Tuesday through Sunday. (910-457-5450)

FORT JOHNSTON

Fort Johnston overlooks the bay where you'll see folks with their fishing poles walking along the small beach. The original fort was burned by Whigs in 1775 but rebuilt between 1794 and 1809. Today, only the brick officers' quarters remain.

Accommodations

For rentals, call **Shannon Real Estate**. (910-278-5251) For a short stay, try the **Sea Captain Motor Lodge** ($$). (910-457-5263)

Dining

The Pharmacy Restaurant & Lounge ($-$$) is a good place for lunch or dinner. This former drugstore was an institution for over 75 years before it started serving soft shell crab sandwiches for lunch—along with Pharmacy fries and prime rib sandwiches for the truly hungry. Its located at 110 East Moore Street.

Photo by Dawn O'Brien

Keziah Memorial Park in Southport.

Not as fancy, but if you want to soak up some local flavor, go to **Yacht Basin Provisions Co.** ($$) at the old yacht basin at the end of Bay Street. Here you'll find great burgers for $2.35, but what it does best is conch fritters. You can also get the freshest steamed clams and shrimp here. Get a cup and move outside to waterfront deck dining. No matter how humid or hot it is, it's cool on the deck and you can watch shrimpers and pleasure boats dock

If you tire of the usual seafood fare, **Thai Peppers** ($$) offers a delicious difference that you won't soon forget. It's at 115 East Moore Street.

For More Information:

N.C. Brunswick Islands
P.O. Box 11352
Southport, NC 28461
800-795-7263

Southport-Oak Island Chamber of Commerce
4841 Long Beach Road SE
Southport, NC 28461
910-457-6964

WILMINGTON

To Get There:
Wilmington sits at the East Coast terminus of I-40.

You know that you've come to a city of old world charm when you come upon 5th and Market Streets and find a working old stone fountain in the middle of the street.

By 1850, Wilmington had become the largest city in North Carolina. Impressive buildings rose in the downtown area, such as the old 1892 red brick courthouse at 24 North 3rd Street. Today you're apt to see TV actor Andy Griffith climbing the stairs of this historic building for his *Matlock* film crew. The building is also home to the **Cape Fear Convention and Visitors Bureau** (800-222-4757), which can supply you with tour times, maps and a short comprehensive film on the area.

Across the street on Chestnut stand **City Hall** and **Thalian Hall**. The ornate Thalian Hall opened in 1858 and remains one of the oldest continuously operating performing arts theaters in the state. This often-restored, turn-of-the-century theater is home to a number of theater companies, drawing from local and regional support. So check out what's playing while you're in the area. There's something going on almost every night. (910-763-3398)

Although Wilmington now bustles with its new movie industry, it has retained its good-mannered, southern dignity. Today's traveler would be hard put to find a city as historically attuned, safe and artistically diverse as Wilmington.

Things To
See and Do _____

THE HISTORIC DISTRICT

Wilmington's historic district covers 200 blocks. You can hit the high points, beginning at the flagpole at Market and Water Streets, with Bob Jenkins' insightfully narrated walking tour (910-763-1785), or take a more leisurely approach in a horse and buggy tour around the central historic district. (910-251-8889)

There are two homes that you can tour for a fee. At 224 Market Street is the 1770 Georgian-style home of the colony's treasurer, John Burgwin, which was also General Cornwallis' headquarters prior to his defeat at Yorktown. The ornate, four-story Italianate Revival **Zebulon-Latimer House** at 126 South 3rd Street was constructed in 1852 and looks as if the family is still living there.

Near the waterfront, there is an intricate network of tunnels, many that ran to private homes.

THE RIVERFRONT

Take a stroll through the **Cotton Exchange** across the street from the Hilton Hotel. This two-block area of historic downtown derived its name from the original Cotton Exchange building which once housed Alexander Sprunt and Sons, at one time the largest purchasers and shippers of cotton in the world. It has now been restored and adapted for shops and restaurants which provide neat pickin's for a rainy day or a respite from the beach.

For a look at the city as it was in the 19th century, continue south treading the old cobblestone streets that lead into **Chandler's Wharf** located on the corner of Water and Ann streets with its quaint picket fences and over-spilling flowers. And train buffs won't want to miss the **Railroad Museum** at Red Cross and Water Streets near the Cotton Exchange. (910-763-2634)

CAPE FEAR MUSEUM

For an innovative and entertaining hour, not to mention a thorough grounding in the social history of the lower Cape Fear region, go up Market Street to the Cape Fear Museum at 1814. Though the museum has the oldest collection of history in the state, it is far from a stuffy place. How many museums let you put a quarter in the juke box to dance? Or when was the last time you saw a boxing match at a museum? You'll enjoy the Fort Fisher light and sound diorama that gives you a better idea of the battle than a visit to the site. And the best news is, it's free, but donations are appreciated.

The museum is open Tuesday through Saturday from 9 a.m. until 5 p.m. and Sunday from 2 until 5 p.m. (910-341-7413)

ST. JOHN'S MUSEUM OF ART

A few blocks to the south at 114 Orange Street is the re-

The Cape Fear Museum in Wilmington is entertaining as well as educational.

stored 1804 St. John's Museum of Art and sculpture garden. The museum houses a good collection of Mary Cassatt color drawings, but concentrates on local artists such as Pender County artist Minnie Evans.

The museum is open Tuesday through Saturday from 10 a.m. until 5 p.m. and on Sunday from 12 noon until 4 p.m. (910-763-0281)

BOAT TOURS

To get a different perspective on the area, book reservations for either a day or midnight sight-seeing cruise or a sunset dinner cruise on **Henrietta II**, a replicated steam paddle boat. Its 1818 predecessor ran the river between Wilmington and Fayetteville for 40 years. Board at the Riverwalk across from the parking deck. (800-676-0162)

BATTLESHIP *NORTH CAROLINA*

You can spend two or more hours on the self-guided tour of this 35,000-ton battleship that is a memorial to the men and women who served in World War II. First, the 10-minute orientation film explains the battleship's important role in 57 battles. Climbing through the hatch down into the ship's belly gives a hands-on feel to daily life, and children especially enjoy exploring the crew's quarters and the large guns. But homesick letters of brave 18-year-old boys who handled deadly torpedoes evokes pride and admiration in visitors.

Photo by William Russ. Courtesy N.C. Travel & Tourism.

Battleship North Carolina is permanently berthed on the Cape Fear River at Wilmington.

The battleship is open daily from 8 a.m. until sunset. Admission for the battleship is $6 for adults and $3 for children. To get there from Wilmington, take N.C. 133 across the Cape Fear River and follow the signs. (910-251-5797)

NORTH CAROLINA AZALEA FESTIVAL

Wilmington's big event of the year is the Azalea Festival, held each year in early April. There's a parade and loads of activities, but the big attraction is the garden tour of selected garden throughout the city.

Accommodations____

BED AND BREAKFAST INNS

Front Street Inn ($$-$$$$) located at 215 South Front Street could not be better located for tourists. Owners Stefany and Jay Rhodes have let their decorating imaginations go wild, and the result ranges from beautiful to funky. They have completely transformed this historic building, but retained its beautiful arched windows, thick walls and old maple floors that look like fresh honey. Each bedroom is individually decorated in a different theme. Guests appreciate the Sol y Sombre bar and breakfast room where you get a light continental breakfast. (910-762-6442)

Catherine's Inn ($$-$$$) is located at 410 South Front Street. Here you feel like you've come to visit a beloved relative when you stay at this 1883 home right on the waterfront. Minutes after ringing the bell, you're brought tea or coffee, with fruit and nibbles. Of course, the pantry is open any time you get a hunger pang, which comes in handy if you are traveling with children. A great breakfast is served either in the dining room or on the screened porch. (800-476-0723)

If you want to hobnob with movie stars, that could happen if you stay at the **Graystone Inn** ($$$$) at 100 South Third Street. This beautifully furnished European-style B & B is the former 1906 Bridgers mansion and one of the favored choices of actors who are brought in to work at Carolco. A continental breakfast is served in the formal dining room. (910-763-5555)

HOTELS/MOTELS

Wilmington's premier hotel is the **Hilton** ($$$-$$$$) downtown on the historic waterfront at 301 N. Water Street. (800-662-9338). An economical option in town is **Park Inn International** ($) at 311 N. 3rd Street. (800-437-7275) For a suite with a kitchen, try **The Inn at St. Thomas Court** ($$) at 101 South Second Street. (800-525-0909)

CAMPING

If you're the outdoors type or traveling on a budget, campsites are available in the park adjacent to Snow's Cut. **Carolina Beach Family Campground** ($) at 9641 River Road in Wilmington has hot showers, wooded tent sites and a swimming pool. (910-392-3322)

Dining

For a taste of night life in Wilmington, wander south to the **Ice House** and sit outside and listen to anything from jazz to bluegrass. Don't be surprised to see a stretch limo discharge the likes of Mel Gibson or other Hollywood notables who are in town making films for the Carolco Film Company.

For great authentic German food try **Nuss Strasse Cafe** ($-$$) at the Cotton Exchange. This is where locals go for lunch or dinner.

If you want to try something a bit more upscale, dinner by the river at **Crooks** ($$$) at 138 South Front Street is worth 4 stars. In addition to great food, you can also get a glimpse of history here.

The old **Pilot House** ($$-$$$) is a good place for seafood, and **Elijah's** ($$) is outstanding too. Both restaurants are located at Chandlers Wharf on the riverfront at the corner of Water and Ann streets.

Caffe Phoenix ($$$) is located at 9 South Front Street. This downtown Wilmington restaurant is reminiscent of New York's Greenwich Village in the '30s. It has a bohemian air of intellectualism that suits the decor. Imported coffees, homemade soups, fresh-baked bread and pasta, plus hot dishes for vegetarians are the items not to be missed here.

For More Information:

Cape Fear Convention and Visitors Bureau
24 N. Third St.
Wilmington, NC 28401
(800-222-4757)

AAA Carolinas
Westridge Shopping Center
3613 Oleander Drive
Wilmington, NC 28403
910-763-8446

Side Trips

BALD HEAD ISLAND

To Get There:

Catch the ferry to Bald Head Island at Southport. It runs hourly and costs $15 for a round trip. You'll need to make reservations (910-457-5003) because the ferry fills up fast. To reach the dock, take East Moore Street to the marked turnoff. Park your car in secured parking for $3 or in nearby free parking.

Photo by William Russ. Courtesy N.C. Travel & Tourism.

"Old Baldy" is the oldest standing lighthouse in North Carolina.

In many ways Bald Head Island is a throw back to primitive times. Until a few years ago, there were no telephones or electricity, and guests had to wade ashore to this 12,000-acre island. Today, there is no crime, no traffic and no noise—only the hum of golf carts to break the occasional honk of Canada geese. A trip here can refine your definition of "natural wild" and "pristine beauty."

Ecologically controlled by the Bald Head Island Conservancy, walking isn't allowed on the windswept dunes that form a spine across the island. Even residents must plant only flowers indigenous to the land. A resident describes Bald Head's beaches as: "...a place of wonder...a kind of religious experience." Fisherman also consider the area's Frying Pan Shoals a religious experience—of blessed abundance.

No matter when you visit—for a weekend or longer, Bald Head will not be on the list of inexpensive getaways. That's because of its inaccessibility. You can only get there by a 20-minute boat ride, and cars aren't allowed on the island. Residents and guests use rented golf carts. There are no fast foods, movies, water slides or motels here. The island attracts a rugged group who could probably afford to stay anywhere they want, but who choose the solitude of unshackled nature.

If you're going for a day of golf or checking out the island's beaches, you shouldn't miss the state's oldest standing lighthouse. **Old Baldy** was built in 1817, after the original 1796 lighthouse was built too close to the Cape Fear River. The lighthouse was part of the earthenworks fort built to help safeguard Wilmington during the Civil War.

Do explore the island's 400-year-old maritime forest. If you are there during August, you'll be on hand for the hatching of the loggerhead turtles.

There are a few rentals, so call ahead to the **Bald Head Island Club** if you want to spend the weekend. (800-722-6450) Dining is at the **Bald Head Island Club** ($$$) as well. For a picnic or snack, you'll find a small grocery store, the **River Pilot Cafe** quite handy.

FORT FISHER

To Get There:

From Wilmington, take U.S. 421; or take the ferry from Southport for $3.

In Fort Fisher there's a beautiful cove with once barricaded beaches where the Union Navy played its most important card of the Civil War. Fort Fisher, a Confederate-controlled, earthenworks fortification, was the major link that defended Wilmington. The Fort kept Federal blockade ships at a distance from the Cape Fear River, allowing the Confederate blockade runners to supply provisions to General Lee's army. These ships came from Nova Scotia, Bermuda and the Bahamas where the British traded clothing and munitions for cotton. When the fort finally fell during the second bombardment of land and sea assaults on January 15, 1865, Wilmington followed shortly thereafter. That defeat cut the supply line to the Confederacy, and sped the Union victory.

Much of the original beach has been eroded, but you can visit the museum (free) and see displays of items from blockade-running ships, plus an informative audiovisual presentation and other interpretive exhibits. There is a gift shop as well. The area is now the state headquarters for underwater archaeology, but you can tour the area's remaining original mounds. You'll enjoy walking through the live oak trees just beyond the beach where you will find ideal picnic spots.

Just north of the fort is the **North Carolina Aquarium at Fort Fisher**,

one of three nationally accredited North Carolina aquariums. This is a busy, program-packed museum that promotes an appreciation of the state's aquatic environments. It has touch tanks that let children stroke living sea stars, and hermit and horseshoe crabs. An interesting exhibit called "Shadows of the Sand" features stingrays and skates that you can go nose to nose with through a 13-foot acrylic viewing panel. You can do the same at the shark and large game fish tank. And, don't miss the sea horse exhibit, the fresh water ponds and the sea turtle exhibit.

For a different slant to your beach getaway, sign up for one of the educational programs at the aquarium. Environmental coastal programs have instituted a committed resolve to protect the mysterious life of the loggerhead turtle with field trip classes; find out about the alligators in North Carolina (which are all over the place); discover just which are the edible marine life in culinary workshops; do a hands-on sand castle class; venture out to sea on board collecting trips; explore the world of marsh birds, wildflowers, etc. The list goes on.

The aquarium, on U.S. 421, is open from 9 a.m. to 5 p.m. Monday through Saturday and from 1 until 5 p.m. on Sunday. It's closed on Thanksgiving, Christmas and New Year's Day. Admission is $3 for adults; $2 for senior citizens and active military personnel and $1 for children ages 6 to 17. (910-458-8257)

PLEASURE ISLAND BEACHES

To Get There:
To reach Kure Beach, Wilmington Beach and Carolina Beach, take U.S. 421 south from Wilmington or take the Fort Fisher toll ferry and go north on U.S. 421.

If education on any level is what you're trying to escape, the beaches in this area offer fun for the entire family. You'll be hard pressed to know when you travel from **Carolina Beach** to **Wilmington Beach** as the two naturally flow together. Stop at the amusement park or build up your courage to try more daring rides at the Boardwalk.

Sports enthusiasts can tackle deep sea fishing, and everyone needs to include a stop at **Carolina Beach State Park,** just north of Carolina Beach, where you may glimpse the Venus Fly Trap in this small region of the world where it grows naturally.

Kure, a not-so-wide, but surprisingly uncrowded beach, is a pleasant place to try your hand at surf fishing, fishing from the Kure Pier (in the center of town) or just swimming and sunning.

ORTON PLANTATION

To Get There:
Take N.C. 133 south from Wilmington.

Orton Plantation is one of North Carolina's best-known Southern plantations. It rivals those in neighboring Virginia and the intricate, white lattice-like patterned bridge that juts out into the former rice fields on the Cape Fear River is reminiscent of Charleston's Middleton Plantation. The Greek Revival home and gardens of this 18th-century rice plantation remain as a window into the past. The garden's walking paths swirl and curl in a paisley-like design through acres of azaleas and camellias. Obviously, the optimum time to visit this fairy tale setting is spring.

Largely due to the home's authenticity, location scouts chose Wilmington for the filming of the movie *Firestarter* a few years ago. A replica of the antebellum house was burned for the movie. This helped establish Wilmington's burgeoning movie industry and persuaded Dino de Laurentis to locate his studio (now owned by Carolco) here.

Photo by Dawn O'Brien.

Like Kure Beach, many of North Carolina's beaches are uncrowded and perfect for family fun.

You can visit the gardens and the plantation's quaint chapel, and even get married there, but the private home is not open to the public. Admission for adults is $7 and for children from 6 to 11 years, $3.50.

BRUNSWICK TOWN

To Get There:
Cross the Cape Fear Bridge on N.C. 133 south from Wilmington and follow roadside directions.

It wasn't until the 1730s, calling itself New Carthage, that Wilmington developed as a commercial rival to the 1725 Brunswick Town. This town already had permanent settlements on the west bank of the Cape Fear River. Elaborate plantations in Brunswick Town became the homes of two North Carolina governors, but were burned, along with the town, by the British in 1776. The Visitors Center provides a (free) film on pre-Revolutionary as well as Civil War life here, and a tour of the ruins is a must for history buffs. A historical footnote: in 1842 the owner of Orton Plantation purchased the entire town of Brunswick for $4.25!

WRIGHTSVILLE BEACH

To Get There:
From Wilmington, follow U.S. 74/76 across the drawbridge.

Unpack the kid's sand pails and inflatable monsters, grab that slightly trashy "beach book," and park your brain for awhile. If you're on a getaway weekend, you may not feel like venturing off the beach. But, if you've overdosed on sun fun, the time may be ripe to try something more adventurous.

Things To See and Do _____

FISHING

You can sign up for wreck and reef diving with **Captain Chris Klingenberger** (910-350-0039), or explore the coast on your own with his boat rental service off Towles Road. You can go out for deep sea fishing with **"Sea Lady" Charters** and reel in a marlin or sailfish. (800-242-2493)

GOLF

If golf is your game, there are plenty of nearby courses from which to choose, including the public course **The Cape** on N.C. 421 south. (910-799-3110) **Porter's Neck**, just minutes from Wrightsville Beach is an 18-hole championship course designed by Tom Fazio. It's at 1202 Porters Neck Road. (800-423-5695)

5658) covers the Intracoastal Waterway beaches, or try **Cabana Del Mar Oceanfront** (800-333-8499) or check with **Walker Realty** (910-458-3388).

Accommodations

RESORTS

One popular choice at Wrightsville Beach is **Shell Island Resort** ($$$$) at the end of Lumina Ave. This all-suite hotel offers miles of picturesque and, because of its secluded location, private beach . In cooler months you can take advantage of its indoor pool. (800-522-8575 or 800-689-6765)

The **Blockade Runner Resort Hotel and Conference Center** ($$$$) at 275 Waynick Boulevard in Wrightsville Beach is truly elegant with oceanfront dining and entertainment. The amenities are plentiful, but it is the wide beach that lures travelers who like nothing more challenging than long evening walks watching the sun take a gentle nose dive. (800-541-1161)

CONDOMINIUMS AND COTTAGES

If you want to rent a cottage or condo at the beach, **Coastal Condo-lets** (910-458-

Dining

For dining at the beach, natives consider **The Oceanic Restaurant & Grill** ($$-$$$) located at 703 South Lumina Avenue on the ocean at Wrightsville the premier restaurant for good fresh seafood. As a bonus, from the upstairs you have a panoramic view of the ocean. The seafood platter is the best way to go with a slice of wonderful cheesecake thrown in for dessert.

There's no shortage of fast-food restaurants on any of the beaches, but with shrimp and fishing boats lining the docks offering fresh shrimp, oysters, Atlantic blue crab and king mackerel, it's hard to imagine dining on a Big Mac.

For More Information:

Cape Fear Convention and Visitors Bureau
24 N. Third St.
Wilmington, NC 28401
(800-222-4757)

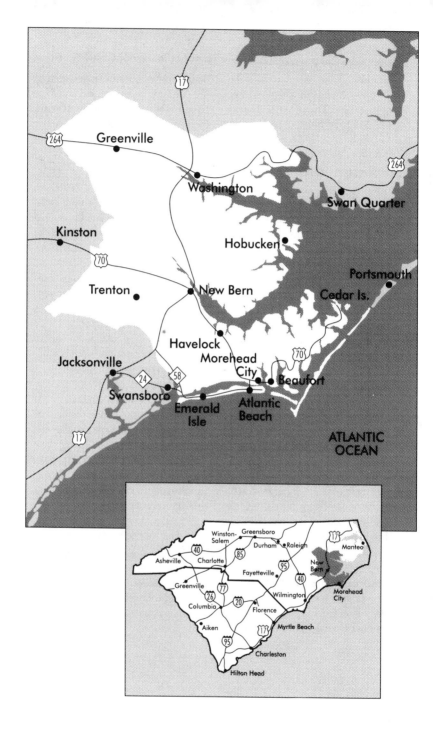

CRYSTAL COAST

The name "The Crystal Coast" was coined within the last 15 years to describe the area around Beaufort, Morehead City and the beaches of Bogue Banks. Today, the area is unified by a convention center in Morehead City, a Crystal Coast Tourism Development Board and a new awareness of the diversity of the area, part of what makes the Crystal Coast such a great place to vacation.

The Neuse River empties into the Pamlico Sound at Beaufort. Winding your way up the river for 50 miles will bring you to the historic town of New Bern, home of the Tryon Palace.

BOGUE BANKS

To Get There:
Go south on N.C. 58.

As you cross the high-rise bridge onto Bogue Banks, you'll get a spectacular view of the ocean intercutting the sandy shores. The Banks is a 30-mile narrow island that stretches from the towns of Emerald Isle to Atlantic Beach with Indian Beach/Salter Path and Pine Knoll Shores sandwiched in between. From the topography you won't know when you leave one beach for the next. Frequent public access points that include showers are on the drawing board.

Bogue Banks comes nearer to unspoiled beaches

than any you'll find in North Carolina, with the possible exception of Bald Head and Ocracoke on the Outer Banks. And we're talking high season—mid-July. When you wade out and see your toes staring up at you through that blue-green water, you know why this is called the Crystal Coast.

Emerald Isle

Originally part of the Theodore Roosevelt estate, this land was sold in 1954 for $50 per acre to four North Carolina businessmen. Emerald Isle is a planned development, originally subdivided by drawing lots from a hat. To ensure that the beach remained easily accessible, each original deed contained a restriction requiring a public access every 1100 feet.

In the beginning, the main road down the Island stopped at Salter Path, but in 1955 it was extended to the fishing pier at Emerald Isle•and later to the ferry landing at the end of the island. The ferry has now been replaced by a high-rise bridge.

A family beach, Emerald Isle got its name from the brilliant green color of the ocean water. This unusual effect is due to a sand bar just off the beach that causes the water to turn from emerald green to a deep azure blue.

Indian Beach/ Salter Path

If you didn't see the sign, you wouldn't know that you'd arrived in Indian Beach/Salter Path. This area is somewhat confusing because Indian Beach surrounds Salter Path. Today, it is both a residential and vacation spot for those who enjoy swimming, surf and pier fishing. It was first settled by staunch pioneers who arrived in 1893 bringing their homes with them on a barge. They had decided to leave Diamond City on Shackleford Banks after weathering harsh storms. Those first families gave a different flavor to this beach area, and would most certainly be amazed at the condos and camp sites that have sprung up here in the past 25 years.

Pine Knoll Shores

This beach area was a planned community by Theodore Roosevelt's heirs and is considered the most ecologically sensitive town in the state. If you're coming for beach fun, this long uncluttered public beach is plenty inviting.

Atlantic Beach

Atlantic Beach, long a favorite beach for repeat visitors, is at the eastern tip of the is-

The North Carolina Aquarium at Pine Knolls shore is one of three nationally accredited state aquariums along the coast.

land. In 1887 shy bathers sailed across the sound from the Atlantic Hotel at Morehead City and walked across the island to the beach. Since that time, travel has been made easier by several bridges that span the sound.

Atlantic Beach is probably the most action-oriented of the Bogue Beaches. **The Circle**, originally the site of its first arcade, is now a central stop to find out what is going on. You'll find some amusement park rides, a terrific volleyball court and a number of night clubs that provide live music and a place to dance.

Things To See and Do

NORTH CAROLINA AQUARIUM AT PINE KNOLL SHORES

This aquarium is one of three nationally accredited state aquariums along the North Carolina coast. You'll learn that yes, we do have alligators in North Carolina. They are found in wetland areas as well as in the White Oak River near

Swansboro. Children will like the Close Encounters Exhibit where they can swish their fingers through the water to tickle crabs and other interesting petable creatures. The aquarium has detailed exhibits of loggerhead turtle hatchlings emerging from their sandy nests, but the most fascinating exhibit is the Living Shipwreck, viewed from below sea level.

The aquarium is located five miles west of Atlantic Beach on N.C. 58 in the Theodore Roosevelt Natural Area. It is open Monday through Saturday from 9 a.m. until 5 p.m. and Sunday from 1 until 5 p.m. The aquarium is closed on Thanksgiving, Christmas and New Year's Day. Admission for adults is $3, for senior citizens and active military personnel, $2, and for children 6 to 17 years of age, $1.

EMERALD ISLE MUSIC FESTIVAL

Two days each May, Emerald Isle is invaded by beach music lovers from all over the Carolinas and the surrounding states. What began as a small, local festival has turned into one of the major annual events on the North Carolina coast.

FORT MACON

One of the most interesting sites to visit here is Fort Macon at the eastern of Bogue Banks. Plundering by the likes

Photo by Bill Russ. Courtesy N.C. Travel & Tourism.

Fort Macon stood guard over Beaufort Inlet
during the Civil War and World War II.

of Blackbeard and other pirates who passed through and raided Beaufort, and from both the British and Spanish convinced North Carolinians that some sort of fortification was needed for protection. Two forts, Dobbs and Hampton were built on this site and washed away by the sea before Fort Macon was completed in 1834. In 1861, at the outbreak of the Civil War, the fort was seized by the Confederacy and armed with 54 cannons, a couple of which you can still see in place on the upper bridge. The fort was purchased by the state and restored in 1936 as a state park.

Fort Macon is the most visited state park in North Carolina with over a million visitors each year. You can fish from the rock jetties, swim at the public beach or enjoy your lunch in the picnic areas. All facilities are handicapped accessible. The park opens daily at 8 a.m. and closes at sunset. The fort is open from 9 a.m. until 5:30 p.m. (919-726-3775)

WORTHY IS THE LAMB

The Passion Play, Worthy *Is The Lamb*, is a powerful musical drama about the life of Christ. The play is performed in the Crystal Coast Amphitheatre where the natural outdoor beauty of the White Oak River provides a spectacular setting for the lifelike replica of the city of Jerusalem. State-of-the-art technology in computer-coordinated sound, lighting and special effects provides outstanding quality for every performance. The play runs from June through September. Call for performance schedule and reservations. (800-662-5960)

GOLF

If golf is your game, some of the better courses are **Brandywine Bay**, accessed by N.C. 24 or U.S. 70 just west of Morehead City (919-247-2541), **Star Hill Golf & Country Club**, located between N.C. 24 and N.C. 58 in Cape Carteret (919-393-8111) and **Bogue Banks Country Club** at 152 Oakleaf Drive in Pine Knoll Shores. (919-726-1034)

ESPECIALLY FOR KIDS

The **Golfin' Dolphin** on N.C. 58 at Cape Carteret has acres of family fun, including 18 holes of miniature golf, a driving range and baseball and softball batting range. (919-393-8131) **Jungleland** is a large amusement park with miniature golf, bumper boats, rides and an arcade. It's located across from the Sheraton on Salter Path Road in Atlantic Beach. (919-247-2148)

Accommodations

CONDOMINIUMS AND COTTAGES

For a list of vacation rentals, call **Emerald Isle Realty** (919-354-3315), **Realty World Clark Realty** (800-722-3006) or **Look Realty** (800-826-6226), all in Emerald Isle. There are a number of condos (2-3-4 bedrooms) for weekly rentals. One is **The Genesis** ($$$-$$$$), located just across from the state aquarium. It has some units on the ocean. (919-247-0388) There are scores of accommodations on Atlantic Beach from week-

end rentals to longer. Try **Alan Shelor Rentals**. (800-786-7368)

HOTELS AND MOTELS

The **Sheraton Resort & Conference Center** on Salter Path Road in Pine Knoll Shores ($$$-$$$$) offers refrigerators, microwaves and some Jacuzzis. (919-240-1155) The **Iron Steamer Oceanfront Family Resort** ($$), also on Salter Path Road, has oceanfront rooms and at low tide, parts of the *Prevensey*, the Civil War blockade runner, can be seen from the pier. (800-332-4221) The **William-Garland Motel** in Salter Path ($) is a clean, no-frills motel with efficiencies and access to the ocean by a lovely nature trail. It also has access to the 20-acre Salter Path Natural Area. (919-247-3733)

The **Islander Motor Inn** ($$-$$$, 919-354-3464) located by but not on the ocean in Emerald Isle, the **Sandra Dee Motel** ($$, 919-354-2755), which faces the ocean and Bogue Inlet Fishing Pier, and the **Holiday Inn** at Atlantic Beach ($$$, 800-726-6570), also on the ocean, are good choices.

The **Show Boat Motel** ($-$$, 919-726-6163) in Atlantic Beach overlooks Bogue Sound, and guests can fish from the motel wharf, rent jet skis and waverunners on-site or board the custom dive boat for a day off shore. All rooms have refrigerators. Also in Atlantic Beach, the **Oceana Family Resort Motel and Fishing Pier** ($$, 919-726-4111) has oceanfront rooms with refrigerators and is near Fort Macon, fishing and the beach. The **John Yancey Motor Hotel** ($$-$$$, 800-682-3700) is located on Salter Path Road. You can have an oceanfront room with a balcony or an efficiency that has a small kitchen .

CAMPING

The **Salter Path Family Campground** ($, 919-247-3525) offers camping on the ocean or the sound and has clam rakes available. The **Beachfront RV Park** ($, 919-354-6400) is on the ocean beside Bogue Inlet Fishing Pier or try **Holiday Trav-L-Park** ($, 919-354-2250) also on the ocean.

Dining

There are a number of excellent seafood restaurants in the Bogue Banks area, but one favorite is **Rucker John's** ($$) at 140 Fairview Drive in Emerald Isle. It offers a bit of everything, including seafood and pasta, but the fried calamari and alligator are really popular.

The **Big Oak Drive-In** ($) beside the William-Garland Motel in Salter Path has perfected the shrimp burger. And if oceanfront dining is what you're looking for, you can literally hang over the water while you swill down steamed clams at the **Crab Shack** ($$) off Salter Path Road. Also in Salter Path, the **Palms Restaurant** in the Holiday Inn is always a good choice and the **Clamdigger Restaurant** at the Ramada Inn is a tasty suggestion for breakfast, lunch or dinner.

Across from the Oceanana is **Man Chun House Restaurant ($$)** just in case you'd like to try the best Chinese food on the island. There's also the **New York Deli** ($) for a great New York Cheesesteak, big fat sandwiches or deli meats that you can take home. And it isn't too far to Morehead City and the legendary **Sanitary Restaurant** that's been here since 1938. Seafood is served (any way you like it) to its 600 guests who come back every year to this not fancy, but wholesome restaurant on the waterfront.

For More Information:

Carteret County Tourism Development Bureau
P.O. Box 1406
Morehead City, NC 28557
800-SUNNYNC

BEAUFORT

> **To Get There:**
> Beaufort is north of Morehead city on U.S. 70 east.

Beaufort, originally called Fishtown, still has that easy old-fashioned charm of the early 18th century although, admittedly, some modernization snaps at its water's edge. There are over 100 historic homes here, some dating as early as 1698.

The homes, constructed with pegs instead of nails, are set back a bit from tree-shaded streets and white picket fences as if awaiting the return of the seafaring men who built them. Many were designed with a widow's walk on the roof. You'll see Greek Revival, gable-hip roofs designed to withstand hurricanes, and a two-story style porch brought over from the Bahamas—not for its attractive design, but for access to cool southern breezes. Most of these ancient homes have passed to succeeding generations. Just think—no mortgage.

You can spend a day—or a week—exploring Beaufort's past, or just sit by the docks waving to fishing and pleasure boats as you watch the changing colors of the sky reflected on the water. Beaufort has the feel of a village where you can ride your bike or roller skate past the waterfront just at the time when the flag is lowered each day at sunset.

Things To See and Do

HISTORICAL HOME TOUR

The **Historical Society** at 305 Turner Street gives a daily tour of a number of homes for $5 (a good deal). This interesting, 50-minute guided tour on a 1936 double-decker English bus points out different architectural styles and where this or that house was moved from (apparently they moved houses in Beaufort as often as you might move your furniture). (919-728-5225)

OLD BURYING GROUND

The 1709 Old Burying Ground on Ann Street comes complete with twisting live oaks which cast eerie shadows over famous and interesting graves. You needn't have a penchant for the macabre to visit this fascinating cemetery. The Historical Society will supply you with a guided map of such notable graves as the British soldier who, not wanting to be buried "with his boots off," was buried standing up facing England. Another is the little girl buried in a barrel of rum because her aggrieved father couldn't bear the thought of burying her at sea.

The Beaufort waterfront at sunset.

CARROT ISLAND

Gazing across Taylor's Creek, you'll see the Rachel Carson Component of the North Carolina Estuarine Research Reserve known locally as Carrot Island. Some 40 feral ponies were taken to the island a hundred years ago and their offspring are the only residents on its uncluttered beaches. You can spend a day swimming, fishing, bird watching, shell collecting, oystering or surfing. Accessible only by boat, a round trip ferry ride is $8 and leaves from the dock at the south end of Orange Street at 10 a.m. and 1 p.m. daily except during winter months. (919-728-7036)

Beaufort's historic Old Burying Ground.

NORTH CAROLINA MARITIME MUSEUM

To find out how this active little fishing village thrived through the years, a visit to the free Maritime Museum on Front Street is informative. This museum has an outstanding international shell collection as well as interesting maritime navigational equipment and rescue equipment that saved many sailors and ships from the "Graveyard of the Atlantic." Here you will find the story of the whaling industry and America's most important industrial fishery—the tiny menhaden fish. The museum strongly stresses that estuaries are a sensitive environment along the coast of North Carolina and are of great ecological value to all of us. (919-728-7317)

CAPE LOOKOUT NATIONAL SEASHORE

If you really want to get close to nature, camping on Cape Lookout National Seashore may be for you. The only cost will be the round-trip ferry fare. **Cape Lookout Tours** (919-728-3491) offers ferry service and beach transportation, and leaves from Morehead City. **Good Fortune** (919-728-7936) offers ferry service and education in coastal ecology, etc., and leaves from the Beaufort waterfront. There is also ferry service from Atlantic Beach. (919-225-4261)

There are no developed campsites and you'll need to bring everything with you, including water and insect repellent because the mosquitoes can be fierce. It's one of the last natural preserves where the only light will be from the light house, the only sound—lapping water against the unspoiled beach. There are a few rustic cabin rentals at North Core Banks on Portsmouth Island.

Accommodations

You won't have any trouble unwinding at the **Inlet Inn Bed & Breakfast** ($$$), located right across from the waterfront with a view of Carrot Island. From your large, attractively appointed bedroom, you can hear the occasional whiny of a pony at night if you leave the French doors open to the balcony. In the fall you can sit by a roaring fire and watch the river boat and people traffic. The inn is located at the corner of Front and Queen streets. (919-728-3600).

If you want to stay in one of Beaufort's restored B & Bs, try **The Cedar's Inn** ($$$-$$$$), circa 1855, at 305 Front Street. (919-728-7036)

The Pecan Tree Inn ($$-$$$$), 116 Queen Street, is a superbly restored Victorian B & B where the owners care about history and good breakfasts. (919-728-6733)

Photo courtesy The Pecan Tree Inn.

The Pecan Tree Inn, one of Beaufort's restored B & Bs.

Dining _____

The atmosphere in **Clawson's 1905 Restaurant** ($$) at 429 Front Street is just what you would expect it to be. Located in the old Clawson's General Store, it's decorated with antiques and wares of the early 1900s. The food, on the other hand, will exceed your expectations. Great lunch selections include overstuffed sandwiches and burgers. You'll find something on the dinner menu to suit any mood, but if you've had your fill of seafood, ribs are the specialty here.

Next door to **The Cedar's Inn** ($$$) on Front Street is its charming restaurant. Located in a restored 1768 home, the owners serve gourmet dinners that are unforgettable.

A good tip for lunch or dinner is the **Beaufort Grocery Co.** ($$-$$$), catty-cornered to the Inlet Inn at 117 Queen Street. The old Owen's Grocery Store was rehabilitated into a wonderfully romantic restaurant with a varied menu. If you like salmon, try the salmon steak served with a dill sauce.

Many visitors enjoy the **Net House Steam & Oyster Bar** ($$-$$$) at 133 Turner Street for its superb steamed seafood and raw oyster bar.

In the evening, you can catch the last rays of the day as you have a drink on the upstairs balcony of the **Dock House** ($) overlooking the water at 500 Front Street.

For More Information:

Carteret County Tourism Development Bureau
P.O. Box 1406
Morehead City, NC 28557
800-SUNNYNC

NEW BERN

To Get There:
New Bern is located at the junction of U.S. 70 East/West and U.S. 17 North/South.

Ideally juxtaposed between the sea and Croatan National Forest makes this historic little town of lacy crape myrtle trees appealing to both history buffs and rugged naturalists. At one time the 157,000-acre forest was home to Tuscarora Native Americans who used the it for hunting and fishing. Today, you can take nature trails through tall pines and ancient hardwoods for an upclose examination of forest life. You may be lucky enough to see a deer or alligator, but bears are seldom visible.

The town of New Bern sits at the confluence of the Neuse and Trent Rivers, which is now known as Union Point Park, and where most of the waterfront activity buzzes. It was New Bern's linkage to the Pamlico Sound and the Atlantic Ocean that made this another ideal shipping port for the sought-after naval stores (tar, pitch and turpentine from the loblolly pine) to Europe, the West Indies and up the coast.

The town was founded in 1710 and named for Baron Christopher DeGraffenried's home of Bern, Switzerland. It became the first colonial capital of North Carolina.

Things To See and Do _____

TRYON PALACE HISTORIC SITES AND GARDENS

Royal Governor William Tryon built his residence/government capitol offices, which took on more the appearance of a palace than a modest government home with offices. The palace burned in 1798, only 28 years after its completion, but was completely rebuilt from architect John Hawks' blueprints. It has been refurbished to its former splendor with a crystal chandelier, a spinet piano like the one Margaret Tryon used to entertain and furnishings authentic to the period.

You can take a guided tour with costumed hosts (admission charged) daily throughout the year. In spring, the formal English gardens are abloom with tulips. During the summer months, historical drama tours are conducted. Actors portray Governor Tryon, cabinet members, his wife and their servants talking about the everyday happenings in the 1700s. There are also daily craft demonstrations. All of these give you a better feel for those early years.

The restoration includes the Tryon Palace, the John Wright Stanly House (another handsome house thought to have been designed by Hawks as well), the Dixon-Stevenson House that was occupied by Union troops during the Civil War and the New Bern Academy, now a museum, that portrays the town's history and role in the Civil War.

The Tryon Palace is located at Pollock and George streets. It is open year-round from 9:30 a.m. to 4:30 p.m. weekdays and from 1:30 to 4 p.m. on Sundays. For a tour of the palace, gardens and Academy Museum, admission is $8 for adults and $4 for children. A combination ticket that includes the Stanly House and the Dixon-Stevenson House is $12 for adults and $6 for children. (919-638-1560)

THE BELLE OF NEW BERN

For a different type of tour, make reservations for the Belle of New Bern's historical cruise. A clever audio presentation with Disney quality describes Eastern North Carolina history in rich detail in its "Tales of Two Rivers." You'll travel from 1710 to the present on this fun cruise. Another option is the dinner cruise offered Thursday, Friday and Saturday.

The Belle of New Bern, an authentic 125-foot paddlewheel riverboat, docks at the Sheraton-New Bern Marina. The historical cruise is Tuesday through Sunday and departs at 1 p.m. Adult fare is $7.95 plus tax and $.95 plus tax for children under 12. The dinner cruise boards at 6:30 p.m. and costs from $29.50 to $31.50 plus tax and gratuity. (919-638-8800)

Accommodations

BED AND BREAKFAST INNS

King's Arms Inn ($$$) at 212 Pollock Street, built in 1847 as a tavern, once hosted members of the First Continental Congress. One of the nicest things about staying here is being served breakfast in bed with the morning paper. Each room, with private bath, is decorated with antiques and good quality reproductions. (800-872-9306)

When you enter the parlor of **The Aerie** ($$$), the old player piano is the first thing you notice, and it takes you back a few years to a gentler time. Bedrooms are attractively decorated with comfortable amenities that travelers have grown to enjoy. Don't skip breakfast because a delicious full meal is served. The Aerie is located at 509 Pollock Street. (800-849-5553)

Harmony House ($$$) is located at 215 Pollock Street. Although you may have come to New Bern to sight-see, the rocking chairs and swing on the front porch of this Greek revival inn

The Tryon Palace was North Carolina's first State Capitol.

The Tryon Palace Gardens.

could induce you to linger here for a spell. The rooms, with private baths, are comfortable and a full breakfast is served each morning in the lovely dining room. (919-636-3810)

HOTELS AND MOTELS

The **Sheraton New Bern** ($$-$$$) at 1 Bicentennial Park has attractive rooms and a knockout view. Its central location makes it within walking distance of the marina, shops and Tryon Palace and Gardens. (800-325-3535)

The **Ziegler Motel** ($) at 1914 Trent Boulevard is a small, older motel set among azaleas and dogwoods in a residential community. (919-637-4498)

CAMPING

There are two rustic campsites for an economical stay in the area. The **Yogi Bear Jellystone Park** on N.C. 17 north is located on the Neuse River. (919-638-2556) **Fisher's Landing** on N.C. 70 east in Riverdale is the more rustic, but affords you the opportunity to walk along the crescent-shaped beach and do some special communing with wildlife. (919-638-5628)

Dining _____

Next door to King's Arms Inn at 216 Pollock Street is the 1799 **Henderson House Res-taurant** ($$$) open for lunch or dinner. The food and history of this beautifully restored award-winning restaurant tie in excellence. The home has ghosts and a secret floor where British loyalists are suspected to have hidden when the colonists got the upper hand. The home was later requisitioned by the Union Army during the Civil War. Try Chef Weaver's seafood casserole or carpetbagger steak.

Located at the back of an old cottage, the **Bagel Cottage** ($) at 712 Pollack Street is another that combines unique food in an old fashioned setting. You can sit inside or outside at a table that overlooks Tryon Palace Cutting Gardens. Bagel lovers appreciate the daily baked variety of bagels with great soups and salads.

The **Harvey Mansion** ($$-$$$), circa 1791, at 221 Tryon Palace Drive was the home and offices of John Harvey. The commanding old home on the Trent River is a romantic place for an elegant dinner of Scallops a la Menthe or Flounder Captain Harvey, deliciously prepared by Chef Beat Zutter of Bern, Switzerland.

For More Information:
Craven County Convention &
Visitors Bureau
P.O. Box 1413
New Bern, NC 28563
800-437-5767

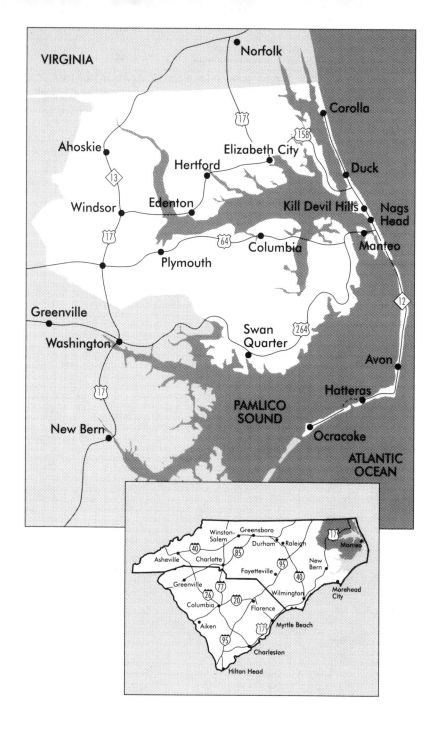

NORTH CAROLINA'S

Outer Banks

SOUTHERN BANKS

OCRACOKE

To Get There:

To reach Ocracoke from the mainland, you must take a toll ferry from either Cedar Island (919-225-3551) or Swan Quarter (919-926-1111). Reservations are strongly advised. From the north, take the free ferry from Hatteras Island.

Ocracoke was explored by two men. Giovanni Verrazano mapped the coasts in 1524 and, later in 1585, Richard Grenville explored the Banks areas but decided they were too harsh and set up colonies inland. Still, rugged English settlers fanned out onto the Banks, finding Ocracoke's then deeper inlet an attractive port for large ships.

Problems arose in the 1700s when pirates also found the inlet attractive. The notorious Black Beard, a.k.a. Edward Teach, was able to terrorize the Banks because it is said that he bought off North Carolina's Governor Eden. Do politics ever change? Resourceful islanders got help from Virginia's Governor Spotswood who sent the Royal Navy to Ocracoke Inlet in 1718 . The navy beat the socks off Black Beard's crew in hand-to-hand combat, severing the pirate's head and hanging it "from the rigging for the trip back..."

The port aided General George Washington during the Revolutionary War, supplying his army through Ocracoke while keeping the patrolling British confused. WWII was a different story. A naval base was set up on Ocracoke in 1942 and Islanders watched German U-boats burn cargo. Dead bodies drifted ashore, not an uncommon sight to natives who, through the centuries, had organized life saving brigades to rescue those who ran aground in the "Graveyard of the Atlantic."

Ocracoke was settled by a small group of English families whose progeny continue to maintain the backbone of the island. Until a few years ago, the natives retained their old English dialect. Progress has unfortunately changed their accent, though not their individuality. They are courteous, if somewhat distant.

A place without movies, fast-foods or crime, "Ocracoke draws a different breed of people, different even from those who choose the northern Outer Banks." As our native hotelier explained, "People who come here either love it or hate it. You'll either never see them again or you'll see them every year." Most folks enjoy walking around the shops and beaches, just soaking up atmosphere at a leisurely pace. As you might imagine Ocracoke has a strong draw for artists, sculptors and photographers.

Things To See and Do

TOURS

To get your bearings, take a short walking tour around the island. Park your car at the lot opposite the **Visitors Center** (919-928-4531), turn left from the parking lot and walk down N.C. 12, along the shores of the lake. You'll pass quaint village shops and a few of the newer motels, but angle off left onto Howard Street, opposite the post office. These homes will give you a flavor of early Ocracoke.

Turn left onto School Street to see the Methodist Church and public school. The cross on the church's altar was carved from a wooden spar from the American freighter, *Caribsea*, sunk offshore by German U-boats in 1942. Turn west and pass the Island Inn where you'll see the beautiful lighthouse, built in 1825, that still guides mariners. Come back to the Methodist Church and head north around the school to the paved road. Turn right after a third of a mile (at the stop sign) and go to the British Cemetery which is shaded by live oak and yaupon trees.

FISHING

Some of the country's best fishing is on or offshore—it's only 30 miles to the Gulf Stream. At **O'Neal's Dockside** (919-928-1111) you can book deep sea fishing charters. Optimum fishing seasons are spring and fall, but after August's full moon the catches increase. Still, you can expect to land both the blue and white marlin plus sailfish all summer long, and dolphin (fish) and wahoo can make a strong showing in the warmer months as well.

WIND SURFING AND KAYAKING

For the super-skilled, wind surfing is ideal when the waves cooperate. When the waves don't cooperate, it's a good time to sea kayak along the Pamlico Sound-side. You can rent kayaks, take lessons and take a guided tour at **Ocracoke Outdoors** (919-928-4061) or **Ride The Wind Surf Shop** (919-928-6311). Paddle through the tidal edge for a closer view of waterfowl and seaside wildlife. If either you or your wallet aren't up for those adventures, it costs nothing on this near-desolate beach to swim, play volleyball or surf fish.

HORSEBACK RIDING

If you want to spend a day or evening horseback riding, call the **Seaside Stables**. (919-928-3778)

Wind Surfing on the Outer Banks.

Photo by William Russ. Courtesy N.C. Travel & Tourism.

PONY PENS

At sometime before records were kept, a ship wrecked on one of the island's ever shifting sand bars, and a herd of cranky-dispositioned Spanish ponies swam to shore. The herd ran wild through the island until civilization impinged. Today, the ponies are penned by the Park Service, about six miles southwest of the Hatteras Ocracoke Ferry landing.

Accommodations___

BED AND BREAKFAST INNS

Oskar's House ($-$$) built by Ocracoke's lighthouse keeper, is a unique 1940's B & B with original beaded board walls and shared bathrooms. Full breakfasts honoring vegetarian or macrobiotic meals are available when requested. (919-928-1311)

Ship's Timbers ($), an over 75-year-old B & B was built from the *Ida Lawrence* ship, which washed up on the beach in 1902. It has lots of personality, shared bathrooms and light breakfasts. Kayakers, wind surfers and sailors will have much in common with owner Erik Mattsson. (919-928-4061)

CONDOMINIUMS AND COTTAGES

For beach cottage rentals, call **Ocracoke Island Realty** (919-928-6261) or **Sharon

Miller Realty (919-928-5711 or 5731).

HOTELS/MOTELS

Boyette House ($-$$) is a folksy motel that has the feel of a B & B. It's centrally located, and offers free ferry or airport pickup. (919-928-4261)

The **Island Inn & Dining Room** ($$) was built as an Odd Fellows Lodge in 1901 and was also used for a school. Recently restored, it offers a variety of accommodations for families and singles. (919-928-4351)

Pirate's Quay ($$$$), located on Silver Lake, is a luxurious all-suite hotel. It provides deep water docking and quiet beaches. (919-928-1921)

CAMPING

If you have a tent, netting and insect repellent, you can listen to the pounding surf while camping beneath the stars for $12. The lure of living this close to nature prompts many who could afford pricier digs to stake their tent at one of these campsites. **Teeter's Campground** (919-928-3511) provides several services including cable TV (for those who need to ease into culture shock gradually). **Beachcomber** (919-928-4031), the newest camp on the island, is close to Silver Lake and the beach. It has hot showers and TV, too. The **National Park Service** operates 136 campsites off N.C. 12 east of town. A bit more rustic, there are no utility hookups here.

Dining

It would be incorrect to say that non-fish eaters are out of luck at Ocracoke restaurants because other offerings do exist. Still, seafood commands the nucleus of the menus—prepared any way you like it: broiled, blackened, raw, steamed, sautéed and stuffed. Fresh, fresh crab meat for Outer Banks versions of She-Crab soup and crab cakes are the kind of staple items appearing on all menus. So—enjoy! Feast!

The Back Porch ($$$) is a restaurant whose chefs make the connoisseur list. Its fresh ingredients and made-from-scratch meals have made this secluded little restaurant a place to investigate. (919-928-6401)

Howard's Pub & Raw Bar ($) is a casual fun place that stays open until 2 a.m. You don't have to go the raw route either; it offers subs, chicken wings, polish sausage, etc. (919-928-4441)

The **Island Inn Restaurant** ($$) is the large dining room located in the Inn. It has been a mainstay on the island through thick and thin times. The cuisine is Southern with the grease and overcooked technique excluded. You'll find friendly food that mamas recommend. (919-928-7821)

The **Pelican Restaurant** ($$) was once the cottage home of Fanny and Billy Howard around the turn-of-the-century. As the story goes, when the robust Billy died, the islanders built his coffin too small. The practical Fanny waved the surprised workers aside and climbed into the coffin which fit her perfectly. Another coffin was built for Billy, and Fanny read *Vogue* and took naps in the first coffin for her remaining 17 years.

Many of the island inns and restaurants provide colorful pages from Ocracoke's past, and this one was too good not to pass on to you. The menu features fish and the inn's blackened technique has won favor. (919-928-7431)

For More Information:

Outer Banks
Chamber of Commerce
P.O. Box 1757
Kill Devil Hills, NC 27948
919-441-8144

HATTERAS ISLAND

To Get There:
Take the free ferry from Ocracoke or from the north travel N.C. 12 south.

To survive on Hatteras, settlers had to be hardy, a char-

Photo by William Russ. Courtesy N.C. Travel & Tourism.

The Cape Hatteras Lighthouse is one of the most famous landmarks on the North Carolina Coast.

acteristic still reflected in its natives. The sea was their life and they had a reverence and respect for its mercurial moods. The ship-snatching currents of the warm, northward-flowing Gulf Stream, and the southbound, inshore Virginia Coastal Drift are what dubbed this the "Graveyard of the Atlantic."

Today, Hatteras combines sports and nature on what many consider the best of the Outer Banks islands. "Best" in terms of sports variety such as fishing from the surf, the pier or on a deep water charter boat in the Gulf. There is swimming, sailing, sea-kayaking or wind surfing at the biggest and most consistent surf on the East Coast; scuba diving through shipwrecks; walking through miles of protected beach; bird watching in the wildlife refuge; horseback riding along the beach; patrolling the beach for loggerhead turtles; golfing, tennis and sight-seeing.

The seven villages on the island, Rodanthe, Waves, Salvo, Avon, Buston, Frisco, and Hatteras provide restaurants, motels, shopping, etc.

Things To See and Do _____

CAPE HATTERAS LIGHTHOUSE
The first **Cape Hatteras Lighthouse** was built in 1802.

Its whale oil beacon warned ships of the eight-mile-long hazardous shoal water until erosion and the Civil War sounded its final toll. The 1870 Lighthouse was built more sturdily, but even with the new lighthouse, ships and crews continued to be lost. In 1874 the federal government built a chain of seven stations along the banks, to rescue the crews of grounded ships. Today, an 800,000 candlepower electric light rotates every 7 1/2 seconds from the Hatteras Lighthouse, signaling to ships 20 miles from shore. Erosion continues to nip at the base of the lighthouse, threatening its very existence and giving rise to campaigns such as "Save our Lighthouse" in an effort to move it to safe harbor.

When you stop by the 1854 **Visitors Center** (north on N.C. 12 near Buxton), take a stroll around the lighthouse. You can also see the remains of a shipwreck. Spend a little time on the nature trail, and if you've come equipped with a four-wheel drive, mosquito netting and repellent, camp at a campground.

FISHING
You can surf fish or fish from the pier at **Hatteras Island Fishing Pier** in Rodanthe, **Avon Fishing Pier** in Avon or the **Cape Hatteras Pier** in Frisco. If deep sea fish-

ing is your choice, you can charter a boat or sign on for a head boat at **Teach's Lair Marina** (919-986-2460), **Hatteras Harbor Marina** (919-986-2166) or **Oden's Dock** (919-986-2733), all located in Hatteras Village.

Etc.

Besides the beaches, there are a number of things to see and do on Hatteras. Kids love the **Waterfall Park** in Rodanthe that has a water slide, go-cart track and miniture golf course. In Buxton, you can ride horseback at **Buxton Stables** (919-995-4659) or wind surf at the "**Canadian Hole**" just outside of town. For a real thrill, take a "Flight Seeing Tour" with **Burrus Flying Service** in Frisco. (919-986-2679)

Accommodations___

Condominiums and Cottages

For cottage rentals on Hatteras, call **Dolphin Realty** (800-338-4775) or **Outer Beaches Realty** (919-995-4477 in Avon or 919-987-2771 in Waves).

Hotels and Motels

The **Falcon Motel** ($) in Buxton is 1 1/2 blocks from the beach, and offers modest family-type rooms. (800-635-6911)

The **Lighthouse View Motel** ($$), also in Buxton, has standard rooms and some cottages on the ocean. (800-225-7651)

Cape Hatteras Motel ($$$) in Buxton appeals to fishermen and wind surfers who come to nearby "Canadian Hole." A popular, no-frills place, some of its guests have been coming here for 30 years. (919-995-5611)

Camping

Rugged campers will enjoy the beautiful **Cape Point Campground** (NPS), near the life saving station. Some of the less rustic campgrounds are: **Camp Woods** (919-995-5850), which is in the woods and has hot showers. **Camp Hatteras** (919-987-2318) is between Rodanthe and Waves on N.C. 12. This full-hookup campground has 1000 feet of ocean and sound footage and lots of recreational facilities.

Dining _____

For a good deli sandwich, try the **Frisco Sandwich Shop** ($) on N. C. 12 in Frisco, or for a good, but inexpensive barbecue, try **Bubba's Bar-B-Q** ($) on N.C. 12 in Frisco.

For a breakfast that will stick to your ribs, try **Diamond Shoals Restaurant** ($$) in Buxton. It also features all-you-can-eat dinners with a variety of seafood.

The **Down Under Restaurant and Lounge** ($-$$) on Rodanthe Pier is the only place in the area that is right on the ocean. Breakfast begins at 7. Also, you won't want to miss its happy hour (3 to 6 p.m.) featuring steamed and spiced shrimp.

The **Waves Edge** ($-$$) on the sound side in Waves offers mesquite-grilled seafood and baby backed ribs, with a side order of light entertainment thrown in.

The **Pilot House** ($$$) in Buxton offers exceptional seafood and soups, especially the seafood bisque. The lounge has a view of the ocean which lends great atmosphere coupled with great food.

For More Information:

**Outer Banks
Chamber of Commerce
P.O. Box 1757
Kill Devil Hills, NC 27948
919-441-8144**

BODIE ISLAND

To Get There:

**From Manteo, take U.S. 64/264
to N.C. 12 south.
From the north, take U.S. 158
south to Whalebone Junction
and U.S. 12 south.
From Hatteras, take N.C. 12
across the Bonner Bridge.**

Bodie (pronounced bahdy) has not changed much in attitude since the 1800s. The change has been physical. Storms depositing shifting sandbars have closed inlets at Whalebone Junction, and like all the Outer Banks barrier islands, it, too, is shifting south and west. If you look over the side of the Bonner Bridge to the north you'll see low, flat marshland, serving as a habitat for waterfowl and wildlife that wasn't there in 1964 when the bridge was built. Due to its incorporation into the National Seashore, the island has maintained its near-virginal state.

Things To See and Do _____

BODIE ISLAND LIGHTHOUSE

The 1872 black and white horizontal striped lighthouse is Bodie's third—the first collapsed due to poor construction and the second was destroyed by the Confederate army in an effort to confuse enemy ships. The lighthouse is just off N.C. 12 about a mile south of Coquina Beach. Although you can't climb to the top of the structure, the base is open to tourists and there is a gift shop on the grounds in the newly restored Keeper's Quarters. (919-441-5711)

THE BEACH

After you've taken a tour of the old lighthouse and the

Photo by William Russ. Courtesy N.C. Travel & Tourism.

The Bodie Island Lighthouse began operation in 1848.

newly restored Keepers' Quarters, go north to **Coquina Beach**, named for the tiny coquina shells found in the surf. This sugar-thin sandy white beach provides one of the best places to stake your umbrella and spend the day swimming. There are public restrooms and showers, but you'll need to bring your own picnic food and drink as the area is delightfully devoid of commercialization. You can get whatever refreshments you need at Nags Head just a few miles north, or cross over the Nags Head causeway onto Roanoke Island.

For More Information:

Outer Banks Chamber of Commerce
P.O. Box 1757
Kill Devil Hills, NC 27948
919-441-8144

ROANOKE ISLAND

Every summer the past comes alive on Roanoke Island when history is reenacted in the outdoor drama, *The Lost Colony*. Before show time, visitors can stroll through the authentic Elizabethan Gardens. A visit to Fort Raleigh, site of both the 1585 and the 1587 colonies, places guests in the midst of the restored fort, and another worthwhile tour is through the reproduction of Elizabeth II, a 16th century English ship

To Get There:
From the mainland, take U.S. 64/264 across the Umstead Bridge.

Things To See and Do _____

THE LOST COLONY

Remember, you can always drive over to Roanoke Island via the causeway for a number of things to do. During the summer, catch a performance of *The Lost Colony* (919-473-3414) at the Waterside Theatre, just off U.S. 64/264 in Manteo. Paul Green's outdoor drama has been entertaining audiences with the history of English colonization of this area since the theater began in 1937. It is professionally performed in a semi-circular bowl with Roanoke Sound as an authentic backdrop.

ELIZABETHAN GARDENS

You can tour the Elizabethan Gardens, adjacent to the Waterside Theatre daily, between 9 a.m. and 5 p.m. This is a spectacular formal garden with curving paths, an abundance of seasonal flowers, and statuary that includes the famous Virginia Dare. History records that Virginia Dare was the first baby born in the colonies and is so commemorated in this worthwhile garden.

FORT RALEIGH

To get a historical feel for North Carolina's first colonial area, stop by the **Fort Raleigh Visitors Center** between 9 a.m. and 6 p.m. daily during the summer, and until 5 p.m. the remainder of the year. The Center is located on the northern end of Roanoke Island in Manteo. You'll see a brief film, a tiny museum, a 400-year old Tudor room from Heronden Hall in Kent, England, a restored fort and a nature trail at the sites of the 1585 and 1587 colonies. No admission is charged.

ELIZABETH II STATE HISTORIC SITE

Elizabeth II State Historic Site in Manteo takes us back to what we consider a more romantic time. But a tour through this authentically reproduced 16th century English sailing ship tells a different story. The 69-foot-long ship, a gift to North Carolina, was built to honor our 400th anniversary that we celebrated for four years. The Visitors Center shows a short film, *Roanoke Village,* which is helpful to see before touring the ship. Admission is $3 for adults, $1.50 for children and $2 for senior citizens. Operating hours are from 10 a.m. until 6 p.m. daily, April through October. From November through March, the ship is open from 10 a.m. until 4 p.m. Tuesday through Sunday. (919-473-1144)

The Lost Colony outdoor drama tells the compelling story of the first English colonists to arrive in the New World.

Photo by William Russ. Courtesy N.C. Travel & Tourism.

NORTH CAROLINA AQUARIUM AT ROANOKE ISLAND

Nationally accredited, the North Carolina Aquarium at Roanoke Island is another must see while you are in the area. It is similar to North Carolina's other two aquariums (at Fort Fisher and Pine Knoll Shores) with lighted tanks filled with beautiful or fascinating sea life and touch and feel tanks that children and adults love to dig into. As do the other N.C. aquariums, this one offers changing exhibits, shark displays, field trips, a gift shop, programs for all ages and interests and various short films. You need to drive north on N.C. 64 and turn left onto N.C. 116, follow the signs to the airport, and you'll find the aquarium on the right. It's open from 9 a.m. to 5 p.m. Monday through Saturday and 1 p.m. to 5 p.m. on Sunday. It's closed on Thanksgiving, Christmas and New Year's Day. Admission is $3 for adults; $2 for senior citizens and active military personnel and $1 for children ages 6 to 17.

THE ISLAND ART GALLERY AND CHRISTMAS SHOP

It's easy to say that you've never seen a shopping complex quite as fantastic as this. Christmas decorations from all over the world are found here in room after room of lighted and decorated trees. Even on a hot summer afternoon, a walk through this fantasy land that also has paintings, pottery, etc., will put you in the Christmas spirit. The seven-building complex is located about a half-mile south of Manteo on U.S. 64.

Accommodations____

BED & BREAKFAST INNS

Mellowing out comes easy at **Tranquil House Inn** ($$$$), named for an old home that once stood in this vicinity. This turn-of-the-century reproduction sits on Shallowbag Bay and you can sit on the inn's long front porch and see the Elizabeth II docked across the bay. This is also a perfect place to sip coffee and enjoy the complimentary breakfast. (800-458-7069)

Roanoke Island Inn ($$$), located on the water front at 305 Fernando Street in ddowntown Manteo offers unhurried hospitality.

HOTELS/MOTELS

The **Duke of Dare** ($) on U.S. 64/264 in Manteo is a family-owned and managed motel that does not fit into today's trendy mode. However, its location just a few blocks from the water front and shopping makes it a good value.

CAMPING

Camping on Bodie, like camping anywhere protected by the National Park Service, is not for the pampered camper. The **Oregon Inlet Campground** is on flat, windswept beaches without utilities.

Dining

The **Weeping Radish** ($$-$$$) is located on U.S. 64 adjacent to the **Christmas Shop.** During warm weather, the ideal place for lunch is its outdoor garden where three different German sausages on buns are served. A favorite is the mild and light bratwurst, which slips down more easily with the restaurant's own-brewed Black Radish (a dark lager). Save time to tour the brewery, which offers scheduled tours. Lunch and dinner are served daily inside. (919-473-1157)

If you like good country cooking, **The Duchess of Dare** ($), located on Budleigh Street in Manteo, is the place to go for a daily breakfast, lunch and dinner.

For More Information:

Dare County Tourist Bureau
P.O. Box 399
Manteo, NC
1-800-446-6262
Outer Banks Chamber of
Commerce
P.O. Box 1757
Kill Devil Hills, NC 27948
919-441-8144

NORTHERN BANKS

NAGS HEAD

To Get There:
From the mainland, take
U.S. 64 from Manteo. From
the north or south,
take N.C. 12.

Since 1838 wealthy sun and sea lovers have been coming to Nags Head, which may make it the earliest beach retreat in North Carolina. The Nags Head Hotel was built back then, and second home cottages became the "in" thing to have for those who could afford the boat fare to this barrier island. That hotel was burned by retreating Confederate forces, but rebuilt in 1870. You'll still see the unpainted homes which were built high on pilings to allow the ocean to wash beneath them.

The early beach goers weren't that different from current ones. They liked to fish, swim, bowl, gamble at a casino (not currently done), kick up their heels and take walks on the beach. The current crop has added golf, scuba diving, kite flying and hang gliding at Jockey's Ridge State Park. Whether you are into those super athletic pursuits or not, a walk on North Carolina's largest (1 mile long, 12,000 feet wide, rising 140 feet above sea level) ridge of sand dunes is an erstwhile adventure in Outer Banks investigation. This ridge forms the tallest medano (isolated hill of sand) on the East Coast, and when you slog your way to the top, there's a great view of the ocean and sound. Along the way you'll enjoy watching classes of would be hang gliders and seeing imaginative and colorful kites flying in all directions.

Local folklore legends insist that the name, "Jockey's Ridge" was so named for the horse races that used to be run on flat sections of the dunes while onlookers sat on the sidelines. Another popular legend spins the story that, on the dune's crest, pirates once hung lanterns from the necks of their horses to trick ships into wrecking on the dangerous shoals along the shore.

Things To See and Do _____

JOCKEY'S RIDGE STATE PARK

Jockey's Ridge has long been the premier place for hang gliders. You will need a permit and you can get that along with lessons at **Kitty Hawk Kites** (919-441-4124). You can't camp at this relatively small (393 acre) park, but it's set up for picnicking with shelters, tables, grills, restrooms and vending machines. And though exploring the dunes is the park's main feature, it's not the only one. "Tracks in the Sand" is a mile-

Photo by T&T. Courtesy N.C. Travel & Tourism.

Hang gliding is a popular sport at Jockey's Ridge State Park at Nags Head.

and-a-half walking trail meandering along the base of the dunes to the park's boundary on Roanoke Sound. You're apt to see fox, opossum, raccoon and varied bird species. During the summer, be sure to sign up for the park's sunset program for some interpretive instruction about the park.

WATER SPORTS

Many people come to Nags Head for water sports. Rentals for almost any kind of sports equipment you want can be found at **Kitty Hawk Sports** (919-261-8770). Today, you'll see jet skis, Hobie Cats, wind surfers, kayakers and piers filled with fisherpersons. And, you can certainly wander across the causeway for the same interests mentioned to Bodie Island visitors.

Accommodations____

There's seemingly no end of accommodations in the area, so we'll list just a few.

For economy's sake **Ocean Veranda** ($-$$) is a good choice because it's on the ocean, offers a continental breakfast and has been partially renovated. (919-441-5858)

Surf Side ($$$) is an attractive ocean front five-story motel with many amenities such as refrigerators, Jacuzzis and king-size beds for ocean front rooms. (800-552-SURF)

Nostalgia buffs may opt for the recently-moved-from-the-ocean and newly-renovated **First Colony Inn** ($$$$). This 1932 landmark harkens back to another era, giving more of an inn feeling. It's graciously appointed with antiques and luxurious amenities and serves a deluxe continental breakfast. (800-368-9390)

Dining _____

Restaurants and night life are also in generous supply in Nags Head.

Casual is capitalized at **Tortuga's Lie** ($-$$) on Beach Road. This restaurant makes everyone feel comfortable. With license tags nailed to the ceiling, it isn't the fanciest place, but it does have good food and some special beers: Bass Ale and Guiness Stout for a start. It serves seafood cooked a variety of ways.

The Pier House Restaurant ($) on Beach Road is the place to go for an early breakfast on the ocean; other meals serve fresh seafood with the trimmings.

There are several **Owen's** restaurants on the beach, but a favorite is the one on Beach Road ($$$) that looks like an old Nags Head Life Saving Station. There's lots of good seafood here, particularly Coconut Shrimp and Crabmeat Remick.

For night life you'll find everything from **The Comedy Club** at the **Carolinian** on Beach Road, to reggae and calypso at **Woody's** on N.C. 158 Bypass at Pirate's Quay.

For More Information:

Dare County Tourist Bureau
P.O. Box 399
Manteo, NC 27954
1-800-446-6262
Outer Banks Chamber of Commerce
P.O. Box 1757
Kill Devil Hills, NC 27948
919-441-8144

KITTY HAWK AND KILL DEVIL HILLS

To Get There:
From Nags Head, follow N.C. 12 seven miles north. From the north, take U.S. 158 or N.C. 12.

Just how Kill Devil got its name depends on whom you talk to, or which history book you read. It may be named after the "Killdeer," a common shore bird; a possible bargain with the devil; or a shipment of Kill Devil rum—take your pick.

The elements (storm and erosion) have taken a toll on the Kitty Hawk beaches, which are not as wide as they once were. You'll find that the Kill Devil beaches attract more families who spend time with their children on the beach and at the Wright Memorial.

Things To See and Do _____

Of course, this area is famous throughout the world as the birthplace of aviation. It was on Kill Devil Hills that Orville and Wilbur Wright flew the first glider-type airplane. A huge, soaring granite monument commemorates the event, or events, that spanned eight years of trial flight experiments. You can visit the memorial center with its interesting exhibits of the planes, engines, notes and reproductions of the original gliders. There are also reconstructed wooden sheds filled with the Wright's tools, reminiscent of the 1900s. Admission is charged.

For an adventure outing, you can take the **Kitty Hawk Aero Tour** in a small plane over the Outer Banks. This worthwhile half-hour flight may give you a glimmer of what the famous brothers experienced.

COLINGTON ISLAND
Another interesting place to visit, Colington Island, seems remote to this half of the 20th century and introduces visitors to another page in coastal living. This is an interesting place to watch the inner workings of commercial fishermen, hang out

at the bait and tackle shops or frequent the small eateries. Colington is ideal for crabbing along the narrow road—as long as you remember to pack your insect repellent. The island has beautiful maritime forests and marshland areas with a variety of plants and great trees draped with the spidery tendrils of Spanish moss.

Accommodations ____

BED AND BREAKFAST INNS

For a stay in a lovely Bed and Breakfast, you might try **The Figurehead B & B** ($) at 417 Helga Street in Kill Devil Hills. This one, located on the sound side, is just a few years old and offers a continental breakfast with other pleasant amenities. (800-221-6929)

CONDOMINIUMS AND COTTAGES

For rental cottages, call **Kitty Hawk Rentals**. (919-441-7166)

HOTELS AND MOTELS

The Mariner ($$) is an oceanfront motel that offers single as well as two- and three-bedroom efficiencies along with recreational activities. (919-441-2021)

The **Day's Inn Orville and Wilbur Wright Motel** ($$) is an old inn designed to resemble a mountain lodge. You'll like the cozy fireplace during off

seasons and the assortment of oriental rugs and furniture from another, more comfortable era. Snorkelers and divers who explore the ship wreck just north of the motel, are frequent guests. (800-325-2525)

CAMPING

You can camp at the heavily wooded **Colington Park Campground**, which has hot showers and other comfortable amenities. (919-441-6128)

Dining _____

There is no ration of good restaurants in this area, and you don't have to be rich to afford them. Certainly, fresh seafood is great, but a wider variety of foods such as Cajun, Mexican, Italian, Thai and barbecue can also be found here.

A favorite haunt is **Awful Arthur's** ($$) on Beach Road in Kill Devil Hills. It's great for steamed seafood, has a casual to robust atmosphere and is a favorite place to hobnob with the locals.

An inexpensive place to take the kids for lunch is **Newby's** ($) on the N.C. 158 Bypass. You can easily put away its delicious subs and sandwiches or cool off with yogurt and ice cream.

With its Victorian decor, the **Port O' Call** ($$$) on Beach Road is something a bit different. This restaurant serves continental cuisine with an emphasis on seafood and service. Like many, it doubles as a good night spot with live entertainment.

On Colington, the best bet is the **Colington Cafe** ($$), nestled in the trees at 999 Colington Road, just a mile west of the Bypass. In a renovated old home with Victorian touches, this charming restaurant is known for its fine French Cuisine. You'll appreciate the homemade soups and pasta dishes.

> **For More Information:**
> **Dare County Travel Bureau**
> **P.O. Box 399**
> **Manteo, NC 27954**
> **1-800-446-6262**
> **Outer Banks Chamber of**
> **Commerce**
> **P.O. Box 1757**
> **Kill Devil Hills, NC 27948**
> **919-441-8144**

DUCK, CAROLLA, SOUTHERN SHORES

> **To Get There:**
> From the mainland, take U.S. 64 east to N.C. 12 north. From the north, take U.S. 158 and turn left onto S.R. 1200. From the south, follow U.S. 12.

Going to the beach on the Northern Banks is as different a beach experience as is going to the beach on Bald Head Island. And the Northern Banks experience is not the same as the Bald Head Island experience either. The Northern Banks is, in general, more environmentally protected and commercially controlled. Unless you stay at the fashionable Sanderling Inn Resort, you have to rent a house because there are no motels or quaint B & Bs. This is where you go when you **really** want to indulge in nature almost as pure as it was when Sir Walter Raleigh arrived.

In the towns of Duck, Carolla, Southern Shores and Monterey Plaza you can get groceries and bait, rent a boat and other recreational equipment, shop and dine. But you will not find the glut of shops and activity here that spoil many beach areas. This is an area where beaches are barren and pure, while its maritime forest on Currituck Sound is so lush that the two don't appear to be part of the same pea pod.

Things To See and Do _____

WATER SPORTS

Water recreation offers the same opportunities as the southern islands for fishing, wind surfing, kayaking, sailing and swimming. If you're the type that doesn't want to lug your boat with you, particularly difficult if flying to the area, then there are rental places that have

Jet Skis, sailboats, catamarans and monohulls, and if you've never tried any of those sports, you can take lessons at the rental places, too.

ETC.

In addition to the usual beach activities, the Northern Banks have two extras. In Corolla, you can hang glide over the beaches and, if you have a four-wheel drive, you can drive on the beach. Naturally, you must watch for sunbathers because this beautiful flat beach is by no means a race strip. You can drive all the way to the Virginia state line but there is no access road into Virginia.

At **Carolla Light Resort Village**, there is miniature golf. You can also play tennis, squash and racquetball at the **Pine Island Indoor Racquet Club** in Pine Island (open to the public), just north of Sanderling on N.C. 12.

Accommodations

CONDOMINIUMS AND COTTAGES

If you choose the cottage rental route, call **Britt Real Estate** for listings from Duck to Carolla. (800-334-6315 for out of state; 919-261-3566 from within North Carolina)

Photo by William Russ. Courtesy N.C. Travel & Tourism.

The Currituck Beach Lighthouse, located at Carolla, serves as the northernmost Outer Banks lighthouse.

RESORTS

The place to stay, and not just because it's the only place to stay, is the luxurious **Sanderling Inn Resort** ($$$$). The owner has carefully designed a resort that does not intrude on the environment. The interior is done in light-colored woods in a simple, yet elegant tone and the suites have varied amenities—including a welcome bottle of wine and a basket of fruit.

Breakfasts are generous and the morning view, on the restaurant's deck, makes you feel that you're close enough to reach out and touch the ocean with one hand and the sound with the other. The resort offers a complete health club with exercise rooms, indoor pool, whirlpool and tennis courts. And if the in-house activities are not enough to keep you busy, you can rent a bike and explore the nearby Audubon Wildlife Sanctuary. (919-261-4111)

Dining _____

Again, the recommended place to dine is the **Sanderling Inn Restaurant** ($$$$), which is a renovated life saving station, known as Caffey's Inlet No. 5. The chef blends continental dishes and great old North Carolina offerings in this upscale casual restaurant. You can go upstairs and see how the early crew members lived on this barrier island. A favorite place for cocktails is the upstairs deck.

The Barrier Island Inn ($$$) on Duck Road in Duck Village is another excellent choice for breakfast, lunch or dinner. The restaurant's view is as spectacular as its food.

Nicoletta's Italian Cafe ($$) in the Carolla Light Village is a good place for Italian food, although it offers a wide selection of other foods as well.

Nicoletta's Pizzeria (in the same area) is new and offers homemade pizzas and subs for lunch or dinner.

For More Information:

Dare County Tourist Bureau
P.O. Box 399
Manteo, NC 27954
1-800-446-6262
Outer Banks Chamber of Commerce
P.O. Box 1757
Kill Devil Hills, NC 27948
919-441-8144

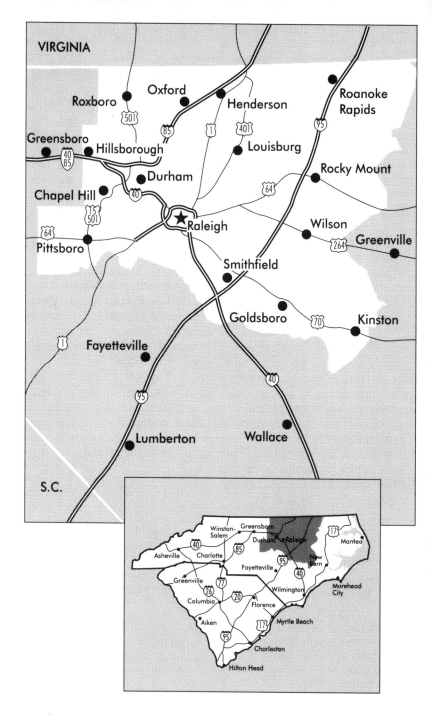

VIRGINIA

Roxboro

Oxford

Henderson

Roanoke
Rapids

501

85

1

401

95

Greensboro

Hillsborough

40
85

Louisburg

Rocky Mount

Durham

40

64

Chapel Hill

15
501

★ Raleigh

Wilson

Greenville

64

Pittsboro

264

Smithfield

Goldsboro

70

Kinston

1

Fayetteville

95

Lumberton

Wallace

40

S.C.

Winston-
Salem

Greensboro

17

40

Durham Raleigh

Manteo

Asheville

Charlotte

85

95

Fayetteville

New
Bern

40

Greenville

26

77

Wilmington

Morehead
City

Columbia

20

Florence

Aiken

17

Myrtle Beach

95

Charleston

Hilton Head

Northern Heartland

THE TRIANGLE

The varied communities of North Carolina's Triangle area, while even more connected than in earlier years by the extension of I-40 from Raleigh through Durham to Chapel Hill and Hillsborough, still retain their distinct identities. There's Raleigh, the state capital, Durham, a one-time tobacco and textile town known today for its high-tech medical research and fine arts programs and Chapel Hill, home of the first public university to open its doors. The area has much to offer and the variety makes it a great destination for families with diverse interests. Because of the close proximity of the cities of the Triangle, Accommodations and Dining are combined.

RALEIGH

> **To Get There:**
> Raleigh is located at the intersection of I-40 and U.S. 64.

Things To See and Do _____

JOEL LANE HOUSE

If Colonel Joel Lane, "father of Raleigh," hadn't been the savvy political mover and shaker of his day, the permanent North Carolina state Capitol would be in another location. You can visit his period furnished home **"Wakefield"** at the corner of St. Mary's Street and W. Hargett Street in downtown Raleigh.

When built in the 1760s, the colonial, farmhouse-style

home was considered the finest within a 100-mile radius and remains in excellent condition today. Costumed guides explain the historic meetings that took place in the dining room of this two-story home, and you can imagine committees of ruddy gentlemen sitting around the hearth warming themselves as they made plans for justice.

It's no secret that they also warmed favorably to alcoholic concoctions, particularly a drink called the Cherry Bounce. Allegedly, they consumed these in great quantities at the plantation tavern of Isaac Hunter the night this committee discussed where the new Capitol should be placed. Shortly thereafter, the assembly passed legislation specifically stipulating that the new Capitol should be located "within ten miles of Isaac Hunter's plantation." The 1,000-acre plot chosen also happened to be part of Joel Lane's 6,000-acre plantation, which he deeded to the state in 1792.

CAPITOL BUILDING

At the State Capitol you can punch up many interesting historical tidbits on a touch-video screen (Capitol Information) that also prints out answers for you to take home. On the video, the Cherry Bounce story asks, "If Fayetteville had the recipe for Cherry Bounce, would the Capitol be there today?

North Carolina is very proud of its forefathers and you'll see evidence of this throughout government buildings and grounds. For instance, opposite the east Capitol entrance is a statue of three U.S. Presidents born in North Carolina: Andrew Jackson, James Knox Polk and Andrew Johnson.

Outgrown and gone is the simple two-story brick Capitol that was built on Union Square in 1792. A fine Greek Revival cross-shaped building with a central, domed rotunda replaces the second Capitol that burned in 1831. When completed in 1840, the Capitol cost $532,682.34, more than three times the yearly general income of the State at that time. Its over-97-foot dome, patterned after a Greek temple, commands your attention. At its center is the copy of Antonio Canova's statue of George Washington (the original burned in the 1831 fire). Only the Governor's and the Lieutenant Governor's offices are housed in the building today.

In such an imposing building as this, you just know there have to be secret tunnels and hidden rooms. Yet the only tunnel served to house heating and electrical equipment; there were, however, secret rooms accessible only through the attic until the 1920's renovation. These rooms were supposedly used by Confederate spies. How-

Photo by Peter Damroth. Courtesy N.C. Travel & Tourism.

The North Carolina State Capitol Building.

ever, during Reconstruction an open bar was set up in the Committee Room where legend has it that "the west stair was chipped by the rolling of whiskey barrels up and down them."

Free tours of the Capitol are offered on Tuesday, Thursday and Friday from 10:00 a.m. until 2:00 p.m. The building is closed each year from December 20th to March 1st.

THE LEGISLATIVE BUILDING

In both the House of Representatives and the Senate, the desks and chairs were handmade by Raleigh cabinetmaker William Thompson in 1840 and are in mint condition today. Folks once sat upstairs on the third floor gallery overlooking the House of Representatives or the Senate. Also on this floor is the State Geologist's Office. It appears today, furnished as it was in the 1850s with minerals on display and packages on the floor, just as if the workers had gone off for lunch.

Free tours are given daily, call for a schedule. (919-733-3456)

GOVERNOR'S MANSION

If the Governor wants to go home for lunch, its only two blocks away to the 1891 Victorian-style Executive Mansion at 200 N. Blount Street. Unfortunately, he or she can't eat in the downstairs dining room without guided tours marching through. The Governor's family

Photo by William Russ. Courtesy N.C. Travel & Tourism.

The Executive Mansion in Raleigh is considered one of the country's outstanding examples of Queen Ann Cottage-style Victorian architecture.

maintains a private apartment upstairs. Of course, State dinners are held in the room around the 1800s English mahogany banquet table.

The Morning Room at the end of the grand hallway is filled with the Governor's choice of past Governors' portraits (subject to change when a different party takes office). The Morning Room's original white wicker furniture and pastel print cushions make it a cheery room where you want to kick off your shoes and curl up with a magazine.

All these beautiful rooms have bouquets of fresh flowers, crystal chandeliers and floor to ceiling windows for good ventilation. The pastel or rich decorating colors, along with the light-filled windows, give the mansion a light, airy feel. Nowhere is there heavy, dark Victorian bric-a-brack. The South Porch, also filled with white wicker and voluminous hanging flower baskets was once accessible to the Governor's friends (before fences were built around the mansion) who came to sit and swap evening stories during warm weather. This was during the same era when children remember roller skating in the mansion's ball room.

An attractive wall of brick and wrought iron encloses the grounds and the Victorian Garden is sheltered by a weeping willow.

Free tours are given of house and garden. (919-733-3456)

HAYWOOD HALL

Back in the good old days, elected officials were required to build a home for their stay in Raleigh. John Haywood, serving as the first elected treasurer of the state, bought land about two blocks from the Capitol. In the 1799 Federal period, he built one of Raleigh's largest classical-style two-story homes, **Haywood Hall**, at 211 New Bern Place. Today, it has the distinction of being the oldest standing home within the original city limits of Raleigh.

Descendants say the 43 year old Haywood wanted the home to be nice enough to keep his 17-year-old wife, Eliza, from spending so much time in her girlhood home in New Hanover County. It kept not only Eliza, who created a diversified garden for her home, and subsequent 12 children, but also 175 years of Haywood descendants who made additions to the graceful home. The house is particularly blessed with 11 family portraits and a large percentage of original family furniture. You'll see the symbols of hospitality: a pineapple and an apple above the ornate, vee-shaped molding at the stairwell, and an upstairs nursery complete with doll furniture.

Descendent, Dr. Fabius Julius Haywood, installed a speaker horn in the upstairs front bedroom so that he could talk with patients who were speaking from the front walk into another speaker horn. Those were the days when doctors still practiced medicine in their homes.

Apparently, those days were also more romantic. Mary Haywood Fowle Stearns had her portrait painted wearing the gown she'd had on when her fiancee, Walter Stearns, first kissed her. It hangs in the dining room.

Haywood Hall offers free tours on Thursday from 10:30 a.m. until 1:30 p.m. (919-832-8357)

MORDECAI HISTORIC PARK

It's just a few blocks away to Mordecai Historic Park at Forest Road and Mimosa Street. Considered a country home when built in 1785, like Haywood Hall this magnificent neoclassical mansion remained in the family for 182 years. Not only was this good for the family, it's good for us who visit today.

There are family portraits and much of the original furniture is in place or being returned. For example, you'll see an old tin bathtub in an upstairs bedroom next to the fireplace. Think of hauling buckets of water upstairs and then heating it over the fire before you could take a bath.

Originally built by Henry Lane, son of the "Father of Raleigh" and his wife, Polly Hinton, it began as a "starter" house of 1 1/2 stories with only a few rooms. Moses Mordecai, a Jewish attorney who converted to Christianity, married the Lane's daughter, Peggy, and moved into the home. Folks didn't have apartments in those days, so along with Peggy came her three sisters and Moses' younger brother, George, to live with them. Following Peggy's death, her sister, Ann, became the second Mrs. Mordecai.

Mordecai's will outlined the changes he'd provided to enlarge his home, which were carried out after his death. The house was restructured along Greek Revival lines and 5 rooms were added as well as the conversion of the north portico to two stories.

Mordecai Park has numerous out buildings that you can visit. Other historical buildings such as a plantation chapel and law office have been moved to the park along with three early town structures arranged along a "village street" such as Raleigh might have had in its first decade. You'll also see the tiny, gambrel-roofed birthplace of our nation's 17th President of the U.S., Andrew Johnson.

Mordecai Historic Park is located on the corner of Forest Road and Mimosa Street. It is open on Monday through Friday from 10:00 a.m. until 3:00 p.m.; weekends, from 1:30 p.m. until 3:30 p.m. (1-hour tour). Admission for adults is $3.00, for children $1 and children under 6 are admitted free. (919-834-4844)

CITY MARKET

In 1914 downtown Raleigh was the farmers' market, with buildings designed along Spanish Mission lines. The buildings are still here, now housing unique restaurants, antique and boutique shops. Adjacent is the art district known as Moore Square that houses 9 different galleries.

Be sure to tour the former Ford dealership at 201 E. Davie Street to visit **Artspace**. Here, you'll find 40 artists working in their studios in a variety of media from oils to stone sculpture. Adjoining this building is **Playspace.** If you have children ages 7 and younger, this is the place to bring them for a 50-minute play/learning period. On child scale size there is a hospital space complete with little x-ray machines, incubators, stethoscopes and varied equipment. You'll also find kids dancing or singing their hearts out on a stage with a video monitor set up so that young performers can watch themselves perform. They can also try out a sports car, child-size grocery store and a pay telephone at their level.

Artspace is open Tuesday through Friday from 9:00 a.m. until 5:00 p.m., Saturday from 10:00 a.m. until 5:00 p.m. and Sunday from 1:00 p.m. until 5:00 p.m.

Playspace is open during the same hours. Visitors are admitted on the hour. Admission is $1.50 per person for 50 minutes and the 4th Sunday of each month is free.

Photo courtesy Playspace.

Playspace at the City Market.

NORTH CAROLINA MUSEUM OF ART

The **North Carolina Museum of Art**, located on the outskirts of Raleigh near I-40 at 2110 Blue Ridge Road, is arguably the finest art museum in the Carolinas. Over 5,000 years of paintings, sculptures, artifacts of ancient civilizations and changing exhibits are housed in this beautiful new (1983) museum building.

This is a museum that blooms with artistic seasons such as its fine collection of German Expressionists and the American artists influenced by that movement. You'll see a Georgia O'Keefe, Thomas Hart Benton, Maurice Sterne and others. The museum has several Andrew Wyeths as well as the works of North Carolinian Minnie Evans, whose inspiration came to her in a dream.

It has a superb Judaic Collection comprising a silver Torah case, silver Hanukkah lamp, silver alms box, Sabbath candles, a silver Torah crown, a silver cup for the Prophet Elijah—even a silver circumcision set and a great deal more. Perhaps, most prominent is the museum's Samuel H. Kress collection of European art that includes: Rembrandt, Van Dyke, Titian and Gainsborough, ranging from the Renaissance to the Baroque.

On the 20th century floor you'll find a wonderful cultural introduction to Africa with ceremonial masks, palace pillars, divination tools and head dresses.

Yes, you could definitely spend the day here and you won't have to bring your own lunch. A terrific restaurant, **Museum Cafe** ($$), is just the thing to break the day for you, and don't think you'll get institutional food here, you won't. Somehow, the cafe has made food that is good for you, also taste good. Don't forget the museum's gift shop.

The museum is open Tuesday, Wednesday, Thursday and Saturday from 9:00 a.m. until 5:00 p.m.; Friday from 9:00 a.m. until 9:00 p.m.; and from 11:00 a.m. until 6:00 p.m. on Sunday. Admission is free; there are free guided tours and the museum is handicap accessible. (919-839-NCMA)

NORTH CAROLINA MUSEUM OF HISTORY

April 1994 saw the celebrated opening of the new $29.3 million North Carolina Museum of History on the corner of Edenton and Wilmington Streets. The new building houses 250,000 artifacts. Visitors can see a replica of the Wright brothers' plane suspended on one side, an early hang glider on the other, and a Gyrocopter above the main stairway. There is a Folklife Gallery beside a 315-seat auditorium. You can also trace North Carolina's past from 12,000 B.C. to today through the Chronological History Gallery and see

Photo by Alan Weed. Courtesy N.C. Museum of Life & Science.

*A musician in the making in Loblolly Park at the
North Carolina Museum of Life and Science.*

the impact women of the state have made in the hall for North Carolina's Women's History.

The third floor holds an exhibition hall for the North Carolina Sports Hall of Fame plus a temporary gallery for traveling exhibits from other museums. This new museum with an architectural feel of openness also features a restaurant on the ground level and there is a parking garage (small fee) beneath the building.

For More Information:

Greater Raleigh Convention and Visitors Bureau
P.O. Box 1879
Raleigh, NC 27602
800-849-8499

AAA Carolinas
2301 Blue Ridge Road
Raleigh, NC 27607
919-832-0543

DURHAM

To Get There:

Durham can be accessed by I-40 from the southwest or from the northeast by I-85

Things To See and Do _____

N.C. MUSEUM OF LIFE AND SCIENCE

Random percussion sounds of drumming and beating on chimes carry from **Loblolly Park**, outside the 70-acre Life and Science Museum, to the parking lot. That's only one aspect of this hand-on, hands-banging, hands-twisting museum that translates difficult-to-comprehend science technology into fun and personal experiences. Take a buddy and play a game of tic-tac-toe through dual telecommunication stations, courtesy of fiber optic technology.

Children (and many adults) enjoy turning cartwheels and dancing in the **Virtual Reality** room as their images are projected upon a giant screen. The screen places them in a journey through an underwater cave or flying through the galaxy.

At exhibits, you can twist a lever and watch sand dunes created; rub a pole and see smoke curl from the base of a 15-foot exhibit and spiral into a tornado; turn a switch to see fluorescent minerals glow into bright blues, greens and yellows; set a square wheel upon a bumpy road and discover how smoothly it rolls along, plus dozens of other interactive exhibits.

Children learn how their bodies function at Bodytech: The Science Behind Medicine, and they can walk through Carolina Wildlife where live North Carolina Animals swim and fly and a few bleat out greetings.

At the Aerospace Development Laboratory, the J-2 Rocket Engine (part of the Saturn booster that sent astronauts to the moon) is ringed with video space information. You'll also see a large re-creation of the Apollo 15 Lunar Module that traveled through mountains on the moon and returned with over billion-year-old moon particles (on exhibit). Push a button at the video center and hear astronaut David Scott describe his lunar exploration, "Man must explore, and this is exploration at its greatest." A visit to this museum is another form of "exploration at its greatest."

The museum is located at 433 Murray Avenue and admission is $5 for adults and $3 for children ages 3 to 12 and seniors. Hours are from 10 a.m. until 5 p.m. Monday through Saturday and 1 to 5 p.m. on Sunday. The museum is open until 6 p.m. during the summer and is wheelchair accessible. A good gift shop is found on the first floor. (919-220-5429)

SARAH P. DUKE MEMORIAL GARDENS

This is a terrific place to take your frisbee. On lazy warm weather afternoons a flurry of varied discs are usually sailing through the air (or someone's picnic lunch) in this 20-acre garden. But the garden is a great place to go anytime of the year because no season is without something beautiful or delicate or rustic blooming. Spring can be counted on for daffodils, tu-

Photo courtesy Durham Chamber of Commerce.

The Sara P. Duke Memorial Gardens offer flowering beauty year-round.

lips and mountains of azaleas, but summer, fall and even winter exhibit a large variety of flowers from roses to pansies. A walk through lacy cherry, dogwood, redbud and crabapple trees can treat the spirit like few other things can, but the fragrant magnolias that bloom in late May will run a close second. The gardens are located on the Duke University Campus, off N.C. 751.

> **For More Information:**
> **Durham Convention & Visitors Bureau**
> **101 E. Morgan St.**
> **Durham, NC 27701**
> **919-687-0288**
>
> **AAA Carolinas**
> **3909 University Drive**
> **Durham, NC 27707**
> **919-489-3306**

CHAPEL HILL

> **To Get There:**
> Chapel Hill is located at the intersection of I-40 and N.C. 54.

Things To See and Do _____

MOREHEAD PLANETARIUM AND SUNDIAL GARDEN

You can park in the specially designated places that border the Sundial Rose Garden, a brilliant and fragrant flowering spectacle from May until November. As you enter the rotunda, filled with Morehead family portraits, note the handsome clock on the wall. This clock was made to order for Mr. Morehead who disliked the sound of constant ticking—this clock ticks only every other second and its repertoire of chimes is glorious.

In the Planetarium's 68-foot domed theater, 8,900 stars can be illuminated upon its perforated dome through the Zeiss Model number 6 projector. That's quite a show. From watching the universe spin above your head to visiting the rare walk-in Copernican Orrery, the Morehead Planetarium offers a day full of activities for the whole family. A triangle treasure for family learning and fun, the Planetarium presents both traveling and original shows about moon landings, space voyages, UFOs and more. Friday evenings, catch Sky Rambles, a live sky show narrated by a Morehead Planetarium staff member, or make a special trip to view a rare wide-angle film stretched across the Planetarium's dome.

The Planetarium is off East Franklin Street beside The Chapel of the Cross Episcopal Church. It's open every day, except December 24 and 25, and there is an evening sky show at least once each day. Admission for adults is $3.00; seniors, kids and students pay $2.50. (919-549-6863)

UNC WALKING TOUR

You can take a half-hour Walkman cassette-guided tour of the historic University of North Carolina, the nation's first university to open its doors. You'll see and hear about the Old Well, the Davie Poplar and the five-acre Coker Arboretum among other sights. The tours begin at the Rotunda of the Morehead Building, Monday through Friday at 2:15 p.m. and on Saturday at 11:30 a.m., March 1 through November 30. A small deposit ensures return of the equipment used on this free tour.

In the Visitors Center of the Rotunda is a new interactive touch-screen computer of information about the campus, and this spring, an outdoor kiosk—the graduation gift of a recent University class—will project this information into the highly-trafficked campus area as well. The Rotunda is well-supplied with informational brochures and pamphlets, but is not always staffed. (919-962-1630)

Triangle Accommodations____

BED AND BREAKFASTS AND COUNTRY INNS

The **Oakwood Inn Bed and Breakfast** ($$-$$$$) at 411

The Morehead Planetarium and surrounding gardens offer visitors a combination of scenic beauty and science.

N. Bloodworth Street in Raleigh's historic Oakwood district has seen a few modernizations such as private baths and air conditioning, but lovely tiled fireplaces remain in each room as does original heart-pine flooring and 12-foot ceilings. Verandahs wrap about the house and the old detached kitchen has been converted into the Innkeeper's quarters. The home bestows a gentle ambiance that defies definition.

Located on three-and-a-half acres north of Durham, the **Arrowhead Inn** ($$-$$$$) features eight guest rooms, including six with private baths, all furnished in antiques and country primitives. Downstairs in the parlor, guests can watch television or relax with an assortment of games and puzzles. Included in the price of a room is a hearty country breakfast of meat and eggs, homemade breads, preserves and coffee. The inn is located at 106 Mason Road in Durham. (919-477-8430)

The luxurious 15-unit **Fearrington House Country Inn** ($$$$) evokes images of an 18th-century country retreat, complete with cozy suites, exquisitely landscaped gardens and Belted Galloway cows grazing in the pasture. Each room is uniquely decorated with antiques, but in addition to the country charm, there are plenty of civilized touches: stereo music, modern baths, afternoon teas in warm sitting rooms, and a complimentary breakfast at the widely acclaimed gourmet **Fearrington House** restaurant right on the premises. The Country Inn is located at **Fearrington Village** about six miles south of Chapel Hill. (919-542-2121)

The century-old **Windy Oaks Inn** ($$) is a farmhouse once occupied by noted playwright Paul Green. It has been lovingly renovated. Located on 25 oak-shaded acres about four miles south of Chapel Hill, the Inn has four guest rooms, including one with a shared bath. Full country breakfasts, featuring delicious homemade biscuits, are included in the price of the room. Guests may take their breakfast on the terrace or in the dining room. Windy Oaks Inn is located on Old Lystra Church Road in Chatham County. (919-942-1001)

HOTELS/MOTELS

The **Velvet Cloak Inn** ($$$$) in Raleigh is a great recommendation. It's been around since the '60s, but recent renovations of the indoor pool and atrium have made the hotel more accommodating than ever. Located at 1505 Hillsborough Street, near North Carolina State University, makes it a good choice for sports weekends. (919-828-0333)

The 171-room, $16-million luxury **Washington Duke Inn and Golf Club** ($$$) is located at the edge of Duke University's west campus. It faces the university's 18-hole golf course, now open to the public, and hotel patrons may use the nearby Duke Forest jogging trails. The inn also offers the **Fairview Restaurant**, **Bull Durham Lounge**. (919-490-0999)

Well situated in the Research Triangle Park between Raleigh and Durham, the **Guest Quarters Suite Hotel** offers travelers the spaciousness of a suite in its 203 rooms, in a conveniently located, first-class hotel. It even offers a guest library and the **Piney Point Grill & Seafood Bar** is a comfortable place to enjoy good food. The hotel is at 2515 Meridian Parkway. (919-361-4660)

The **Radisson Governors Inn** ($$$$) is adjacent to Research Triangle Park and convenient to RDU International Airport. Recently renovated, it offers 193 rooms with queen-size beds and color satellite TV. The Radisson Governors Inn also features an elegant restaurant and a lounge. A swimming pool, tennis courts and exercise trails are on the property as well. (919-549-8631)

Named for a small Italian city, **The Sienna** ($$$$) is a luxurious addition to Chapel Hill. It was designed to recall the intimate hotels of Europe. Rooms range from doubles with king-size beds to the two-bedroom Presidential Suite, with traditional furnishings, spacious marble-tiled baths (including whirlpools) and nine-foot ceilings. The Sienna's restaurant, features Northern Italian and Mediterranean cuisine and nightly piano entertainment. (919-929-4000)

CAMPING

Raleigh is one of the most inexpensive places you can visit because so many attractions are free. To trim your lodging costs as well, there are several good, accessible parks. Downtown, **College Park** ($) at 4208 New Bern Avenue has RV hookups, water and electricity. (919-231-8710) Another very scenic place to camp is at **William B. Umstead State Park** in the Crabtree Creek section on N.C. 8. (919-787-3033)

Triangle Dining ____

Try to be in Raleigh's City Market area around lunch for a visit to **Big Ed's City Market Restaurant** ($). For down-home cooking this is **the place** to go, and we're not talking over cooked, either. Fresh limas with corn, broccoli and cheese, okra, mashed potatoes and gravy, cornbread and biscuits (with homemade blackberry jelly), the best chicken salad in Raleigh, eastern barbecue, burgers and such old fashioned desserts as banana pudding and apple cobbler. Located in the City Market's old produce building, the walls are bedecked with old-timey toys, photos of earlier days, farm implements and memorabilia. It, too, has become a Raleigh hangout for those interested in good food at a reasonable price. **The Farmers Market Restaurant** located at the New State Farmers Market is quite popular for good reason, Big Ed's son runs it with equally excellent country cooking at a reasonable price. Added bonuses to both restaurants are their locations, you can enjoy shopping at either the City Market or the N.C. State Farmers Market before you eat!

The Angus Barn ($$-$$$$) located on U.S. 70 west at Airport Road in Raleigh is the place to go for a steak dinner. For years it has consistently served the best beef in the state. The choice is wide, too. Chateaubriand, kabobs, filet mignon, and lobster combinations. And though you wouldn't ordinarily think of ordering seafood at this venerable old restaurant, which is a composite of old slave cabins, barns and ship's ballast, its seafood can match any of the local seafood houses.

This is upscale rusticity. (919-781-2444)

If you shop at **Crabtree Mall** while you're in the Triangle, don't miss **The Kanki Japanese House of Steaks** ($$), where an enjoyable lunch or dinner is prepared tableside by chefs who put on quite a show. (919-782-9708)

The **Magnolia Grill** ($$$$), located at the corner of Knox and Ninth streets in west Durham, is one of the Triangle's finest places to dine, with its commitment to innovative and absolutely delicious food. Chef-owner Ben Barker was one of 14 chefs nationally recognized by a panel of food experts, including Julia Child and Craig Claiborne, at the third annual American Chefs' Tribute to James Beard (they particularly liked his grits cakes with fresh morels).

This charming bistro features a daily menu composed of fresh ingredients of the season. You're likely to find anything from pumpkin soup to grilled quail with bleu cheese and walnuts—tantalizing, eclectic fare that defies labeling. Each menu features six to nine appetizers (like asparagus in raspberry-hazelnut vinaigrette), just as many entrees, and incredible desserts. (919-286-3609)

Chapel Hill seems to have more fine restaurants per capita than either of the two other larger cities of the Triangle. It is certainly safe to say that there is no restaurant like **Crook's Corner** ($$$) anywhere in the Triangle.

First, the food. A changing menu features a wide choice of seasonal entrees, including specialties from South America to North Carolina. This means you can get everything from jambalaya to shrimp and grits, all from the same kitchen. Crook's has put together ethnically and regionally authentic dishes. The influence of the late Bill Neal, the chef and cookbook author who moved the tastebuds and won the praise of food critics such as Craig Claiborne, is still felt.

Crook's is located at 610 W. Franklin Street in Chapel Hill. (919-929-7643)

411 West ($$-$$$), at 411 W. Franklin Street in Chapel Hill, opened to rave reviews. The restaurant's woodburning pizza oven gives an authentic touch to the "pizzettes," or individual pizzas made with toppings like four cheeses or prosciutto and peppers. Homemade pasta and fresh seafood are other good choices here. (919-967-2782)

A downtown Chapel Hill landmark, **Spanky's** ($-$$) specialties include burgers, grilled chicken sandwiches, pasta and sautees. Live music several nights a week makes this a popular spot where you will mingle with UNC students, faculty, sports fans and alumni, as well as locals. This is the restaurant at which you can run into such well-known personalities as Susan Lucci or Judd Hirsch, among others, who eat here when in town. (919-967-2678)

Who would have "thunk" that Chapel Hill connoisseurs would pack a restaurant featuring squid? If you're hungry and thirsty, you can kill two birds with one stone at **Squid's** ($$) raw bar which features the Spiked Oyster Shot: an oyster nestled in a shot glass of Stolichnaya vodka, designed to be consumed in one gulp. The bar also offers freshly shucked oysters, peel-your-own shrimp, and littleneck clams.

The menu of fresh seafood features specialties such as shrimp curry, blackened salmon, smoked salmon manicotti, grilled fresh tuna with fresh fruit salsa, salt and pepper catfish and even squid fradiavlo on linguini. In addition to fish, you'll find steak, poultry, burgers, salads, chowders and an array of desserts. Squid's is at 1201 N. Fordham Boulevard, a.k.a. U.S. Highway 15-501 Bypass. (919-942-8757)

The Weathervane Cafe ($-$$$) located at **A Southern Season** is a delightful place to dine for lunch or dinner. Casual to gourmet foods can be found on their menu. Its new outdoor cafe adds another dimension to a charming restaurant located in one of the most incredible places to shop for gourmet foods, wines and gifts in the Triangle. (919-929-9466)

HILLSBOROUGH

To Get There:

Hillsborough is located 12 miles north of Chapel Hill on N.C. 86.

The word is overused, but quaint is how Hillsborough looks. And maybe that's because it doesn't capitalize on it's 1754 status as much as it could. Over 200 years of architectural styles span everything from Piedmont farmhouses to classic Federal with an interesting mix of Tidewater thrown in. Just beyond the Eno River, the town is about one square mile of historic buildings and homes with more markers commemorating events and heroes than any town in the state.

Things To See and Do _____

Orange County Historical Museum
At the Orange County Historical Museum you'll learn that the clock above the Orange County Courthouse, a gift from

King George III in 1769, has been shuffled about town, and legend declares that part of it was thrown into the Eno River to prevent it from becoming British contraband. And if you think taxes are unjust now, look at the Regulator movement that formed to protest them in 1768. Downtown, you'll see the marker to the five Regulator men who were hanged after the battle at Alamance rather than pay taxes to a corrupt government.

Obviously, no one was thrilled to have Gen. Cornwallis winter here at the Colonial Inn. Ironically, at the same time, Hillsborough was the home of William Hooper (Nash-Hooper house) who signed the Declaration of Independence. Although, both Union and Confederate forces quartered here temporarily, Hillsborough prefers to be known for its Revolutionary history.

Historic Churches
The architecture of Hillsborough churches is quite significant. The 1816 **Hillsborough Presbyterian Church** is the oldest Presbyterian Church in continuous use in North Carolina, and you can tour the church's interior by asking the church secretary for the key. Admission is free. Adjacent to the church lies the **Old Town Cemetery**. Hillsborough's burial grounds from pre-Revolutionary War

days were originally connected to the Anglican Church that burned. The remains of William Hooper, William Graham, John Berry, Archibald DeBow Murphy and many others are buried here, some whose gravestones can no longer be read. **St. Matthew's Episcopal Church**, circa 1825, is known for its outstanding stained-glass windows, but particularly for the Angel Window, created and signed by Louis Tiffany. On the outskirts of the city on Barracks Road, look for an 1859 gray clapboard Anglican church. It is directly across the street from Hillsborough's former Military Academy's commandant's home.

Tours
The Colonial Guides at 125 East King Street provides 5 different walking tours (fees range from $4-$14) that take you to prominent homes such as the Rochester home, supposed namesake for Rochester, New York, and the Ashe home, the origin of Asheville, North Carolina's name. They'll also take you inside the 1821 Burwell School and brick "necessary" at 319 North Churton Street, which has been restored to its former intention, an 18th century home. Originally, it was the home of Presbyterian minister, Robert and his wife, M.A., whose portrait is above the mantel. They turned it into a fine girl's school.

Accommodations and Dining

You can spend the night at the 1759 **Colonial Inn** ($$) at 153 West King Street, the oldest continuously operating inn in America. This venerable old inn weathered both the Revolutionary War and the Civil War. When Union soldiers began ransacking the inn, its clever innkeeper, Sara Stroud, ran to the upstairs porch balcony and waved her husband's Masonic apron. The flag's symbol captured the eye of a sergeant who was a Mason. He ordered his soldiers to return their looting. It was a tavern back in early times, but today its known as a fine county-type-food restaurant that serves bountiful meals and breakfasts. Its baked ham with raisin sauce rivals its fried chicken and home-cooked vegetables. (919-732-2461)

If you're looking for a really romantic honeymoon B & B, then check out the oldest brick "summer kitchen" in Hillsborough. The **Hillsborough House Inn** ($$$$) at the corner of Tryon and St. Mary's roads has converted the summer kitchen into a luxurious cottage loft. The bed is under an arching canopy of just-budding tree branches facing the original 1790 fireplace. (919-644-1600)

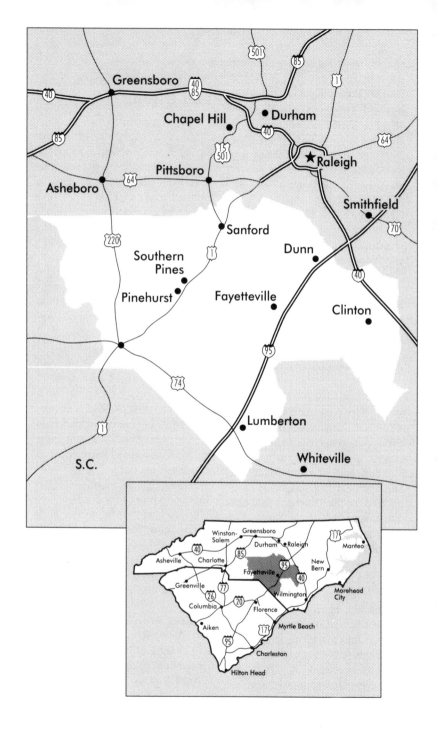

NORTH CAROLINA'S
Southern Heartland

THE SANDHILLS

PINEHURST/
SOUTHERN PINES

To Get There:

Southern Pines is located
near the southern intersection
of U.S. 1 and U.S. 15-501.
Pinehurst is 4 miles west
at the intersection of
N.C. 5 and N.C. 2.

Few people realize that
this golfers' utopia was once
barren wilderness. The tract
was nothing but leveled tree
stumps when James G. Tufts
bought the land in 1895 and
hired landscape architect
Frederick Law Olmstead to design a resort for convalescents.
Olmstead was already famous
for his design of New York's
Central Park and the gardens
of Biltmore House in Asheville,

N.C. You might say that golf
was born in Pinehurst when
Tufts found his healthier pa-
trons disturbing the cattle in
his fields by hitting little white
balls with clubs. Swimming
against the tide that viewed golf
as a passing fad, Tufts built a
nine-hole golf course, and the
rest is history. In 1900 Scottish
golf pro Donald Ross came to
Pinehurst and designed more
courses, which eventually
earned the area an international
reputation. Today, it is considered one of the "golf capitals of
the world."

For many years the
Pinehurst-Southern Pines area
has been a favorite of visitors
who enjoy golf, tennis, horseback riding, polo, croquet, water sports, trap and skeet shooting and other sports. Like
Camden, S.C., Southern Pines
has a long tradition of harness
racing and steeplechase as well.
The annual Stoneybrook Race

is here. Happily, in this fast-track world the area has retained its quiet charm. There are approximately 35 golf courses, including Pinehurst's Number 2, which was voted by *Golf Magazine* as one of the "golden dozen" golf courses in the world.

Most of the golf courses in the area are attached to resort hotels. What that means is that, although they are billed as "public" you must be a member, a guest of the resort or an invited guest of one of the above to play. Some of the most popular of the courses are:

PINEHURST RESORT AND COUNTRY CLUB

Pinehurst Resort and Country Club has 7 courses, all designed by such respected golf designers as Donald Ross, Ellis Maples, Robert Trent Jones, George and Tom Fazio and Rees Jones. Each course has its own personality and many challenge the skills of the best golfers. No. 1 and No. 3 are both short courses and remain favorites of the club members. No. 2 was designed by Donald Ross who called it "the fairest test of championship golf I have ever designed." Although efforts have been made several times to toughen the course, No. 4 remains the least challenging and the Par-3 15th hole of No. 5 is the most recognizable hole in Pinehurst as it is the most photographed. With its undulating fairways and unforgiving water hazards, No. 6 presents dra-

The majestic pounding of hooves can be heard nearly as often as the call of "Fore!" in the horse country of the Sandhills.

Photo courtesy Pinehurst Area Convention and Visitors Bureau.

matic challenges. The infamous No. 7 is without compare and will challenge players from tee to green. With a length of 7,114 yards from the back tees, this is a driver's course.

Fees are rated high for all 7 courses, with No. 7 carrying the highest price tag. Pinehurst Resort and Country Club is located on U.S. 15-501 north. (910-295-8141)

The Pit

This 1985 course has won high praise from both *Golf Digest* and *Golf Magazine* that regards its Par-5 8th hole to be one of the top golf holes in the country. This Dan Maples original, compares favorably with his designs along the Grand Strand. The Par-71 course has a wild beauty and its curving fairways and bent grass greens demand accuracy from even the pros.

Located on N.C. 5 in Aberdeen, The Pit is expensive to play. (910-944-1600)

Mid Pines Resort

This is an easygoing resort that doesn't put on airs and strives to make everyone comfortable. The Mid Pines Golf Course is a mental challenge as Donald Ross has designed this course to demand a thoughtful approach to each and every shot. The Par-72 course is expensive to play.

Mid Pines Resort is located on Midland Road, 1 mile from Southern Pines. (910-692-2114)

Pine Needles Golf Club

This still-authentic 1920's course roams across the undulating sand hills. Built with the use of oxen in 1927, the Par-71 course is weathered but remains well-groomed and is known as a "shot makers" course. It will host the 1996 Women's U.S. Open. It is located on Midland Road in Southern Pines and it is rated expensive. (910-692-7111)

Other nearby sites of interest include **Historic Aberdeen**, the **Malcom Blue Farm**, **Weymouth Center** and the **House in the Horseshoe** (near Carthage).

Accommodations

BED & BREAKFAST INNS

If you'd rather stay in a B & B, the lovely **"Finally," The O'Connor House** ($, 919-281-5622) in Pine Bluff has Sandhill's charm and great food. The present owners retired from military service after 33 moves around the world, hence the unusual name. A full homemade breakfast is standard fare in this 1909 home.

Another excellent choice in nearby Aberdeen is the **Inn at the Bryant House** ($-$$$, 919-944-3300) with continental breakfast in a beautifully refurbished 1914 home.

*The tradition of excellence continues on the more than
30 courses in the Pinehurst Area.*

A super choice is the **Magnolia Inn** in Pinehurst ($$$—$$$$, 919-295-6900) that offers a complete country breakfast. The inn also has an on-site restaurant—the 726 Pub, open for lunch and dinner.

RESORTS

For golfers, ideal stays are **Pinehurst Resort and Country Club** ($$$$, 800-ITS-GOLF) or **Mid Pine Resort** ($$$-$$$$, 800-323-2114).

HOTELS/MOTELS

A long-time favorite since it opened its doors in 1895 is the **Holly Inn** ($$$, 800-682-6901) on Cherokee Road in Pinehurst. The **Pine Crest Inn** ($$-$$$, 919-295-6121) on Dogwood Road in Pinehurst is so comfortable that it's like slipping on an old shoe, or you may want to try the **Manor Inn** ($$-$$$, 919-295-2700) on Magnolia Road.

Dining _____

Recommended restaurants include **Barrister's Steak House** on U.S. 1 in Pinehurst, the **Lob Steer** and **The Barn,** both on U.S. 1 in Southern Pines.

For More Information:

Pinehurst Area Convention & Visitors Bureau
P.O. Box 2270
Southern Pines, NC 28388
800-346-5362

SEAGROVE AREA POTTERIES

To Get There:

Seagrove is on U.S. 220 about 30 miles south of Greensboro. Most of the potteries are off N.C. 705 between Seagrove and Robbins and all potteries have maps of the area.

In this day of plastic and throw-away paper dinnerware, there are still among us potters who dig the clay, throw the pot and carefully shape the vessel with their bare hands, sometimes on the same type of manual, foot-spun potter's wheel used by their predecessors. These potters are treasured by those who respect and care about their ancient way of earning a living.

Varied accounts date pottery at Seagrove to Native American pottery of the 1500s, and Quaker potters to 1750. Mrs. Ben Owen, Sr., says a parcel of the southern Piedmont, near Seagrove, North Carolina, was granted to James Owen from Staffordshire, England, in 1756. Owen, and others like him, lured by the area's heavy red clay and abundant firewood, used to keep the kilns firing, brought their skills to fashion pitchers, bowls, demijohns with corn cob stoppers and churns then found in everyone's kitchen.

In time, an entire potting culture grew in the area where whole families worked to produce their specialized shapes, distinctive designs and secret mix of glazes. In 1923, descendant Ben Owen's dirt dishes, as they called the orange pottery, were discovered by artist Jacques Busbee and his wife Lucille, who saw a future for the utilitarian ware. Now, original pieces of that famous pottery reside in many museums. Today, Ben-Three proudly carries on the family tradition. He also works in stoneware and porcelain down the road from where Busbee and his grandfather set up Jugtown, the original studio.

Most of the original families such as Cole, Owen, Garner and others have passed down their individual styles and continue to be represented in this Sandhills conclave. Today, your choices range from raku to bright colored crystalline pottery to traditional earthenware that carries a rougher look. Prices range too, from modest to expensive, stopping just short of exorbitant. This late infusion of talent gives you over 60 potters with different styles and tastes to choose from: traditional, original, contemporary and custom order pottery.

Blissfully, the Seagrove area has not become a neon sign, tourist-type environment. Most of the studio cabins are unpretentious and hard to spot.

POTTERIES

If coming in from the south, you might stop at **Beaumont Pottery** right on U.S. 220 just north of Seagrove. (Don't even think of leaving here without a map of the area's potteries. Although maps are available at most potters, the various potteries are tricky to find and can become a true time waster if you try to wing it.) This was the **Seagrove Pottery** until owners, Dorothy and Walter Auman, were tragically killed in a car accident in 1991. Friends, Jerry and Sally Beaumont, now operate the pottery with the Auman's sign still hanging above their own. Here, you'll see Early American saltglaze and stoneware.

If this is your first visit to the area, make sure to stop next at **Turn and Burn** near the intersection of U.S. 220 and N.C. 705 in downtown Seagrove (the only potter located in town). David Garner, a soft-spoken potter who also teaches Bible classes at a nearby prison, continues to throw his family's 1600's styles that satirize politics with both hand carved face and snake jugs. You may see the current politician that folks are poking fun at. Garner says, "My family on both sides in every direction has been in pottery." But Garner has also branched beyond his traditional heritage, making bird feeders and glasses with a sgraffito technique (carving through one color of clay into another). He works in traditional salt glaze, contemporary stoneware and some raku, and on the base of all but the smallest pieces, notes Bible scripture numbers and the Christian fish symbol.

The DirtWorks Pottery on U.S. 220 in Seagrove is known for Dan Triece's copper luster raku ware. His stoneware glazes range from soft pastels to deep blues. You can also see the artistry of other North Carolina crafts people here such as Mike Mewborn's wood-turning bowls and goblets from varied rich

Potter Ben Cole at work.

woods. The shop also displays works of weavers and basket makers.

Go to the intersection of U.S. 220 and N.C. 705 (1 block away) and turn south onto N.C. 705. Stop at **Phil Morgan's Pottery** on your right where you'll discover the rainbow brilliance of Morgan's unique crystalline glazed porcelain vases. They have a museum quality about them that tempts you to take home half the shop.

Continue south on N.C. 705 and turn left at Fork Creek Mill Road to reach **Potts Town Potters**. Co-owner, Linda Potts' grandmother was a Cole, another well-known potting family. She and husband Jeff use local clay (not used by many potters anymore) to produce traditional earthenware, tableware and serving pieces.

The potteries are scattered throughout these beautiful rural roads, that lie on the fringes of the Uhwarrie National Forest, so don't think you're lost—enjoy the scenery. There can be quite a distance between potteries. Look for Dover Road and turn west there for the **Dover Pottery**. At its sign, wind down the dirt road to an old weathered barn with beautiful plates dotted across its front. Reminds you a little of the Pennsylvania Dutch barns with their protective hex signs, and looks like a Bob Timberlake painting.

A dog announces you. Inside the barn, with antique stained-glass windows, you'll see the traditional slip-painted pottery of Milly and Al McCanless who use the Majolica technique. Some pieces are done with intricate fish and rabbit designs. Their crystalline vases are displayed on a wall shelf.

Back out on N.C. 705 south, stop at **Ben Owen Pottery**. Here, three generations work in either throwing, glazing, selling or just taking the time to get to know you. Grandson, Ben-Three, devotes the bulk of his creativity to crafting individual pieces rather than production type works. Now working in porcelain, he describes it as, "Like having cream cheese in your hands. It's a real challenge to throw it. If you get the walls thin enough it will be translucent." A showroom displays the variety of his work.

If your interest is in Old Salem style pottery, then check out the work of Westmoore and Cole. Turn east onto Busbee Road for **Westmoore Pottery** found in a new, rustic-styled studio-house. You'll see redware as historically accurate as is feasible here. Since no pottery had interior glazes in Seagrove before 1920, Westmore uses none, which means containers won't hold liquid for an extended period without seeping. You'll also see many green glazes at this pottery.

Continue down Busbee Road and turn left after **Owens Pottery** for **Jugtown Pottery**. It dates to 1923 and, in its little log cabin museum, you'll see the works of some early potters. Its stoneware reflects many local styles and glazes with a preference for blues and grays. Expect a larger operation here than at most potters. Stone picnic tables under its trees provide a nice place to bring your picnic basket. Soft drink machines are nearby.

It can take a full day to visit the shops and you might want to spend two if you've come from a distance. Most potters are open from 9 a.m.-5 p.m., Monday-Saturday, but never on Sunday. Once a year you can check out all the potters at the Seagrove School, usually the Sunday before Thanksgiving, when Seagrove holds its **Seagrove Pottery Festival**. A limited edition of signed and dated pieces from local potters is auctioned. Other traditional crafts people demonstrate and display their crafts. Barbecue is served. Admission is $2 and free for children under 12 accompanied by an adult.

Accommodations and Dining

There are three restaurants in the area, but you can get a good down home meal that includes an entree, two vegetables, salad and dessert for a reasonable price at either **The Jugtown Cafe** ($) or **Seagrove Family Restaurant** ($), open only until 3 p.m. You might also try the **Dairy Breeze** ($). The restaurants are all along the main street of Seagrove.

For lodging you will have to go to Pinehurst (about 30 miles away), or go north on U.S. 220 to Asheboro.

For more information:

Pinehurst Area
Convention and Visitors Bureau
P.O. Box 2270
Southern Pines, NC 28387
800-346-5362 or 919-692-3330

PISGAH COVERED BRIDGE

To Get There:
From Seagrove go north on U.S. 220 and turn west on Burney Road. Go for nearly 8 miles to Pisgah Covered Bridge Road and turn left. Be sure to bear right around the sharp curve. Go past a cross roads. The bridge will be on your left, off the road, and can easily be mistaken for an old weathered house. The covered bridge is only a few yards from a small bridge that you'll pass over.

Of course, it was romance that made *The Bridges of Madi-*

Photo by clay Nolen. Courtesy N.C. Travel & Tourism.

The Jugtown Pottery near Seagrove produces 18th Century-style pottery made entirely of native clays.

son County a roaring success. This covered bridge perched over a beautiful creek among ancient trees bestows its own kind of romance. After a day of browsing and talking with potters, who live a far simpler life than most of us, watching the sun set over this 100-year-old bridge can make you rethink your lifestyle. You can still walk through the bridge and view the graffiti of who loved whom throughout the years. Used heavily between 1890 and 1930, this bridge was one of 40 covered bridges in Randolph County and is one of only two left standing in North Carolina.

UWHARRIE NATIONAL FOREST

To Get There:
Take N.C. 24/27 7 miles east of Albemarle.

No one will verify it, but it is believed that "Uwharrie" comes from a Native American tribe indigenous to the area. They were pushed out by Germans, French, Irish and English who came here for good logging and setting up stone quarries. In 1961, President John F. Kennedy established the Uwharrie National Forest, and our government bought 50 tracts of land from Piedmont farmers.

Some scientists believe the Uwharries to be the oldest peaks in North America. These 900-foot-high, rounded hills in the Uwharries are the remains of once ancient volcanoes. Those volcanoes erupted many moons before Native Americans searched this rich hunting ground for the prized mineral rhyolite to make their arrows and tools. Today, this smallest of America's national forests is truly the happy hunting ground for hunters and anglers alike. Bass is abundant in the 5,973-acre Badin Lake, and the Uwharries has some of the best hunting in North Carolina. Hunters, from all over the southeast, come to these low-lying mountains for dove, quail, squirrel, raccoons, rabbits and, of course, deer—the biggest draw. The bow-and-arrow season is from the first weekend in September to the first weekend in November; the muzzle-loading season is usually the second week in November; the regular gun season is from the middle of October to January 1. In past years, this 47,000-acre forest has had the largest number of deer to come through the check-in station at Donnie Mullinix' Grocery on N.C. 109 (heart of the Uwharrie Forest) than any other national forest.

Camera hunters also find this a happy hunting ground where the threatened red-cockaded woodpecker is occasionally glimpsed and hawks, chickadees, titmice, cardinals and many other birds are seen throughout the forest. During the late spring and early summer, the Uhwarrie comes alive with over 40 different kinds of wildflowers. Beginning the season with azalea, wild iris and laurel, the grounds later become resplendent with wild indigo, wild geranium, wild larkspur, trillium and hydrangea.

Located in parts of Montgomery, Randolph and Davidson counties, this quiet forest makes an ideal place to pitch your tent for a night or so of camping. Besides hunting, fishing, bird watching and photography, you can also ride horseback, swim and hike, which makes the Uwharrie's slogan, "Land of Many Uses," most appropriate.

CAMPING

Badin Lake Campground ($), **Uhwarrie Hunt Camp** ($) and **Uhwarrie Group Camp** ($) have showers. There're also picnic tables and other facilities at **Denizen's Creek Trailhead** and **Holt's Cabin Picnic Area** ($).

For More Information:

Uwharrie National Forest
District Ranger
U.S. Forest Service
Route 3, Box 470
Troy, NC 27371
919-576-6391

MORROW MOUNTAIN STATE PARK

To Get There:
Take N.C. 740 seven miles east of Albemarle.

Winter, which is not always the kindest time to parks, is the ideal time to hike the Sugarloaf Mountain Trail at Morrow Mountain State Park. This is the time that offers extraordinary views of the park's 4,700 acres and lets you escape cabin fever doldrums. Out here, you can enjoy 15 miles of hiking and 16 miles of bridle trails through the Uhwarrie Mountains, which is one of the oldest mountain ranges in the east. Hikers have a choice of 9 trails that range from a half to 4 miles, with varying stages of difficulty. (Some are a snap.) Even though there aren't any bike trails, you can ride your bike along the hilly to rough roads. You might also want to check out the park's Natural History Museum before exploring the park. Nature and ecology programs are offered daily during the summer and on weekends for school children the remainder of the year.

And although the pool and boat house are closed during the winter, there is still a boat ramp available at the northern end of the park. This is where the Pee Dee, Yadkin and Lake Tillery Rivers form the park's boundaries. You can catch striped, largemouth and white bass as well as catfish, bluegill, crappie and perch.

If you want to make this a day trip, pack a picnic basket and bring some charcoal for the grills beside the picnic tables. Hikers like the summit area, which has a shelter and comfort station near the parking areas and offers a panoramic view of an area that's hard to beat.

CAMPING

Like most of the park's over 300,000 visitors, spring, summer and fall are the likely times you'll choose to sign up for one of the park's three camping areas. The first, a 106-site area, can accommodate your RV and although no hookups are available, a water station is nearby. A second, smaller camping area is available and reservations are requested. For hearty souls who don't mind lugging in their own water, the third is a beautiful primitive camping area along a two-mile trail. Two-bedroom cabins are also available to rent from March through November by the week or weekend. (704-982-4402)

For More Information:

**Morrow Mountain State Park
Rt. 5, Box 430
Albemarle, NC 28001
704-982-4402**

NORTH CAROLINA ZOOLOGICAL PARK

To Get There:
Follow the signs from U.S. 220 south of Asheboro. The Zoo is located on Zoo Parkway, 6 miles southeast of Asheboro.

It would cost big bucks to go on an African Safari and could flatten your wallet to explore North America's Sonora Desert, but you can see both at North Carolina's Zoo for a fraction of that cost. The zoo covers over 2 gorgeous miles of trails through the Uhwarrie Mountains. Don't panic, trams transport you to most exhibits, saving shoe leather and energy. And helpful tram attendants will load and unload strollers or wheelchairs and assist elderly citizens, too.

The first of the North American habitats, Sonora Dessert, opened in 1993 and the swamps and grassland exhibit is scheduled for September 1994. The moment you enter the Sonora Desert habitat you'll feel dry heat (75-85 degrees Fahrenheit) and notice the fragrant hint of jojoba in the air. Pockets of boulders build mountain-like toward its domed roof with mesquite and cacti jutting over outcroppings of rocks beside the looping path. Flying free overhead or plodding their way through desert underbrush, you'll see cactus wrens, quail

Photo by Blair Callicutt. Courtesy N.C. Zoo.

A mother communicates with her young gorilla at the N.C. Zoo.

and doves that act almost tame. Reptiles, spiders, ocelots and 37 other creatures are sheltered behind either the habitat's glass partitions or moat-like barricades that let you see (upclose) how animals navigate in the wild. Because of the dessert's extreme heat, much of the wildlife has become nocturnal. You'll loop down into a darkened, 10-degree cooler area where kangaroo rats, rattlesnakes and bats readjust their predatory prowls.

The tram can deposit you next at the R.J. Reynolds Forest Aviary (another terrific place to visit during winter's bleak months). Moist warmth, so different from the Sahara Desert's dry, welcomes you inside this lush, Technicolor rain forest. Often, stationed like a flaming sentinel at the top of a tropical fig tree perches a scarlet ibis. At feeding time you're bound to find amethyst starlings and other electric-colored beauties splashing through the clear, ground level pond below. Listen for the speckled crested barbet piercing through the other birds' musical twittering with its loud, repeated call. Yes, you can picture Tarzan swooping down vines hanging amidst the blood banana and mangrove trees. Look closely for a bromeliad plant, hidden in a tree's crevice. The plant catches water in its vase-like center and offers the water for birds to drink. And its fronds have twisted into a funnel making it perfect for frogs. Around the center's waterfall-fed pond, a circular walkway introduces you to giant tortoises and 150 other birds and ducks. Outside, you'll see dozens of shrimp-pink flamingos standing on one spindly leg. The joint that looks like a knee is actually their ankle. They're standing on their toes!

Hop aboard the tram for the African Pavilion where a baby Gerenuk (deer-like animal) can be playing either outside or in the pavilion. Children delight in the red and blue faced baboons in the center that jump from cage to bare branched trees. Surrounding them are meerkats, pacing servals, bat-eared foxes, cuddly looking Kirk's dik-diks and many others. Outside a family of gorillas lumber along like a Sunday afternoon. Take the foot paths to visit the chimpanzees, lions, giraffes and zebras, but the tram will take you past the 37-acre African Plains where antelopes and gazelles leap in unison with impalas. Get off the tram for a better look at elephants snorting then spraying water from their thigh-high pond and see the bigger-than-life rhino looking more placid than he is.

When hungry, stop by one of the refreshment centers or picnic beside the lake. And along pathways take time out to investigate the zoo's "smart carts" that explain varied species of plants and animals.

The North Carolina Zoological Park is open April through October from 9 a.m. until 5 p.m., Monday through Friday; 10 a.m. until 6 p.m. weekends and holidays. November through March, the hours are from 9 a.m. until 4 p.m. daily. Admission is $6 for adults; $4 for senior citizens and children 2 to 12. (919-879-7000)

For More Information:
North Carolina Zoological Park
Asheboro, NC 27203
910-879-7000

Photo courtesy N.C. Zoo.

Bath time at the zoo.

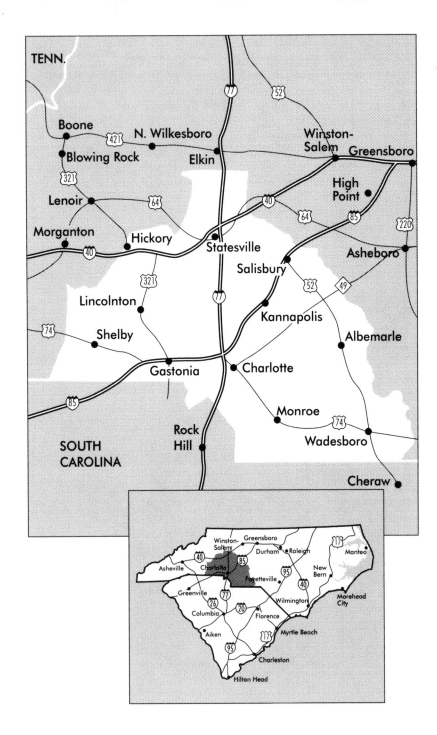

TENN.

Boone
421
N. Wilkesboro
Blowing Rock
Elkin
Winston-Salem
Greensboro
321
High Point
Lenoir
64
40
64
85
220
Morganton
Hickory
Statesville
Asheboro
40
Salisbury
321
52
49
Lincolnton
Kannapolis
74
Shelby
Albemarle
Gastonia
Charlotte
85
Monroe
Rock Hill
Wadesboro
74
SOUTH CAROLINA
Cheraw

Winston-Salem
Greensboro
Durham
Raleigh
Manteo
17
40
Asheville
85
Charlotte
Fayetteville
95
New Bern
Greenville
77
40
Wilmington
Morehead City
26
Columbia
20
Florence
Aiken
17
Myrtle Beach
95
Charleston
Hilton Head

SOUTHERN FOOTHILLS

CHARLOTTE

To Get There:

Charlotte is located at the juncture of I-85 and I-77.

Charlotte is becoming known as a "World Class" city and its recreational offerings are headed toward the same status. This beautiful city, known as both the "City of Trees" and the "Queen City," makes an ideal day or weekend trip. It pleases with sophisticated city offerings such as museums and historic homes and tops out with "rockem-sockem" country doings and spectator sporting events.

There are attractions from the participant, family-kind found at **Paramount's Carowinds** theme park and

New Heritage USA to the visually exhilarating type at **Discovery Place's Omnimax Theatre** and the **Charlotte Motor Speedway**, which has enough excitement to relocate your heart and push it up into your throat. There are folks who come here just to see the **Charlotte Hornets** play at the **Coliseum** or the **Charlotte Knights** play at beautiful **Knights Castle.**

But "World Class" applies to the whole picture, which includes the exploratory offerings at **Reed Gold Mine** (the first gold mine to send Charlotte on its economic path) where you can spend a day panning for gold. And you can go through the **James K. Polk Memorial** (11th president of the U.S.), or the **Hezekiah Alexander's Homesite Museum**, a 1744 pioneer who helped shape the city along with James Latta at **Latta Plantation**, or try a little sight-seeing at the **Mint Museum of Art.**

Things To See and Do _____

PARAMOUNT'S CAROWINDS

TO GET THERE:
Carowinds straddles the boundary between North and South Carolina. Accessed from I-77, it is 13 miles north of Rock Hill, S.C. and 10 miles south of Charlotte, N.C. at exit 90.

Carowinds has gone Hollywood—literally. But that's not bad. In fact, it's more fun than ever because it gives timid types another reason to spend a day at the park. And for the stalwart among us, its new Days of Thunder ride, can give us the sensation (with motion simulation) of being behind the wheel of a race car. Add that to its ripsnorting roller coasters such as Thunder Road, Frenzoid and Vortex, and you're off to a thrilling start. Cool off with Rip Roarin' Rapids and White Water Falls or the wave pool.

This new park marriage with Hollywood has incorporated a professional ice skating show, an MTV-style choreographed show and Richard Scarry's *Huckle, The Cat.* Walk-

ing around the park you'll see such characters as Klingons, Romulans, Vulcans and Race Track Star notables, and you will find scads of movie paraphernalia to buy in the stores. Look for the Paramount Walk of Fame that lists prominent movies and their stars. The new motto is: "Where the Magic of the movies meets the thrills of a lifetime." They could be right. Check it out.

Carowinds' one-price ticket covers all rides and park shows. Palladium concerts, featuring big-name entertainers, are extra. Carowinds is located off I-77 at exit 90. General admission to Paramount's Carowinds for ages 7-59 is $24.95 and $13.50 for children ages 4 to 6 and senior citizens 60 years and older. Children ages 3 and younger are admitted free.

The park has a new restaurant called "Wings" honoring Paramount's 1927 academy award winning film. It is decorated with props from famous movies of the 1900's era .

At Paramount's Carowinds, you can camp at 207 sites ($). Facilities include: hot showers, a laundry, a grocery at the Trading Post Lodge and a game room. There are electrical hookups and water for pull-through and primitive sites. Transportation is provided from the campground to the theme park.

Photo courtesy Paramount's Carowinds.

Paramount's Carowinds' thrilling stand-up roller coaster, VORTEX.

The campground also has a swimming pool, a miniature golf course, a softball field and an outdoor movie theater. (704-588-2606)

NEW HERITAGE USA

> **To Get There:**
> **From I-77, take S.C. 160 east toward Ft. Mill.**

Reopened in June, 1992, this Christian resort and theme park features its famous water park, a working farm, horseback riding, carriage rides, tennis courts, swimming pools, game rooms, miniature golf, fishing, canoeing, go-cart rides, batting cages and a Passion Play. Admission is charged for individual rides and attractions. New Heritage USA is located at 3000 Heritage Parkway in Fort Mill, South Carolina. Campsites ($) are available as well as hotel and motel accommodations ($$-$$$$). (803-548-7800 or 800-374-1234)

DISCOVERY PLACE

Discovery Place has long been considered one of the top 10 science museums in the country. With lights flashing and a continual stream of children and adults chattering enthusiastically, excitement rivets through this hands-on science and technology museum. Almost every exhibit is designed to be inter-

Staff photo.

Charlotte's Discovery Place is one of the top ten science museums in the country.

active—from the **Aquarium Touch Pool** to the **Science Circus** to the **Computer Center**.

For many, the museum's *piece de resistance* is its **Observer/Omnimax Theatre,** featuring a tilted dome screen and a wraparound sound system. The **Space Voyager Planetarium**, sharing the same space, features a "Starball" that projects over 10,000 stars on the largest dome in the United States and promises to take you on an incredible journey through space.

Downstairs in the museum, birds and sea life thrive in the **Knight Rain Forest**. You can really imagine yourself in a forest jungle on the bottom floor with birds flying overhead.

The museum is open every day of the year except Thanksgiving and Christmas. Hours are 9 a.m. until 5 p.m. weekdays (9 a.m. until 6 p.m., June through August), 9 a.m. until 6 p.m. Saturdays, and 1 until 6 p.m. Sundays. Admission is $5 for adults, $4 for students 6 to 18 years old and senior citizens 60 and over. When accompanied by a parent, admission for children ages 3 to 5 is $2.50 and children under 3 get in free. Admission is free after 2 p.m. on "Wonderful Wednesday," the first Wednesday of each month. Discovery Place is located at 301 North Tryon Street in downtown Charlotte. (800-935-0553)

CHARLOTTE MOTOR SPEEDWAY

Just 12 miles northeast of Charlotte lies the nation's hottest and most up-to-date racing facility. The now lighted NASCAR facility is home to 4 annual events: **Coca-Cola 600** and **Winston Select 300** in May, **Mello Yello 500** and **All Pro Auto Parts 300** in October. Biannually, April and September, the speedway holds the **AutoFair**, considered the largest antique car show and flea market in the South.

If you've never gone to a stock car race, make plans to visit on one of the qualifying days. Find a place next to the fence that separates you from the comet-charging cars when they decelerate from the 170-mph-and-over speeds to make their bank turn. Right here is where you get the feel of how fast these mega engines are firing. And right here is where many a fan is born. The qualifying day for the Coca-Cola 600 is the Wednesday prior to Memorial Day weekend. Qualifying day for the Mello Yello 500 is the first Wednesday in October.

The first of the major race weekends begins with the Winston, the kickoff race for the "Eight Days in May" that ends with the famed Coco-Cola 600. The Coca-Cola has become the

Photo courtesy Charlotte Motor Speedway.

The Charlotte Motor Speedway draws millions of visitors to the area each year.

second-largest single-day paid spectator event in the United States, bringing in over 160,000 fans.

The Speedway has a gift shop that is open year-round and group and individual tours are available. CMS is located near Concord. (704-455-3200)

REED GOLD MINE

Long before the famous California Gold Rush, the Reed Gold Mine, just outside Charlotte in Cabarrus County, became the site of the first authenticated gold find in the United States. This initiated a regional gold rush that resulted in around 100 operating gold mines in the Charlotte area. Conrad Reed discovered a 17-pound gold nugget in 1799, which his family used for a doorstop for several years before selling it to a Fayetteville jeweler for the unprincely sum of $3.50.

Reed Gold Mine is one of the area's significant contributions to history. The museum has a number of interesting mining artifacts and you can watch a 20-minute film that will give a good grounding in gold mining. During the April-October panning season, you can try your luck at finding a piece of the glittery stuff. But first you need to take the 30-minute underground tour (50 feet below the surface) as well as the 20-minute tour to the mill to watch the stamp machine pulverize large rock into fine textured sand.

No restaurant is available, but there are picnic tables and vending machines. Hours are 9:00 a.m. until 5:00 p.m. Monday through Saturday, April through October; 10:00 p.m until 4:00 p.m. Tuesday through Saturday, November through March. Sunday hours are 1:00 until 5:00 p.m. during the summer season, but are one hour shorter during the winter. No admission is charged, but if you pan for gold, you will pay about $3 for two pans of dirt.

Reed Gold Mine is located at Stanfield, North Carolina. From Charlotte, take N.C. 24/27 to Reed Mine Road. (704-786-8337)

JAMES K. POLK MEMORIAL

The 11th president of the United States, James K. Polk, came into the world in a little log cabin near Pineville in 1795. His home has been reconstructed and several out buildings have been moved to the state historic site. The Visitors Center has an interesting display of his early beginnings and what life was like in the area.

Free guided tours are available throughout the year. The Polk Memorial is open from 9:00 a.m. until 5:00 p.m. Monday through Saturday, April through October; 10:00 a.m. until 4:00 p.m. Tuesday through Saturday, November through March. Sunday hours are from 1:00 until 5:00 p.m.

HEZEKIAH ALEXANDER HOMESITE & HISTORY MUSEUM

Charlotte's oldest dwelling, built in 1774, served as the home of Hezekiah and Mary

Photo courtesy Reed Gold Mine.

Panning for gold at the Reed Gold Mine.

Alexander and their 10 children. Alexander was a blacksmith and planter by trade and assumed a leadership role in the new community called Charlotte, eventually becoming a signer of the Mecklenburg Declaration of Independence. Today his homesite—plus a replicated kitchen and reconstructed springhouse—can be toured.

Guided tours are given. The house and museum are open 10:00 a.m. until 5:00 p.m. Tuesday through Friday and 2:00 p.m. until 5:00 p.m. on weekends. Tours of the homesite are given at 1:15 p.m. and 3:15 p.m. Tuesday through Friday; 2:15 p.m. and 3:15 p.m. Saturday and Sunday. You can see the museum free of charge, but there is a $2 charge for adults and $1 for children 6 to 16 for the homesite. Hezekiah Alexander Homesite & History Museum is located at 3500 Shamrock Drive. (704-568-1774)

ST. PETER'S CATHOLIC CHURCH

The ancient art form of fresco, which means fresh, can be seen in the magnificent work of North Carolina native Ben Long in this beautiful old 1893 Charlotte church. The fresco is a triptych depicting: The Agony, The Resurrection and The Pentecost. Long, who apprenticed with Pietro Annigoni of Florence, Italy for seven years, has two fresco works in Italy, and

several in West Jefferson and Glendale Springs, North Carolina. The church is located at 507 South Tryon Street and is open to visitors from 10:00 a.m. until noon and from 1:00 p.m. until 4:00 p.m. Monday through Saturday; from 1:00 until 4:00 p.m. on Sunday. Visitors are asked to respect masses and weddings. (704-332-2901)

LATTA PLACE

In the early 1800s, settlers chose the good bottom land beside Charlotte's many rivers and creeks. James Latta built his plantation beside the Catawba River in what is now called Huntersville, about 12 miles north of Charlotte.

Latta was a prosperous traveling salesman who bought wares in Charleston and Philadelphia and peddled them throughout the Piedmont area. You can tour his furnished home, slave house, barn, smokehouse, well house and experience a demonstration kitchen, plus see farm animals on a tour with costumed guides. The house is on the National Register of Historic Places and is part of Latta Plantation Park, a 760-acre nature preserve on Mountain Island Lake that includes an **Equestrian Center** and the **Carolina Raptor Center**. This facility cares for injured and orphaned birds of prey. The park also features nature trails, bridle paths, fishing, canoe access to the lake and a Visitors Center.

Tours are given at 1:30 and 3:30 p.m. Tuesday through Friday; Saturday and Sunday at 1:30, 2:30 and 3:30 p.m. Admission for adults is $2.00, for seniors, $1.50, for children $1 and children under 5 are admitted free.

MINT MUSEUM OF ART

One of the Southeast's most prominent museums is known as the Mint Museum due to the building's original function. Built in 1836 on West Trade Street, the building processed gold that came from the 75 to 100 gold mines located around Charlotte. Piece by numbered piece, the building was moved to its Eastover location in 1933 when preservationists fought to save it. Reconstructed, the classic structure opened in 1936 as the first art museum in North Carolina.

This museum draws a wide spectrum of people because, in addition to mounting its own shows, it now accommodates larger and more nationally prominent exhibits such as "Rameses the Great."

There is always something fun to see or do at the Mint. You can also plan on afternoon tea, Sunday brunch and daily lunch at the newly opened **Classical Taste Cafe**. Hours are: Tuesday and Friday from 10 a.m. until 10:00 p.m.; Wednesday, Thursday and Saturday from 10:00 a.m. until 5:00 p.m.; Sunday from 12:00 until 5:00 p.m. Admission for adults is $6.00, for seniors, $5.00, for

Photo courtesy Mint Museum of Art.

The Mint Museum of Art's pottery and porcelain collection ranks among the finest in the nation.

students, $4.00 and children 12 and under are admitted free. Admission is free on the first Tuesday evening of the month. The Mint Museum of Art is located at 2730 Randolph Road. (704-337-2000)

Accommodations

BED & BREAKFAST INNS
The Inn Uptown ($$$-$$$$) is located at 129 N. Poplar Street in uptown Charlotte. Hornet's Nest Liniment, concocted by one of the original owners, Walter Mullen, in 1897 is no longer available at this beautifully restored B & B. However, the whirlpool bath at the top of a spiral iron staircase in the romantic Tower Suite is bound to soothe your muscle aches.

Less romantic souls will appreciate the inn's showers (with three body sprays), which

The Inn Uptown.

kind of gives the feeling of being in an automatic car wash. Four of the handsomely appointed rooms have fireplaces, and all have writing desks and phones with modem capabilities. Guests receive a complimentary full breakfast at this three-story brick home, historically known as the Bagley-Mullen house. (704-342-2800 or 800-959-1990)

HOTELS/MOTELS
Days Inn ($) is located at 1408 Sugar Creek Road off I-85 north. It is convenient to the Charlotte Motor Speedway and University City; others are located at the Airport, Carowinds and Woodlawn Road.

Homewood Suites ($$$) is located at 8340 U.S. 29 near the University of North Carolina at Charlotte. This spacious, apartment-style suite hotel is comfortably furnished with all the features and amenities you expect, and some that may surprise you. Separate sleeping and living areas, two remote controlled color TVs and a video cassette player are the standard. A complimentary Deluxe Breakfast Buffet is served daily with an evening social hour with a light meal Monday through Thursday. You can work off stress by working out at the exercise center, sports/activity court, swimming pool or whirlpool. (704-549-8800)

Located at 237 N. Tryon Street, the 1929 **Dunhill Hotel**

($$$$), which originally opened as Mayfair Manor, is one of Charlotte's few remaining landmark hotels. Completely updated in 1987, it had the distinction of housing Beattle, Paul McCartney, last year. Its 60 guest rooms are elegantly furnished in 18th century decor. Some rooms have a Jacuzzi and a sitting area. Room service is available from its **Monticello Restaurant**. (704-332-4141)

The **Hyatt Hotel** ($$$$) located at 5501 Carnegie Boulevard in SouthPark is one of Charlotte's most elegant new hotels. It has an indoor pool, hot tub, sauna and fitness club. You can request an in-room refrigerator, a hair dryer, etc., without being charged an extra fee. You will appreciate its free valet parking or, if you are traveling by air, the hotel provides complimentary shuttle service. It's also convenient to **SouthPark Shopping Center**. (704-554-1234)

As the name suggests, the **Ramada Inn Carowinds** ($$) is conveniently located for visitors to Carowinds. It has all the amenities—including an outdoor pool—and if you're a guest Monday through Friday, breakfast is free. **Chow's** restaurant, located on the premises, features Chinese and American cuisine and it has a lounge that is open from 5 p.m. until 2 a.m. The Ramada is located at 225 Carowinds Boulevard in Fort Mill, South Carolina. (South Carolina: 803-548-2400, North Carolina: 704-334-4450)

Dining

It's not unusual to see a line of people all the way to the parking lot of **Gus's Sir Beef Restaurant** ($-$$) at 4104 Monroe Road. This family-style restaurant has been serving vegetables, fresh from its garden, for over 29 years. No fats are used to cook the delicious squash, greens and other good veggies—a heart healthy way to dine. You'll also appreciate the lean roast beef. Actress Elizabeth Taylor said Gus's fried chicken was the best ever. Meals are served from 11 a.m. until 9 p.m. Monday through Saturday.

At **La Bibliotheque** ($$-$$$$), 1901 Roxborough Road, even lunch is an elegant affair. La Bibliotheque means library in French, and the cuisine is prepared using traditional French techniques in a library setting. Bookcases line most of the walls, making you feel like you're dining in a friend's lavish walnut library. Dining is available on the new patio during warmer seasons. Your taste buds can enjoy a diversity of tastes from Escargo a la Chablisienne (snails baked in wine and garlic butter) as an appetizer to D'agneau (lamb), Canard (duck) to a N.Y. strip steak for your dinner entree.

For those who love authentic Northern Italian food, **Scallini** ($$$$), located in the Hyatt Hotel at SouthPark, is one of Charlotte's most highly rated restaurants. At lunch, prepare to feast on its oversized salads and sandwiches, and you'll never forget the country breakfasts served on the weekends.

Spratt's Kitchen & Market ($-$$) is located Uptown in Founders Hall at 100 North Tryon Street. If it's a busy day of sight-seeing and you don't want to waste a minute, stop by Spratt's cafeteria-type deli for a scrumptious quick meal. You can build your own sandwich from a vast array of deli selections and homemade breads, or a salad, charged by the pound, from the cold salad bar. (704-334-0864)

Lizzie's Restaurant ($$-$$$) at 4809 South Tryon Street is a smooth combination of nightclub and gourmet restaurant. Live bands play jazz and Top 40 hits nightly, and the wide selection of entrees should please even the most finicky palate. (704-527-3064)

For More Information:
Charlotte
Convention & Visitors Bureau
122 E. Stonewall St.
Charlotte, NC 28202-1838
800-231-4636

AAA Carolinas
720 East Morehead St.
Charlotte, NC 28202
704-377-3600

Side Trips _____

SCHIELE MUSEUM OF NATURAL HISTORY AND PLANETARIUM

To Get There:
From Charlotte, take I-85 south and take the New Hope Road exit. Follow N.C. 179 east to Garrison Blvd.

This gem of a little museum, located at 1500 Garrison Boulevard in Gastonia, has the reputation of being the most visited museum in North Carolina. It offers an outstanding exhibit on the state's natural history, an extensive collection of North American land mammals and a planetarium. Both children and adults enjoy the 18th century pioneer site, where living history demonstrations are staged throughout the year. The museum is open from 9 a.m. until 5 p.m. Tuesday through Friday and from 2 p.m. until 5 p.m. on Saturday and Sunday. It is closed Thanksgiving Day and Christmas week. (704-866-6900)

TOWN CREEK INDIAN MOUND

To Get There:

Take N.C. 27 east from Charlotte to N.C. 73 south.

This state historic site, near Mount Gilead in the Uwharrie Mountains, commemorates the life of the Pee Dee Indians who inhabited the area hundreds of years ago. Town Creek was a fortified place of refuge and counsel where religious ceremonies and feasts took place. The reconstruction is based on archaeological excavations.

A Visitors Center provides more insight into this Indian culture. Guided tours are available. For more information, contact Town Creek Indian Mound, Rt. 3, Box 50, Mount Gilead, NC 27306. (919-439-6802)

CROWDER'S MOUNTAIN STATE PARK

To Get There:

Take I-85 south to the Edgewood Road exit (13) and turn west on U.S. 29/74. Follow the signs to the park on Sparrows Springs Road.

Since the late '60s Crowder's Mountain, located in Gaston and Cleveland counties,

Photo courtesy Spencer Shops.

Visitors have the opportunity to "ride the rails" at Spencer Shops.

has been a rock climber's haven. Crowder's Mountain, the survivor of the ancient Kings Mountain range, geologically known as a monadnock (mountain protruding from a plane rather than a range), used to be much higher than those climbers tackle today.

On just about any given nice weather weekend, the side of its vertical cliff-face looks like a human stone anthill. Dozens of rock climbers scale the sheer crag and practice rappelling with nary a thought of the scary 150-foot drop. Even though the 2,500-acre park has posted signs warning about the dangers of this perilous sport, accidents which spell injury happen every year due to inexperience or lack of attention to detail. Climbers tell you it's a man/woman-against-nature kind of thing that builds self-esteem, trust and a camaraderie that's hard to put into words.

Of course, the park also draws about 160,000 annual visitors who come here to fish or canoe the lake, hike through its 15 winding trails, picnic and watch the "climb show" as they walk along the mountain's 1,625-foot summit. You can also participate in the park's Nature Study programs throughout the year. Primitive camping is available on a first-come, first-served basis for a nominal fee. (704-867-1181)

SPENCER SHOPS
NORTH CAROLINA
TRANSPORTATION MUSEUM

To Get There:
From Charlotte, take I-85 north. The exit for Spencer Shops is well marked, just north of Salisbury.

Unlike Steve Brody, the famous brakeman in the "Wreck of the Old 97," you can get to Spencer on time. In fact, in no time at all you can see what was once Southern Railway's largest repair facility between Washington, D.C., and Atlanta, Georgia. You might even be lucky enough to run into some old engineers who work on the rusty engines and meet for coffee in the **Spencer Ties Room**.

In the last few years, visitors have had the opportunity of "riding the rails" from Spencer to Salisbury. The museum also houses other artifacts that relate to transportation.

This state historic site is open year-round except for major holidays. Hours are 9 a.m. until 5 p.m. Monday through Saturday and 1 p.m. until 5 p.m. on Sunday, April through October; 9 a.m. until 4 p.m. and 1 p.m. until 4 p.m., November through March. Train rides are offered at 11, 1, 2, and 3 Monday through Saturday and 1:30, 2:30, and 3:30 on Sunday. There is a nominal fee of $1 - $3 for train rides. (704-636-2889)

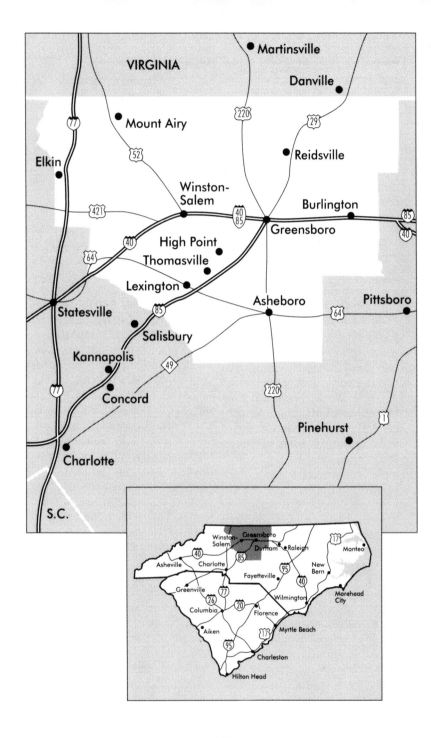

VIRGINIA

Martinsville

Danville

220

77

Mount Airy

29

52

Reidsville

Elkin

Winston-
Salem

421

40
85

Burlington

Greensboro

85

40

40

High Point

64

Thomasville

Lexington

Asheboro

Pittsboro

Statesville

85

64

Salisbury

Kannapolis

49

77

Concord

220

Pinehurst

1

Charlotte

S.C.

Winston-
Salem

Greensboro

17

40

Durham

Raleigh

Manteo

Asheville

Charlotte

85

New
Bern

Fayetteville

95

40

Greenville

77

Morehead
City

26

Wilmington

Columbia

20

Florence

Aiken

95

17

Myrtle Beach

Charleston

Hilton Head

NORTH CAROLINA'S

Northern Foothills

THE TRIAD

The area of North Carolina called The Triad is comprised of the cities of Greensboro, Winston-Salem and High Point and points in between. The Triad has a full range of drawing cards to entice visitors, including museums, historical sites, sports, shopping and a host of festivals and other events of interest.

Greensboro

To Get There:
Greensboro is at the junction of I-85 and I-40.

Greensboro was named for General Nathanael Greene who led the battle at Guilford Battleground, one of the most decisive battles of the Revolutionary War. The Battleground is just the beginning of the historical treasures of Greensboro. But Greensboro is about the present too. Art lovers will enjoy browsing through the galleries at the Greensboro Cultural Center or a visit to the Weatherspoon Art Gallery. Kids can immerse themselves at the Carolina's largest water park, Emerald Pointe.

To get the feel of Greensboro, drive downtown along Elm, Greene, Davie and Washington streets. The 600 block of Elm Street has great antique shops. Take a walk through **Fordham's Drug Store** where its original fountain's "Soda Jerker" still makes ice cream floats the way they should be made. You can pick up a self-guided tour brochure from the

Old Greensborough Preservation Society. (919-272-6617)

Things To
See and Do _____

GUILFORD COURTHOUSE
NATIONAL MILITARY PARK

On this site, March 15, 1781, Revolutionary War General Nathanael Greene's ragtag group of soldiers met General Cornwallis' British army in a battle that changed the momentum of the war. The Battle at Guilford Courthouse was fought on uneven, scrabble farmland scored by a deep ravine and tangled woods beside what is now Spring Garden Road in Greensboro. Today, you can walk through the marked paths where each line of troops stood, push a button at an audio station and hear a compelling narration that chronicles the battle, segment by segment. It's almost as if you were there.

Be sure to take time to see the excellent 20-minute video slide presentation in the Visitors Center's theater. This gives some background about the months and conditions that led up to the Battle at Guilford Courthouse. The film includes informative and touching letters from Continental soldier, Benjamin West, to his wife. It's hard to imagine 20th century soldiers enduring such hardships as lack of warm clothing, boots and food, and it makes you realize to what extent our forefathers were willing to go for freedom.

Guilford Courthouse Military Park is open daily from 8:30 a.m. until 4:30 p.m., closed on Christmas and New Year's day. There is no admission charged. (910-288-1776)

Tannenbaum Park

Located at the corners of Battleground and New Garden roads, only blocks away from Guilford Courthouse National Military Park, is Tannenbaum Park, the site of the British battle line. A new Colonial Carolina Heritage Center has been built here. This is a participatory museum that encourages folks, particularly children, to touch, smell and investigate the way 18th century "back country" people lived. Among the many hands-on experiences, children can try their hand at the spinning wheel or find out how iron making was done by Quakers, Moravians and Presbyterians who settled the area. The **Guilford Sutler**, an 18th century gift shop with fine reproductions, is part of the center.

Outside, visit the 2-story 1778 **Hoskins House**, requisitioned by Cornwallis as his command post and also used to treat wounded soldiers from both sides after the battle. Constructed of chestnut, poplar and oak logs, the cabin has remained in excellent condition because it stayed in the family until 1925. It has since been restored to the 18th century period.

Living history weekend reenactments take place almost monthly, depicting how people lived and worked throughout the Revolutionary War period. Many skills of the period are demonstrated by performers dressed in authentically recreated uniforms.

Tannenbaum Park is open from 8:00 a.m. until 5:00 p.m, Monday through Saturday, and from 1:00 p.m. until 5:00 p.m. on Sunday. The Colonial Heritage Center is open from 9:00 a.m. until 5:00 p.m. Tuesday through Saturday, and 2:00

Living history weekend reenactments take place monthly at Tannenbaum Park.

p.m. until 5:00 p.m. on Sunday. There is no admission charged. (910-288-8259)

NATURAL SCIENCE CENTER

This is a museum kids will love! They will see reproduction dinosaur skeletons—which don't resemble Barney at all. The Tyrannosaurus is big enough to scare the begebbers out of any dinosaur-adoring youngster and the Triceratops and Stegosaurus look as if they could scoop you up like an ant. In the geology section, children will be surprised to see what and how some of those North Carolina rocks and minerals are used to produce things that make our lives easier.

The **Edward R. Zane Planetarium** will give kids a better idea of the space program through its multimedia shows. This steady transfusion of information keeps kids involved and asking more questions on the way home. As at SciWorks, the Science Museum in Winston-Salem, there's a Foucault pendulum here, but this one is much larger. It extends from the top of the ceiling to the basement and shows the rotation of the earth's movement around the sun. The Thesaurus Shoppell features many fun gifts and educational items.

Before leaving, take a walk through the nature trails where you'll see an enclosed jaguar, a North Carolina black bear, bobcats and other animals from both the U.S. and South America.

Natural Science Center is open from 9:00 a.m. until 5:00 p.m. Monday through Saturday, and from 12:30 p.m. until 5:00 p.m. on Sunday. Admission for adults is $3.50, for children $2.50 and children under 3 are free. The Planetarium charges $1 additional. The Center is located at 4301 Lawndale Drive, right behind the Guilford Battleground in Country Park. (910-288-3769)

OLD MILL OF GUILFORD

The Old Mill is ongoing history. Here, workers grind corn into grits and wheat into flour just as workers did at this 1764 water-powered mill before Cornwallis took possession in 1781. As the story goes, the night before Cornwallis' arrival, Mill owner James Dillon dreamed that his toe was on fire. Upon awakening, he found British soldiers at his mill. When the shooting began, Dillon took cover behind a tree, but his protruding foot was hit by a shot that ignited a pain in —you guessed it—the toe he dreamed about.

In an adjacent small shop, the shelves resemble contents you might see at a country store. Here, you'll find respect for the region's culinary talents in homemade relishes, jams and jellies made by a North Carolina Amish family. The molasses and honey, dried apples and pork side meat also come from local talent.

Current owners, Charles and Heidi Parnell, have researched historic recipes and made special mixes using their milled flours with honey or molasses. You can choose from 19 different mixes that are only sold at the Old Mill and in museum shops. Wouldn't you like to have a mix of the gingerbread recipe that George Washington's mother made for General Lafayette? Old Mill of Guilford is open daily (including Sunday) from 9:00 a.m. until 6:00 p.m. (910-643-4783)

WEATHERSPOON ART GALLERY

For those interested in 20th century American art, the place to go is the Weatherspoon Art Gallery. Six galleries showcase traveling exhibits plus house their own permanent collection of Henri Matisse lithographs and bronzes, a Willem de Kooning, a Robert Rauschenberg screen paining, a Louise Nevel, postwar paintings and many other paintings by noted artists. The gallery, located in the Cone Building on the University of North Carolina at Greensboro campus, is open every day except Monday. (910-334-5770)

The Old Mill of Guilford is a working water-powered mill listed
on the National Register of Historic Places.

GREENSBORO HISTORICAL MUSEUM

Not many museums have a cemetery dating back to the 18th century, but this Romanesque Revival-designed building was once the First Presbyterian Church. Graves date its existence back to the Revolutionary War and bronze markers designate veterans from the War of 1812 and the Civil War.

One of the favorite exhibits features the life of Greensboro native O. Henry (a.k.a. William Sidney Porter), and vignettes of five of his short stories were staged here in celebration of his birthday. On the main level, Dolley Madison, wife of U.S. President, James Madison, is honored with two reconstructions of "the magnificent doll's" gowns. A velvet rust-colored gown is said to have come from White House draperies that the resourceful Dolley allegedly tore down to make her gown. The museum has a great gift shop that celebrates North Carolina inventiveness and skill.

Greensboro Historical Museum is open from Tuesday through Saturday from 10:00 a.m. until 5:00 p.m. and on Sunday from 2:00 p.m. until 5:00 p.m. No admission is charged. The museum is located at 130 Summit Avenue in downtown Greensboro. (910-373-2043)

GREENSBORO CULTURAL CENTER

Five individual art galleries are housed in this center. Each gallery is distinctly different in purpose and ethnicity from the others, which makes this a diversified visit. The galleries include: **Green Hill Center for North Carolina Art, Greensboro Artist's League Gallery & Gift Shop, African American Atelier, Guilford Native American Art Gallery** and the **Mattye Reed African Heritage Center Satellite Gallery**.

Located at 200 North Davie Street downtown, the galleries within the Cultural Center are open from 10:00 a.m. until 5:00 p.m., Tuesday through Saturday. The African American Atelier is open Sunday from 3:00 p.m. until 6:00 p.m. and the Mattye Reed African Heritage Center is also open on Sunday from 1:00 p.m. until 5:00 p.m.

RICHARD PETTY MUSEUM

Located just 10 minutes south of Greensboro on Branson Mill Road, off U.S. 220 south in Level Cross, North Carolina, this museum is a real treat for race car fans. A short video background describes what made the King of NASCAR Racing, Richard Petty, the king. Some of Petty's famous race cars are on exhibit along with Petty's signature cowboy hats and sunglasses. Awards and photos will take you back to the 7 Winston Cup Championships that Petty has won. The museum is open from 9:00 a.m. until 5:00 p.m., Monday through Saturday. Admission is $3 for adults, $1.50 for students and children under 6 are free. (910-495-1143)

FESTIVALS

If you are anywhere near Greensboro, do make a point of coming to its annual **Fun Fourth**, held downtown. This fourth of July festival is the old-fashioned kind that begins with a parade. Crafts and cotton candy, dances, games, and sidewalk art spill into an evening of jazz bands, gospel sings and

The Richard Petty Museum features memorabilia from the "King of NASCAR Racing."

Greensboro's Symphony orchestra signing off with a $25,000 fireworks show.

During the summer season, there are over 60 concerts at the **Eastern Music Festival** held at the Guilford College Campus and other locations. You can hear music from symphonic to chamber by professional and talented students from all over the world. (910-333-7450 or 800-772-5568).

Accommodations ____

Hotels/Motels

Since so much that you'll want to see and do fans outward from downtown Greensboro, the recently renovated **The Biltmore Greensboro Hotel** ($$-$$$$) is an excellent place to stay. High ceilings, canopy beds and hardwood floors are attractive, and a continental breakfast is served each morning. There's also a stretch limo to take you out to dinner. It's located downtown at 111 West Washington Street. (910-272-3474)

CAMPING

Then again you could camp out. **Greensboro KOA** is located at 2300 Montreal Avenue, exit 128 from I-85 & N.C. 6. It has hot showers, electrical and water hookups, a swimming pool, a grocery store, etc. (910-274-4143)

Dining _____

Stamey's Barbecue ($) is located at 2812 Battleground Avenue. In North Carolina people have been known to fight over which barbecue is the best. The old-fashioned "Lexington style" barbecue served up on paper plates in this casual atmosphere is wood-cooked pork, prepared in the same delicious way since 1930.

Fran's Front Porch ($) is 20-30 minutes from Greensboro, but this old farmhouse restaurant is worth the drive if you're looking for authentic Southern cooking. People actually fly in to a small private airport across the road and walk a quarter of a mile to eat at this no-frills buffet-style restaurant. You can't miss with the chicken pie or any of the 30-plus desserts. Fran's is located in Liberty, North Carolina at 6139 Smithwood Road and is open Thursday through Sunday only. (910-685-4104)

Madison Park ($$$$), located at 616 Dolley Madison Road, is a super restaurant featuring dishes from the provinces of France and Northern Italy. A seafood tray appetizer laden with smoked salmon, shrimp, etc., lets you immediately know what you can expect from this elegant restaurant.

At the back of the Greensboro Cultural Center is an ex-cellent restaurant for lunch or dinner. Schedule sight-seeing so that you can stop by **Paisley's** ($-$$) during meal time. The restaurant's art deco theme fits with the rhythm of the center. Pasta's and seafood are standouts.

For More Information:

Greensboro Area Convention & Visitors Bureau 317 S. Greene St. Greensboro, NC 27401 800-344-2282

AAA Carolinas Oak Hollow Business Park 14-A Oak Branch Drive Greensboro, NC 27407 910-852-0506

WINSTON-SALEM

To Get There: Winston-Salem is at the intersection of I-40 and U.S. 52.

Winston-Salem offers a broad variety of activities. The historic Moravian village, Old Salem, Reynolda House, SciWorks museum and Tanglewood Park make this a city for repeat visits.

BETHABARA PARK

The Moravians, an industrious religious group, came to America from the states of Moravia and Bohemia. These settlers came to escape religious persecution and seek a better home. Calling their new home Wachovia, the Moravian pioneers made their first settlement north of their tract's center. It was given the name, **Bethabara,** which means House of Passage, but was never intended as a permanent settlement. From Bethabara's inception, the church's controlling head dictated that the central village be placed in the center.

Today, you'll see sections of a rebuilt palisade wall that the Moravians erected to protect their new village from Native American attacks. Recent excavations have unearthed the basics of that early village. In the restored **Brewster House Museum**, you'll see a display of farm tools, kitchen utensils and unusually well-crafted china. Do visit the restored place of worship—**Gemeinhaus**. Here,

Photo by Dawn O'Brien.

The Gemeinhaus at Bethabara Park.

you'll see one of those handsome tile stoves that kept the church warm for parishioners who sat on those backless benches. Try sitting here for awhile and you'll appreciate the depth of Moravian religious convictions.

The park's grounds are open throughout the year, but guided tours are available from April through December 15 from 9:30 a.m. to 4:30 p.m., Monday through Friday, and from 1:30 to 4:30 p.m. Saturday and Sunday. No admissions charged. (910-724-8191.

OLD SALEM

The restored Moravian Village of Old Salem is often preferred to Williamsburg because you can tour the entire community in one day. They began building this new section of their tract in 1766 in what is now known as Old Salem.

When the Bethabara settlers moved to this area they instituted commune living until the village could become established. You'll see evidence of that at your visit to the **Single Brothers House**. This is where young men from age 14 lived and learned various trades from master craftsmen. Today, guides and craftspeople dress in colonial costumes. It will give you the feeling of being back in the 18th century when you walk though this two-story building.

The rooms have been converted into work areas where you'll see tinsmiths cutting and crafting butterfly candle sconces and others making various tools used in the homes. Upstairs, you'll see costumed women spinning yarn and weaving fabric. The costumed tour guides introduce you to craftsmen and women at work in their shops.

Visit the shoemaker shop and see how they worked with an ingenious candle lighting system. It took 30 hours to produce one pair of shoes, a task still accomplished by current shoemakers. Then visit the shops of other distinguished artisans. Visit the bakery that almost always has homemade bread or delicious Moravian cookies. Natives know that they sell out early each day, so you may want to make that your first stop.

At the **Boy's School** you'll see a display of musical instruments, a significant feature of this progressive group. Music still plays a festive role in Christmas and Easter celebrations each year.

The **Easter Sunrise Service**, beginning on Old Salem's square, is a worship service that now draws crowds of 5,000. A Moravian minister opens the

Photo by Clay Nolen. Courtesy N.C. Travel & Tourism.

Old Salem is a restored 18th century Moravian congregational town founded in 1766.

service with a brief sermon. Then Moravian brass bands, stationed along the two-block route to the Moravian Cemetery, play somber pieces that musically answer each other as the congregation silently files past. This awe-inspiring pilgrimage leads to the cemetery where you'll see fresh-scrubbed gravestones, each adorned with flowers. People of all faiths are welcome, but if going, you should arrive no later than 3:00 a.m. in order to find a place to stand.

You can watch a 17-minute film in the reception center that will orient you to Moravian history and give you a tease of what you are about to see. Open Monday through Saturday from 9:30 a.m. to 4:30 p.m., Sunday from 1:30 p.m. to 4:30 p.m. Admission: adults, $12, children (6-14) $6. (910-721-7300 or 800-441-5305)

MUSEUM OF EARLY SOUTHERN DECORATIVE ARTS (MESDA)

While giving a lecture in reference to the Colonial period, the late Joseph Down said, " . . . nothing of merit was made south of Baltimore." A woman in the audience asked, "Sir, are you speaking from ignorance or prejudice?" The horror of that remark persuaded Frank Horton and his mother to contribute their vast collection of Southern furnishings to build a museum that now displays 19 furnished period rooms and 6 galleries. You'll see rare examples of 150 years of Southern furniture, silver, paintings and needlework from 1640 to 1820 that have been reassembled here, just as they were in their original locations. This is the only museum dedicated to exhibiting and researching the regional decorative arts of the early South.

They designed a great deal of tall southern furniture in order to give the appropriate scale ratio to high ceilings built for cool breezes. If you've heard the Piedmont region referred to as the Back Country, take no offence. The term merely designated the area back from the coast and had no bearing on sophistication or life-style, as is evident from much of the ornate Piedmont furnishings displayed at the museum.

MESDA is more appropriate for adults and older children. Located in Old Salem at 924 Main Street, the museum is open Monday through Saturday from 10:30 a.m. until 4:3 0 p.m., and from 1:30 p.m. until 4:30 p.m. on Sunday. Admission for adults is $5 and for children, $3. Tickets can be purchased at a discount in combination with admission to Old Salem. (910-721-7360)

REYNOLDA HOUSE

Reynolda House, the bungalow-style former home of R.J.

Reynolds of tobacco fame, is now a museum of American art. The collection features paintings that range from works by 19th century landscape painter Frederic Church to those of Thomas Eakin and Mary Cassatt. Also represented are contemporary painters, including Georgia O'Keeffe, Andrew Wyeth and Frank Stella. Out of the whole collection, the painting that garners more awe and surprise is Frederic Church's dramatic cross lighting used in *Andes of Ecuador*. And the more recent acquisition of sculpture includes pieces by Alexander Calder, David Smith and Paul Manship.

The attic displays many of Katherine Reynolds clothes, including her 1905 hand-sewn wedding dress and other elegant gowns. Reynolds children clothing and toys are also included in the display. The second-floor balcony overlooks the living room from all four sides. The house contains many of its original furnishings, and you're sure to appreciate the basement floor, complete with bowling alley, shooting range, night club area and enclosed swimming pool.

You may tour the gardens on the grounds, which are a mass of daffodils in springtime. And in the formal gardens, roses are a fragrant delight throughout the summer. When the Reynolds family lived here Reynolda was a self-contained estate with its own dairy barn (which you can visit), boiler room (now the great French restaurant, **La Chaudiere**) and other shops of Reynolda Village.

Reynolda House, located on Reynolda Road, is open Tuesday through Saturday from 9:30 a.m. to 4:30 p.m. and from 1:30 to 4:30 p.m. on Sunday. Admission: adults, $6, seniors, $5, children $3. (910-725-325)

SOUTHEASTERN CENTER FOR CONTEMPORARY ART (SECCA)

From the Reynolds mansion, turn left onto Reynolda Road, then right onto Margarite Drive and proceed to the end. Walk down the fan-designed brick path to the former Hanes home. Children are intrigued with the unusual sculpture here. The house, now devoid of furnishings, has been expanded to house several galleries for SECCA. Works by contemporary Southern artists and educational programs are the museum's mission. Don't become so absorbed with the galleries that you decide to skip the gift shop. It's a find.

Located at 750 Marguerite Drive, off Reynolda Road, SECCA is open Tuesday through Saturday 10:00 a.m. to 5:00 p.m. and Sunday 1:00 to 5:00 p.m. Admission: adults, $3, students and seniors, $2, children under 12 are free. (910-725-1904)

SciWorks

It's become overworked to say, "Children of all ages will enjoy…" but in the case of SciWorks, the phrase is true. Adults need to be as willing to tap into fun as are children. So, don't be afraid to try out the procedure that lets you make a shadow and then walk away from it. Oh, sure, SciWorks is educational, but not the boring lecture variety. You won't hear someone **tell** you what a tornado is, you press a button and watch the elements go into action that whirl a mass of fluid to build into a vortex. You can whisper into a parabolic whisper dish and be heard clearly by someone standing 40 feet away. Or stand up close and watch how the Foucault Pendulum demonstrates the rotation of the earth.

Norman Tuck's different magnetic sculptures bring a chuckle from all types in this interactive, "touch me" museum. Be sure to take a trip through the African exhibit and the Carolina Piedmont Wildlife exhibit that offers an upclose video look at special animal exhibits. Before scheduling a trip here, be sure to call first for Planetarium show times. The Planetarium theater is a 50-foot tilted dome with a Spitz star machine that produces eye-boggling laser effects.

Drawing by Jeanette Smith.

The Henry F. Shaffner House

This museum isn't geared only for older children. There's a huge room for toddlers and preschool children filled with big, floppy climbing bars, slides and cushions to roll around upon. And outside you can become acquainted with Jacob sheep, an otter swimming in his tank and a few other animal exhibits.

SciWorks is located north of downtown. Take U.S. 52 north, exit at Hanes Mill Road and follow the signs. It's across from Sara Lee Offices on Museum Drive. It is open Monday through Saturday from 10 a.m. to 5 p.m. and on Sunday from 1 to 5:00 p.m. Admission: adults, $3.50, students and seniors, $2.50, children under 3 are free. (910-767-6730)

Accommodations___

BED AND BREAKFAST INNS

The **Brookstown Inn** ($$$$) is a magnificent renovation of an old cotton mill that once made Confederate soldiers' uniforms. The rooms are attractively appointed and many show exposed brick walls and rough-hewn beams. A continental breakfast that includes delicious Moravian buns is a standout. The inn is located at 200 Brookstown Avenue, very convenient to Old Salem. (910-725-1120)

The **Henry F. Schaffner House** ($$$-$$$$) at 150 South Marshall Street is ideally located near downtown and Old Salem. A visit to this former home of the co-founder of what is now Wachovia Bank & Trust Company takes you on a visual journey to the Victorian era, which was copied when this house was built in 1907. The handsome tiger-oak panelled walls have been meticulously restored and set the tone for this very elegant home. Each room and private bath is individually decorated, but the home's *piece de resistance* is its honeymoon suite decorated in 18th century Biedermeier. The suite features a whirlpool and wet bar. A continental deluxe breakfast is served that includes either quiche, omelette or waffles with all the trimmings. (910-777-0052)

Old Salem's latest offering is the **Augustus T. Zevely Bed and Breakfast** ($$$$), located at 803 South Main Street. This recently renovated and designed B & B has been restored to museum quality. Its rooms and suites overlook Old Salem, and the home is decorated using Moravian-style furnishings. Each room has a private bath, and some have either a whirlpool or steambath. Complimentary breakfast is served in the dining room as is wine and cheese each evening. (910-748-9299)

HOTELS/MOTELS

The **Comfort Inn-Cloverdale** ($$) at 110 Miller Street is also convenient to Old Salem and is a comfortable place to stay. It has a fitness room with a whirlpool and sauna, and an outdoor swimming pool. Continental breakfast is served daily. (910-721-0220)

Dining _____

A good place for lunch or dinner in Old Salem is historic **Old Salem Tavern Dining Room** ($$-$$$$) at 736 South Main Street. Most people order the Moravian chicken pie, which is excellent, but save room for the chocolate amaretto pie.

La Chaudiere ($$$$) is located at 120 Reynolda Village. You won't believe that this quaint country-French restaurant was the Reynolds Estate's former boiler room. The very best authentic French cuisine can be experienced here. It serves lunch and dinner and reservations are suggested. (910-748-0269)

Noble's Grill ($$$) is at 380 Knollwood Street, just off I-40 Business. This very California-contemporary-looking restaurant has managed to make healthy food taste like a gourmet offering. Lunch and dinner are served.

Leon's Cafe ($$) is located at 924 South Marshall Street. Leon's has become not only a standby, but a hangout because of its exceptionally good offerings at affordable prices. Dinner is served daily.

> **For More Information:**
> **Winston-Salem Convention & Visitors Bureau**
> P.O. Box 1408
> Winston-Salem, NC 27102
> 800-331-7018

Side Trips _____

TANGLEWOOD

> **To Get There:**
> Take the Tanglewood exit from I-40 west of Winston-Salem, and follow the signs.

Photo by Dawn O'Brien.

The Christmas light show at Tanglewood Park.

Photo courtesy Tanglewood.

Tanglewood Park has two championship golf courses.

Tanglewood's hardwood forest was so tangled with gnarled overgrowth back in the 1900s that it looked like a mythical place from Hawthorne's *Tanglewood—Tales*. The idyllic lake, now called Mallard Lake, completed this fantasy setting for Margaret Griffith who gave the park its name. In 1921, new owners Kate and William Reynolds, added wings onto the original 1848 home, now known as the **Manor House Bed and Breakfast Inn**.

Thirty years later, Tanglewood was left to the people of Forsyth County for use as a park. Tanglewood's brambling undergrowth has now been cut back to provide for horseback riding trails, a swimming pool, 9 tennis courts, a fenced area for deer, a steeplechase course, nature trails, a rose garden, a lake filled with canoes and paddleboats, camp grounds, golf driving ranges, a Championship Golf Course where the Senior PGA Vantage is played and the popular William Neal Reynolds Golf Course that runs along the forest.

This park has a multitude of events from lavish tailgate parties for the annual **Spring Steeplechase** to the new **Festival of Lights** program during the Christmas season. Begun in 1992, the Festival of Lights more than quadrupled by 1993. There are now 45 fanciful light exhibits. It's worth a trip to the area just to drive through the fantasy snow storm. But golfers and equestrians will love the ingenious, moving light representations of their sport. To be sure, children will enjoy snowmen, candy cane figures, etc., that are liberally sprinkled over the drive.

One of the best things about Tanglewood is that people of a variety of incomes can enjoy staying here. You can camp out ($) at one of the 100 tent and trailer sites that offer good camping facilities, including hot water showers, firewood and picnic tables. Camping is conveniently located near nature trails and the riding stable, or you could stay at one of the secluded cottages ($$$) that overlook the lake, or in the historic Reynolds Manor House Bed and Breakfast Inn ($$$-$$$$). The inn's bedrooms have private baths, TVs, telephones, and attractive decor. You can breakfast beside the original old stone fireplace with a big continental breakfast of fruit muffins, cereals, and a large fruit plate.

Tanglewood Park is open year-round from dawn to dusk. Admission to the park is $1. Golf fees for the Championship Course range from $24 to $50; for the Reynolds Course, $8 to $26. Tennis fees are from $6 to $8 per hour. Horseback riding fees are $14 per hour. (910-766-0591)

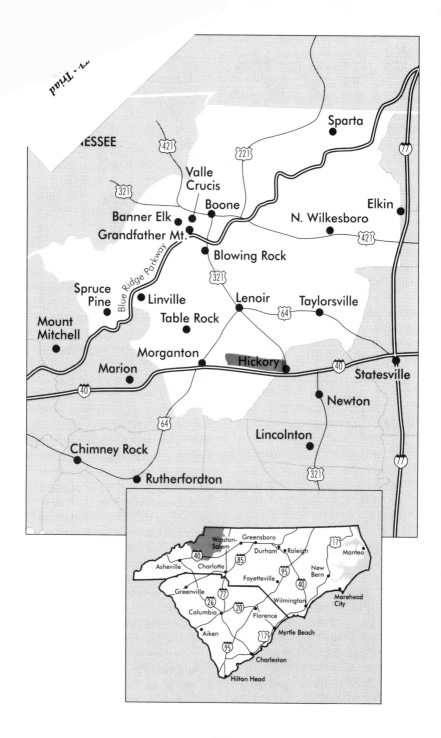

The Mtns. / Triad

TENNESSEE

Sparta

421

221

77

Valle
Crucis

321

Boone

Elkin

Banner Elk

N. Wilkesboro

421

Grandfather Mt.

Blowing Rock

Blue Ridge Parkway

321

Spruce
Pine

Linville

Lenoir

Taylorsville

64

Mount
Mitchell

Table Rock

Morganton

Hickory

40

Statesville

Marion

40

Newton

64

Lincolnton

Chimney Rock

321

77

Rutherfordton

Winston-
Salem

Greensboro

40

85

Durham

Raleigh

77

Manteo

Asheville

Charlotte

95

New
Bern

Greenville

77

Fayetteville

40

26

Morehead
City

Columbia

20

Wilmington

Aiken

Florence

77

95

Myrtle Beach

Charleston

Hilton Head

Northern Mountains

BLUE RIDGE PARKWAY

The Blue Ridge Mountains formed about a billion years ago from "sediment at the bottom of a long-vanished sea." More recently, just 300 million years back, the "continents collided and our ridges and mountains rose from the depths" to provide a ridge that has been engineered to become one of America's most scenic parkways.

The frequent overlooks afford breathtaking panoramas of high peaks, waterfalls and lakes tucked into verdant valleys, and thousands of visitors are drawn to the colorful displays nature provides in the spring and the fall. Mountain laurel, flaming azaleas and red rhododendron are in awesome abundance beginning in April.

The red and gold beauty of fall foilage varies according to the weather, but color is usually at its height in mid-October.

The Parkway twists and turns for 250 miles through the North Carolina mountains and you will want to take time for side excursions or you will miss many of the highlights of the area. You will find Visitor Centers along the way that offer food, fuel and restroom facilities. There are plenty of accommodations in the towns just off the Parkway, but in North Carolina only two on the Parkway itself. The **Bluffs Lodge** (910-372-4499) at Milepost 241 near Winston-Salem is open from May through October and offers a coffee shop, service station and gift shop. The **Pisgah Inn** (704-235-8228) outside of Asheville at Milepost 408.6 has a rustic feel and each room boasts a beautiful view of the surrounding mountains.

THE HIGH COUNTRY

The area around Boone, Blowing Rock, Banner Elk and Spruce Pine is known as the North Carolina High Country. An abundance of attractions for adults and children, a number of excellent ski resorts and spectacular scenery combine to create a near-perfect vacation spot year-round. The towns are close together, which makes it easy to enjoy it all, even if your trip is a short one.

> **For More Information:**
>
> **High Country Hosts**
> **701 Blowing Rock Road**
> **Boone, NC 28607**
> **704-264-1299 or 800-438-7500**

BOONE

> **To Get There:**
> From I-40 take U.S. 321 north.
> From I-77 take U.S. 421 north.

Boone is the county seat of Watauga County and the home of Appalachian State University. Due in large part to the presence of the university, Boone has a large number of accommodations and restaurants and serves as a good base from which to visit the surrounding towns and attractions.

Things To See and Do _____

APPALACHIAN CULTURAL MUSEUM

The evolving lifestyle of mountain people is attractively displayed with artifacts plus information on the Appalachia's abundant variety of rare and unusual herbs and plants (some medicinal). The relationship between man and (not versus) environment is a prevailing theme. An 8-minute film is accompanied by sweet mountain music. Admission for adults is $2, $1.75 for seniors and $1 for children ages 12 to 18. (704-262-3117)

HORN IN THE WEST

During the summer (mid-June to mid-August) make evening reservations for the outdoor drama, *Horn In The West,* now going into its 42nd season. The play, a musical drama, revolves around life in Appalachia during the days of Daniel Boone. Admission for adults is $8 and for children $4.50. (704-264-2120)

HICKORY RIDGE HOMESTEAD

Adjacent to *Horn In The West,* you'll find **Hickory Ridge Homestead,** which was an interesting tour of five representative home sites of the 1800s. Admission is $2.

Accommodations

Overlook Lodge ($$) is a comfortable B & B two miles outside Boone off U.S. 105 on Poplar Grove Road (704-963-5785); or try **Lovill House Inn** ($$-$$$$) at 404 Old Bristol Road. (704-264-4204)

In winter, the large water wheel fronting the **High Country Inn** ($$-$$$) on U.S. 105 bears a cascade of icicles, which gives a false impression of its rustic but cozy interior. After a day of skiing, there is nothing so soothing as relaxing in the hot tub or sauna. During the summer months, you can enjoy either the indoor or the outdoor pool. On the premises, the **Water Wheel Restaurant** serves both breakfast and dinner, and **Geno's Lounge** is a great place to unwind. (800-334-5605)

Many of the chains have a presence in Boone, such as the **Hampton Inn** at 208 Linville Road. (704-264-0077)

Dining

The place the natives go for a quick snack is the **Appalachian Soda Shop** ($). Ask for Carolina Pharmacy Doughnuts.

Vacationers like the **Daniel Boone Inn** ($) for lots of food served country-style for the whole family to enjoy. **Peppers** ($-$$) is also a favorite of locals and visitors alike. Its onion rings are the greatest!

Frequent overlooks afford views from the Blue Ridge Parkway.

Photo by William Russ. Courtesy N.C. Travel & Tourism.

Side Trips

LAUREL SPRINGS

To Get There:
From Boone, take the Blue Ridge Parkway north, exit at Milepost 246. Turn right onto N.C. 1143 for 3 miles and follow signs.

Some Hurricane Hugo victims overcame disaster ingeniously. Because Tom and Nancy Burgiss' 200-year-old farm yielded enough "Hugo" lumber to build a dancing barn, the popular **Mountain Music Jamboree** took up new residence here. Folks from near and far come to dance the Texas Two-Step, and old-time mountain dances. Dance classes are Monday and Tuesday nights; Texas Two-Step dances are on Friday and there are two alternating live Blue Grass and Old Time Music bands on Saturday.

Staying at the **Burgiss B & B** ($$) can be restful or exhilarating, and no matter your choice, it's a win-win deal. Overnight guests are treated to a two-bedroom suite with private hot tub, private den with fireplace and piped in spring-fed water that lulls you to sleep like a trickling brook. The full breakfast offers a unique menu of choices. (910-359-2995)

GLENDALE SPRINGS

To Get There:
From Boone, take N.C. 105 north to U.S. 221 north to 163 south. Or, take the Blue Ridge Parkway north to the Glendale Springs exit at Milepost 259.

It's a toss-up to know whether people go to Glendale Springs for the wonderful gourmet food at the inn or to see the Frescoes. The 1895 **Glendale Springs Inn** ($$-$$$, 910-982-2101), intact with convivial ghost, is a sophisticated country inn that attracts discriminating visitors from around the country. And, Ben Long's controversial **frescoes at Episcopal Holy Trinity Chapel**, a block away, are among the most highly visited in the state. A number of craft shops have sprung up, which changes the area's once "hidden away" flavor but does not diminish its overall appeal.

VALLE CRUCIS

To Get There:
From Boone, take N.C. 105 to N.C. 194.

While you're in Valle Crucis, make it a point to check out the over-100-year-old **Mast Store**. The original post office is still inside along with a trap door in the floor where bartered chickens were once deposited. Locals still play checkers with Coke and Pepsi bottle tops beside an original pot-bellied stove. The store's motto is "If we don't have it, you don't need it anyway." Very few browsers leave empty handed as the prices are better than any known to this writer anywhere. And for a totally different (non-winter) type adventure, investigate a wilderness camping weekend where you trek with llamas. Yep, that's right, llamas carrying the gear through the Blue Ridge on guided trips from Valle Crucis (704-297-2171).

The Mast Farm Inn ($$$) is a popular place to stay in Valle Crucis and it serves fabulous, from scratch country dinners included in the price. (704-963-5857)

For More Information:

Boone Chamber of Commerce

112 W. Howard St.
Boone, NC 28607
704-264-2225

Boone Convention & Visitors Bureau
112 W. Howard St.
Boone, NC 28607
800-852-9506

BLOWING ROCK

To Get There:

Blowing Rock is 8 miles south of Boone at the junction of U.S. 321 and U.S. 221. Or exit the Blue Ridge Parkway at Milepost 291.9, onto U.S. 221, 2 miles north of Blowing Rock.

The Blowing Rock overhangs the Johns River Gorge.

Photo by William Russ. Courtesy N.C. Travel & Tourism.

A lot of towns are dressed up to look quaint these days—Blowing Rock is the genuine thing. In summer, the main street is lined with pyramid-shaped planters spilling over with pink and white begonias. Since the days the rambling hundred-year-old **Green Park Inn** was built over the center of the Continental Divide, the town took on an aristocratic appeal.

Window shopping down Main Street is a favorite pursuit with lots of antiques, oriental rug houses and classy mountain wear. Evenings find folks at the auction house, which is a show in itself. The park on Main Street is a gathering place for tennis, people watching, craft shows, etc.

Things To See and Do

THE BLOWING ROCK

No one knows why the wind blows stronger at the Blowing Rock than in any other spot in this area, but it does. Light objects tossed from this rock formation are returned by air currents from the 3,000-foot-deep gorge. Take a walk through the site's lovely gift shop and out on the trail that leads to the lookout platform. From here you get the most dramatic view of the overhanging rock and the view is breathtaking. On clear days, you can see both Grandfather

and Grandmother Mountains as well as Table Rock. Hours are from 8 a.m. until 8 p.m., June through September, and 8 a.m. until 7 p.m. during October. The attraction is open during the winter when the weather cooperates. Admission is $4 for adults, $1 for children ages 6 to 11 and $3 for senior citizens. The Blowing Rock is located off U.S. 321 south of the town. (704-295-7111)

HORSEBACK RIDING

The more athletically inclined can enjoy horseback riding along the trails of Moses Cone Estate on the Blue Ridge Parkway. Make reservations with **Blowing Rock Stables.** (704-295-7847)

WHITE WATER RAFTING

The adventurous will enjoy canoeing and white water rafting through class III to V rapids down the Nolichucky. Use **Wahoo's Adventures** on U.S. 321 between Blowing Rock and Boone. (800-444-RAFT)

TWEETSIE RAILROAD

Children in N. C. grow up on trips to **Tweetsie Railroad** on U.S. 321/221 between Blowing Rock and Boone. The drawing card is a 3-mile adventurous train ride on an original mountain train with interruptions of Indian attacks and settler rescues. The attraction has amusement rides, live entertainment, crafts, shops and picnic tables. Open from May through October; weekends in November. Admission for adults is $12.95, children ages 4 to 12 and seniors are admitted for $10.95. (800-526-5740)

Accommodations and Dining

The **Green Park Inn** ($$$$) is a great place to stay as many of our U.S. presidents will attest. (704-295-3141)

Another romantic B & B is the **Ragged Garden Inn** ($$-$$$$)it has great food. (704-295-9703)

A favorite restaurant with some of the best food in the mountains is **Best Cellars** ($$-

$$$), the **Speckled Trout** ($$-$$$) is also good.

For More Information:
Blowing Rock Chamber of Commerce
P.O. Box 406
Blowing Rock, NC 28605
704-295-7851

BANNER ELK/ LINVILLE

To Get There:
From Boone, take N.C.105 west and turn right on N.C. 184 .

Nature, in its rawest form of beauty, unfolds on many levels throughout this area as the Blue Ridge Parkway ribbons its way through unspoiled scenery.

Photo by Clay Nolen. Courtesy N.C. Travel & Tourism.

Visitors love the 3-mile adventurous train ride at Tweetsie Railroad.

Linville Gorge, Linville Caverns and Grandfather Mountain provide diversified recreational opportunities. Each summer, Grandfather Mountain draws thousands of visitors to celebrate two events, **Singing On The Mountain** and the **Highland Games**.

Things To See and Do

GRANDFATHER MOUNTAIN

The soaring peaks of 6,000-foot Grandfather Mountain can be seen from miles around. It looks like a giant sleeping grandfather and is considered North Carolina's top scenic attraction. A few years ago, UNESCO recognized the mountain as one of 311 Biosphere Reserves in 81 countries around the world. The program is a worldwide effort to identify and designate areas that are considered critical to the continued integrity and richness of the global environment.

Grandfather Mountain connects Linville's peak with the Visitors Center. The famous swinging bridge, for those brave enough to cross it, rewards you with a spectacular view. You'll want to visit the natural habitats to see native black bear, white-tailed deer, cougars, and bald and golden eagles. Stop in at the new nature museum that offers state-of-the-art displays and entertaining movies on native wildlife (especially the redtailed hawk film) shot at Grandfather Mountain. The museum's restaurant is a good bet for lunch featuring—what else? A dynamite view. You can also picnic on the mountain. Grandfather Mountain is open daily from 8 a.m.- 7 p.m.

What better place to hold such wholesome entertainment as **Singing on the Mountain** and the **Highland Games**? One of the most fun Grandfather Mountain experiences is the annual **Highland Games**, held the second weekend in July. From the moment you walk up the hill onto Macrae Meadow, the sound of bagpipes stirs your blood, whether you are Scottish or not.

On Saturday morning the games begin at 9:00 a.m., but long before that time you can hear varied clan bands tuning up all over the mountain. Like a three ring circus, you watch several games or activities taking place at the same time. Scots, proudly dressed in their clan's bright plaids, hale from all over the U.S. and Scotland. You'll overhear discussions concerning the merits of the sheaf toss, a game that originated when early Scot farmers stuck their pitchforks through sheaves and tossed them upward into their silos. Naturally, the bit of good

Photo by Dawn O'Brien.

*One of the most fun Grandfather Mountain experiences is
the annual Highland Games held each July.*

natured rivalry that resulted was channeled into athletic competition. Today, the sheaves are tossed over a bar raised higher for each player's succeeding turn.

At the same time, out of the corner of your eye, you'll see a band marching toward the center field to accompany young lassies clad in swinging kilts. You may want to get closer to watch them compete in such intricate dances as the Sword Dance and Highland Fling.

Clan-represented tent stalls with an interesting mix of clan literature and trinkets ring the playing field. While moving from one end of the field to the other checking out these different clans, you learn something about each clan's history and location in Scotland. It's kind of like milling through a European country fair.

By the time you return, other athletes are throwing the iron discus. This new competition seems to be equally balanced between strength and skill as is the cabal toss taking place simultaneously at the other end of the field.

Clan groups have front row seats in front of or inside their stalls, but there is a lovely hill at one end of the field where "wannabe" Scots, and even native Highlanders, spread their quilts or set up folding chairs under shade trees. Picnic baskets and coolers for drinks are everywhere but so are food stands. Some stands offer traditional Scottish foods, which is your chance to try shepherd's pie or Scottish sausages. Hot dogs, barbecue and soft drinks are available, too. Throughout the day you'll be serenaded by some of the best Scottish voices singing lilting melodies and folk songs.

Just beyond the entrance gate, large tents are set up selling Scottish jewelry, kilts, and books. There are few T-shirts and sweat shirts about, which makes this excursion pleasantly devoid of junky tourist wares.

This is a full weekend of merrymaking, with private and public dances and storytellers scattered about. And don't leave the kids at home, booths and entertainment areas are set up with storytellers who spin old and new tales with puppets and songs.

Another popular yearly event that comes the fourth Sunday in June on Grandfather Mountain is **Singing on the Mountain**.

Grandfather Mountain is located two miles north of Linville off U.S. 221. From the Blue Ridge Parkway, exit at Milepost 305.9.

Accommodations and Dining

(See Ski Country below.)

For More Information:

Banner Elk
Chamber of Commerce
High Country Square
Banner Elk, NC 28604
704-898-5605

Beech Mountain
Chamber of Commerce
403-A Beech Mountain Parkway
Beech Mountain, NC 28604
704-387-9283

Side Trips _____

LINVILLE FALLS AND LINVILLE GORGE

To Get There:
Exit Blue Ridge Parkway at
Milepost 317.4.

At Linville Falls and Gorge, there are three trail options from easy to rugged, depending on your energy level and your time. All are exquisite windows of nature that date back a half billion years. That was when the great rock folds tipped so far that they broke and pushed older sandstone beds on top of quartz. Erosion cut through the older rocks leaving openings to expose nature's handiwork.

The gorge is the deepest slash in the earth's crust east of the Grand Canyon. And the river tumbles into the gorge from its head to form a 90-foot fall of water. To reach the falls, you'll walk through a half-mile tunnel of towering trees so dense that spatters of sunlight are rare. Waterfalls take on many personalities—these are gushing high-drama ones, particularly at the peak which affords an unparalleled view.

This is not a picnic area, you'll have to go further up the Blue Ridge Parkway for food, but restrooms are available and the park is open year-round, depending on weather.

LINVILLE CAVERNS

To Get There:
Exit Blue Ridge Parkway at
Milepost 317.4 and go 4 miles
south on U.S. 221.

Undiscovered caves connect and almost interconnect throughout the mountains. But, Linville, like other caves, was discovered by accident in 1822 when curious fishermen followed trout disappearing into the side of a mountain. The current trout in this 20 million year old limestone cave have become blind due to low light source.

Both Confederate and Union soldiers hid out in this cave during the Civil War, but it wasn't opened to the public until 1939. The knowledgeable tour guide shows visitors the difference between stalagmite and stalactite formations, which is nature's slow sculpting process that makes this phenomenon so eerily attractive to us. Don't expect Carlsbad or Luray splendors, but the cavern, on 3 levels, is an interesting and enjoyable half-hour experience. The caverns are open year-round, but check times. Admission for adults is $4, and for children from ages 6 to 12, $2.50. (704-756-4171)

SPRUCE PINE

To Get There:

Exit the Blue Ridge Parkway at Milepost 331. Spruce Pine is at the intersection of U.S. 19E and N.C. 226.

Several different adventurous appetites are served in the Spruce Pine area: Nature—view from Mount Mitchell; Gem exploration—mines and museum; Artistic education—Penland School.

Things To See and Do

MOUNT MITCHELL STATE PARK

Mount Mitchell State Park is located at milepost 355. Mount Mitchell is the highest peak east of the Mississippi River, and you can hike through the park's many nature trails and see a spectacular mountain view from the lookout tower. If you want to camp here, call (704) 675-4611 to reserve one of the 9 campsites.

NORTH CAROLINA MINERAL MUSEUM

This is a small museum is located at Blue Ridge Parkway Milepost 331. The self-guided tour provides information on many native North Carolina minerals, such as feldspar, kaolin and mica, that are used to produce products that we use every day. The museum has over 300 varieties of minerals on display.

EMERALD VILLAGE AND CAROLINA MINING MUSEUM

The 3-hour museum tour includes a 45-minute underground tour of the mine, a gallery gemstone identification explanation (20 minutes) and an hour to do some prospecting of your own. Working at the flume, you can unearth gemstones from a salted bucket. This is a truly fun way to have a hands-on educational experience, and who knows, you could come home with one of North Carolina's emeralds, rubies, sapphires, aquamarines or garnets, as well as the native mix of feldspar, mica and smoky quartz.

In addition, Emerald Village has a tobacco and music exhibit and a gift shop full of reasonably priced native gemstone jewelry just in case the Village's "finds" are preferable to yours. Emerald Village is on McKinney Mine Road in Little Switzerland, exit Milepost 334 from the Blue Ridge Parkway.

PENLAND

The Penland Gallery, now located in the newly renovated Horner Hall, houses representative works of Penland artists and instructors. You are welcome to picnic on the grounds or rock on the front porch chatting with instructors and students. But we weren't about to spend time rocking when the "for sale" gallery was just inside. This gallery collection of glass, fiber, pottery, woodworking, metal and jewelry is like walking through a contemporary art museum with a wish list in hand. The work is so exceptional that it gives you goosebumps. It's obvious that this 1929 school, started by Lucy Morgan, challenges serious artists to focus their individuality in this hard working environment.

It's a good idea to view the Penland audio/visual film that explains the history and mission of this unique arts and craft school tucked away in this secluded mountain community of artists. After visiting the gallery, if you want to see more of an individual artist's work, a map of community artists' studios is available. And you can take a tour of the school on Tuesdays and Thursdays at 10:30 a.m. or 1 p.m. from March 15 through November 20.

To get to the Penland School, take N.C. 226 north from Spruce Pine and turn left onto S.R. 1164.

Accommodations ____

HOTELS/MOTELS

For those who want to spend the night, the **Pinebridge Inn and Executive Center** ($$) at 101 Pinebridge Avenue in Spruce Pine compliments the school environment you've experienced at Penland because it is a recycled and totally renovated elementary school building. (800-356-5059)

CAMPING

If you are on a budget or like to camp, the area has several good recreational options. **Springmaid Mountain Lodging and Campground** (803-547-1006) on Henredon Road in Spruce Pine offers horseback riding, canoeing, hiking and tubing. The **Blue Ridge Gemstone Mine and Campground** (704-765-5264) on McKinney Mine Road in Little Switzerland is close to the gem mines. The **Mountain Cove Campground and Trout Pond** (704-675-5362) on U.S. 80 at 800 Still Fork Road in Burnsville provides bait and tackle.

Dining ____

The restaurant in the Pinebridge Inn, **The Meeting Place**, is a nice but casual place for dinner and breakfast.

For More Information:
Mitchell County Chamber of
Commerce
Route 1, Box 796
Spruce Pine, NC 28777
704-765-9483

SKI COUNTRY

BANNER ELK, SKI BEECH, SUGAR MOUNTAIN SKI RESORT, SKI HAWKSNEST, APPALACHIAN SKI MOUNTAIN

Remember those "Think Snow" bumper stickers? Those are from thousands of Georgia, Tennessee, North and South Carolina skiers who listen to weather reports, watch the sky, send up snow prayers and wax skis in hope of bringing on the first winter's snow. And when mother nature cooperates, snow guns whirl into action adding and packing ski resort bases. That's when you'll see packed car ski rack's headed for one of the high country's downhill ski resorts. If you are new to the sport you can rent equipment at any of the resorts, but you can save time by renting locally before you go.

Appalachian Ski Mountain, home of the French Swiss Ski College, is off U.S. 321 between Blowing Rock and Boone and has one of the best teaching schools around for beginners. It has 8 slopes with a peak elevation of 4,000 feet and a vertical drop of 365 feet. (704-295-7828)

Of course, both **Ski Beech** (704-387-2011) and **Sugar Mountain Ski Resort** (704-898-4521) have good ski schools, particularly for very young children, and both offer challenging slopes. Beech, north of Banner Elk, has 14 slopes and a peak elevation of 5,505 feet, making it the highest in the East with a vertical drop of 830 feet. The resort also has a charming Swiss village appearance with an outdoor ice skating rink encircled with shops and restaurants. Sugar, just to the south of Banner Elk on N.C. 184, boasts 18 slopes, peak elevation of 5,300 feet with a vertical drop of 1,200 feet, and needless to say, fairyland views.

Ski Hawksnest (704-963-6561) reopened two years ago, is sometimes less crowded, and has 7 slopes, a peak of 4,819 feet, and vertical drop of 619 feet, plus night skiing. All of these resorts have chair lifts, rope tows, lockers and restaurants, plus nurseries on Beech and Sugar. You can get a ski report by calling **High Country Hosts** at (800-438-7500), also a good source for mountain area information.

You can cross country ski at **Moses Cone Park** on the Blue Ridge Parkway just outside of Blowing Rock and other gated-off areas by calling the Ranger's office: (704-295-7591); or on **Roan Mountain,** you can ski cross country with guided trips, including instruction. (615-772-3303)

Accommodations and Dining

What skier has not dreamed of that idyllic mountain ski lodge with roaring fireplace and happy apres ski bums tippling hot cider. You and yours can do just that at the **Beech Alpen Inn** ($$$-$$$$, 704-387-2252), or bring your family to an on-the-slopes condo at **Sugar Ski and Country Club** ($$$-$$$$, 800-634-1320).

On Beech, **Kat's Overlook Pub** ($$) is a good place to dine with an enviable mountain view. And a few yards down Beech Mountain is **Fred's General Mercantile Store** where **Fred's Backside Deli** ($) offers good deli food. An exceptional dining option in Banner Elk is the **Louisiana Purchase** ($$) with to-die-for Cajun and Creole food.

Cross country is gaining popularity in the North Carolina mountains.

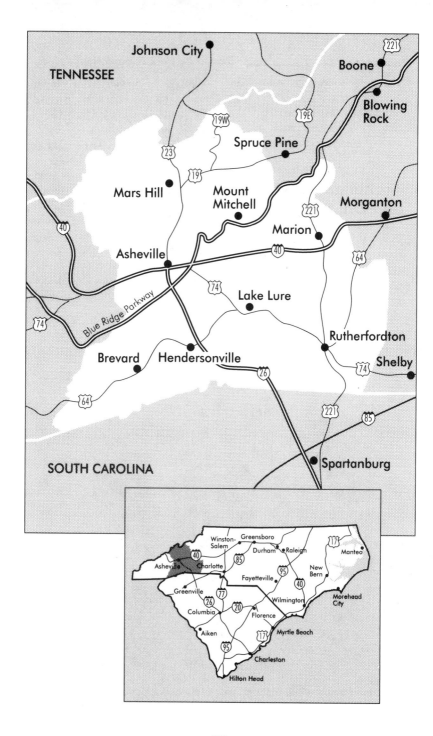

TENNESSEE

Johnson City

Boone

Blowing
Rock

Spruce Pine

Mars Hill

Mount
Mitchell

Morganton

Marion

Asheville

Blue Ridge Parkway

Lake Lure

Rutherfordton

Brevard

Hendersonville

Shelby

SOUTH CAROLINA

Spartanburg

Winston-Salem
Greensboro
Durham
Raleigh
Manteo
Asheville
Charlotte
Fayetteville
New Bern
Greenville
Wilmington
Morehead City
Columbia
Florence
Aiken
Myrtle Beach
Charleston
Hilton Head

The North Carolina central mountains tiptoe between the arts-centered sophistication of Asheville and the profound and homespun wit found at Connemara, outside Flat Rock.

HENDERSONVILLE, FLAT ROCK

To Get There:
Hendersonville is located at the intersection of I-26 and U.S. 64.

The cream always rises to the top. **Jump Off Mountain** wears a halo of cream each day when the afternoon clouds roll in. From the look out at **Jump Off Rock**, you can see almost 28 miles past Mount Pisgah, the Blue Ridge and into Tennessee. This represents only one area of the scenic mountain plateau called Hendersonville that rises some 2200 feet above sea level.

Folks who've been coming to Hendersonville and Flat Rock to vacation all their lives say the air is crisper here, easier to breathe. They come here for refreshment, recreation, rest and entertainment. Sparkling, sunshiny days of playing tennis or golf or hiking through Mount Pisgah, exploring the area's rich history and taking in a live theater play at night at the Flat Rock Playhouse are only the beginning of things to do in these mountains.

Things To See and Do _____

JOHNSON FARM

You can take a historical tour of the over 100-year-old Johnson Farm. Located off N.C. 191, you can tour the original faux painted red clay brick Italianate-style two-story home built by Oliver Moss in 1880. Moss came to the area to grow tobacco in the fertile valley of the French Broad River, but soon learned that tobacco was not well suited for this region. A few years later the home came into the hands of the tiny widow, Sallie Johnson and her two sons, Leander and Vernon. Aunt Sallie, as she was called, made the home into a boarding house for those who wanted to escape the dread malaria of the South Carolina Lowcountry as well as northern neighbors who discovered the peace of North Carolina's lush green mountains. Aunt Sallie's fame as a wonderful cook soon spread throughout the area and brought whole families to stay at her unpretentiously furnished boarding house for 4 to 6 months at a time. Even though she only accepted boarders through referrals, so many had to be turned away that she built a two-story white clapboard house next door. You can almost hear the music on the front verandah where callers once called square dances and folks shucked corn and snapped beans for entertainment.

Walking through both boarding houses and the kitchen where Sallie prepared meals for 75 people a day is a lesson in economics. Outside, you can visit the barn museum where tools and history of the eras is kept and also see where the pigs and chickens were kept in this self-sufficient operation.

Johnson Farm is a slice of history frozen in time and exposed each year on festival day for a hands-on experience.

Admission is $3 for adults and $1.50 for children. For operating hours call 800-828-4244.

JACKSON PARK

Located at the end of Fourth Avenue East and covering 212 acres, this is the largest county-owned park in Western North Carolina. What you'll like here is the 1.5-mile nature trail that lazily winds through a hardwood forest and wetland meadow. Another nature trail can be found at William H. King Park on Ashe Street. This easy-for-tenderfoots 1-mile trail also includes an 800-foot boardwalk.

ST. JOHN IN THE WILDERNESS EPISCOPAL CHURCH

The time is 1833. Try to imagine handing your prayer book to the maid who places it on a velvet pillow while you, Susan Baring from England, alight onto the carriage step at your own personal church, St. John in the Wilderness. Inside, are your best friends—all from Charleston, South Carolina. They are the wealthy summer people your husband, Rice planter, Charles Baring and Judge Mitchell lured to Flat Rock. These first land developers purchased all of Flat Rock for $.25 to $1 an acre. Then sold tracts of land for the luxurious homes tucked away in these sylvan retreats. In a few years the area became known as "Little Charleston." Services are held regularly in this still-operating Episcopalian church, and the lovely cemetery that rings the church reads like the who's who of Charleston's elite. When the church was enlarged in 1852, one old grave became part of the new addition, and you can see its flat marble marker in the chapel's center aisle.

FLAT ROCK PLAYHOUSE

St. John's lies catty corner from state theater of North Carolina Flat Rock Playhouse, begun by Robroy Farquhar in 1952. The Vagabond Players' summer stock performances have entertained thousands of visitors from all over the United States. The theater is now be-

ing operated by son, Robin Farquhar. Call the box office early for tickets as seasonal hits are soon sold out. (704-693-0731)

CONNEMARA

You can often hear the goats abrupt baa-braying before you get to **Connemara**, the antebellum oasis home of Pulitzer prize winning poet and biographer, Carl Sandburg and his wife, Lillian. Sandburg devoted his life to empowering and understanding the common man, so you won't see a fancy house here. You'll see the special breed of goats and the basement area where his wife kept her baby goats until the weather was kinder to them. She became a known pioneer in goat raising, so much so that a native making a delivery to these

The Flat Rock Playhouse is the oldest professional summer theatre in the state.

idyllic grounds remarked to her: "You've got a nice place here, what does your husband do, Mrs. Sandburg?"

Today, you can tour the grounds and house, see the "dizzy corner" where Sandburg typed on top of an orange crate and the bedroom where he slept by day so that he could work at night. In the downstairs basement you can watch an excellent video of Edward R. Murrow's interview with Sandburg. Sandburg's books are also available for sale as well as goat cheese and deliciously rich goat cheese fudge. Try it, you might like it.

Admission for adults is $2, children are admitted free of charge.

FARMERS MARKET

Folks enjoy the **Curb Market** (Farmers Market) in downtown Hendersonville on Tuesday and Saturday mornings. You'll find reasonable to downright cheap handmade articles, jellies, fresh vegetables and the like.

HOLMES STATE FOREST

Holmes State Forest looks like, acts like and smells like a park in the mountains, but it isn't. This is a managed forest with 7 talking trees that come with accompanying posts. You push a button and mountain music sails across the crisp air

as a narrator identifies the tree and tells you something about it in a folksy manner. Designed as an educational tool for children, adults get a kick out of it too.

You can take 3 trails that vary in length and difficulty. The most difficult one winds to the top of the mountain. If you call ahead for reservations, semi-primitive camping is available for free. In fact, everything in the Holmes Forest is free. This includes the picnic tables and shelter that folks often use for parties, volleyball and a game of horseshoes. Pleasant and friendly Forest Rangers are happy to help you understand the concept of a managed forest and how it benefits us economically, environmentally, and obviously, recreationally. The view from the mountain top overlook is spectacular, particularly in the fall when the mountains are still humming with color, but enough leaves have fallen to clear the view for you.

Holmes State Forest is located on Kanuga Road (S.R. 1127). The Forest is open from mid-March through the day after Thanksgiving. It's closed on Monday. (704-692-0100)

Accommodations___

Mountain Home Inn ($$-$$$) is located at 10 Courtland Boulevard in Hendersonville. If Robin Leach had been looking for the "rich and famous" when the Wyckham Hotel stood on this site, he would have been well supplied. This was then known as "Little St. Petersburg Colony."

After the hotel burned in a fire that could be seen as far away as Asheville, Dr. Troutman built a sturdy stone home here for his family. The home was completely renovated and redecorated a few years back and is now known to travelers as their "home away from home." But it's doubtful that many guests' homes are so fancifully decorated or kept as shiny clean. Then too, how many guests serve a full breakfast of blintz soufflé sauced with fresh blueberries and accented with a tiny pansy in a candlelit dining room?

Rarer still is the separate kitchen for guests who wish to prepare their own lunch or dinner. The kitchen is adjacent to a washer and dryer for guests' use.

The decor for each bedroom is different with a warm touch of whimsy here and there. There is a TV and telephone in each bedroom. You may choose a private bath with Jacuzzi. Another telephone sits near the tub so you won't miss that important call while showering. Innkeepers, Lynn and Bob Romera are gracious hosts who think of everything—even

where to go for dinner. (800-397-0066 or 704-697-9090)

Highland Lake Inn ($$$) on Highland Lake Road in Flat Rock, one of the oldest resorts in the area, has been recently renovated. Both the inn and cabins now have lovely antiques, oriental rugs and a multitude of activities to keep you busy. The resort's restaurant is a four-star choice. (704-693-6812)

CAMPING

Creekside Mountain Camping Resort ($), located 3 miles from Bat Cave, off U.S. Highway 74 has modern facilities plus a clubhouse and swimming pool in a true mountain setting. (800-248-8118)

Big Willow Campground ($) is located on Willow Road, off Cummings Road west of Hendersonville. This campground has full hookup, hot showers, a laundromat, square dancing and is next door to Cummings Cove Golf Course. (704-693-0187)

Dining

Expressions ($$$$) located at 114 North Main Street is Hendersonville's best choice for a gourmet dinner. The award-winning chef never disappoints whether it's seafood, lamb or veal or some brand new creation.

The Park Deli Cafe ($) at 437 North Main Street serves a very filling lunch using old favorites, such as tuna fish salad, chicken salad and Waldorf salad. But they mix some "oomph" into the ingredients.

Side Trips _____

CHIMNEY ROCK/LAKE LURE

To Get There:

Chimney Rock is located 15 miles east of Hendersonville. Take U.S. 64 east to Bat Cave and turn right onto U.S. 74.

Hollywood doesn't scout in locations that are less than picturesque. They've made three movies in this area in the past few years. Remember *Dirty Dancing*? It was shot in Lake Lure. Lake Lure is a tranquil lake that is ideal for swimming, fishing and boating. A must in the area is a climb to Chimney Rock Park (admission fee). The town, with the river running beside it, gives a nice rural atmosphere, but it is a touch on the "touristy" side. You can forgive a lot though as you wind up to the spectacular Chimney Rock or ride in a 26-story elevator inside the mountain. It deposits you at the top of the chimney-shaped rock. This renders a panoramic view that, all by itself, is worth the trip. Below is

Hickory Nut Gorge, which includes the **Rocky Broad River** and **Lake Lure**. Pack a picnic lunch or grab some take out food to enjoy at one of the park's many picnic areas.

Admission to Chimney Rock Park is $9 for adults and $4.50 for children ages 6 to 15.

You can stay at the refurbished art deco **Lake Lure Inn** ($$$) for a truly restful weekend. A favorite stay in Chimney Rock (not "touristy") is the **Ginger Bread Inn** ($$) right on Main Street with every room looking like a page out of *Country* magazine.

For More Information:

Henderson County Travel & Tourism
P.O. Box 721
Hendersonville, NC 28793
800-828-4244

ASHEVILLE

To Get There:

Asheville is easily accessible at the juncture of I-40 and I-26.

On the surface, Asheville, with its abundance of Art Deco architecture, looks sleepy—it isn't. Asheville simply waltzes to a classier tune. Rich folks once came here to rock on hotel verandahs and don formal wear for dinner. Folks still rock on the verandahs, but now it's usu-

Photo by William Russ. Courtesy N.C. Travel & Tourism.

*Chimney Rock is a unique rock formation that overlooks
Hickory Nut Gorge and Lake Lure.*

ally after a challenging game of golf, a trail hike on the Blue Ridge Parkway, a mountain trek with llamas, a day spent at Biltmore or antiqueing, or visiting the Folk Art Gallery and Pack Place.

Things To
See and Do _____

PACK PLACE

In Asheville's downtown square, Pack Place sits directly opposite to the memorial obelisk of Zebulon Vance. This historic structure houses four distinctly different museums in one setting. Not yet two years old, Pack Place is making a name for itself.

The former **Young Men's Institute**, commissioned by George Vanderbilt in 1893, commemorates African-American art, culture and history traditions. The whooping and hollering you may hear from the **Health Adventure Center** come from smallfry, ages 3 to 10, sliding down a pink tongue or dressing up in "Let's Pretend" costumes to perform in this interactive creative PlaySpace. They learn nutrition and how their bodies function in a game-type program that looks like recess time. At any visit you'll enjoy the amazing collection of native gems in the **Colburn Gem and Mineral Museum**. Throughout the year,

the 520-seat **Diana Wortham Theatre** offers performances ranging from plays to musicals and pageants. Pack Place also offers a super **Gift Shop** and **Courtyard Cafe**.

Pack Place is located at 2 South Pack Square in Asheville, and is open Tuesday through Saturday, from 10 a.m. until 5 p.m.; Sundays, from 1 p.m. until 5 p.m. The cost of admission depends on how many museums you choose to visit. For adults the range is $3.00 to $5.50; for seniors and students: $2.50 to $4.50; and for children $2.00 to $3.50.

THOMAS WOLFE MEMORIAL

The house, Dixieland, where writer Thomas Wolfe grew up has been kept in much the same "...bleak, cold and run down" fashion that Wolfe described in *Look Homeward Angel*.

Downstairs in the parlor, sister Mabel's cut crystal lamp is the sparkling centerpiece in an otherwise dreary setting. You'll see the large dining room with four separate tables set for dinner as if the writer's mother, Julia, expected her boarders to appear for dinner. The kitchen with two old stoves, is filled with mismatched crockery, a cherry pitter, apple peeler, and various other items that have become historical footnotes themselves.

Neither Tom nor his brothers and sisters ever had a permanent room of their own, "No place sacred to themselves against the invasion of the boarders." However, on his last visit before his premature death at age 37, he stayed in a spacious upstairs bedroom where he wrote, *Return.*

The guided tour gives a thorough explanation of life at the boarding house, including the cubbyhole of a room off the kitchen, where his mother stayed. True Wolfians can easily identify the various rooms and pieces of furniture that the author described. Half an hour

here and you'll feel like you, too, have come home again.

The Thomas Wolfe Memorial, located at 48 Spruce Street downtown, is open Tuesday through Saturday from 10 a.m. until 4 p.m; Sunday from 1 p.m. until 4 p.m. Admission is $1.00 for adults and $.50 for students. (704-253-8304)

BILTMORE ESTATE
HOUSE-GARDEN-WINERY

Biltmore is the sole purpose that many people visit Asheville, and may be responsible for making the city internationally known. There's been so much hoopla written and

Photo courtesy Pack Place.

Pack Place, in downtown Asheville, is four museums in one.

filmed about Biltmore that you may think the estate has lost its mystique. Never! Yearly, people come for a Christmas visit when the mansion is filled with poinsettias, old-time festive decorations, music and commemorative wine. Many buy an annual pass in order to see the gardens in their seasonal variety, have lunch in the **Stable Cafe** or dinner at **Deerpark Restaurant,** try a new wine at the Winery or point out favorite rooms in the mansion to their guests.

Wouldn't you love to have been at the first Christmas party in 1895? After seven years of work, European-imported artisans had recreated a 250-room

Photo courtesy N.C. Travel & Tourism.

The Banquet Hall at the Biltmore Estate.

French chateau-styled mansion atop a hill with a view of Mount Pisgah. The chateau, commissioned by George Vanderbilt, grandson of railroad industrialist, "Commodore" Cornelius Vanderbilt was designed by architect Richard Morris Hunt and landscaped by Frederick Law Olmstead.

Vanderbilt, an extremely well-educated man of vision made this estate famous as the "cradle of forestry." The tour is self-guided which means you can move at your own pace, lingering as long as you like in the skylit winter garden with its center fountain or the library. The Tapestry Gallery features Flemish tapestries and a John Singer Sargent portrait of George Vanderbilt over the library door. Inside, you'll find a nothing-like-it-anywhere-else library with a fresco ceiling and 10,000 priceless books.

Mount Pisgah can be seen from Mr. Vanderbilt's bedroom, a very masculine room with ornate Portuguese, Italian and Spanish pieces. Mrs. Vanderbilt's bedroom, decorated in Louis XV, has bright gold satin wall covering that commands a bit of drama. But no more so than the downstairs banquet hall with its three stone fireplaces and 16th century Flemish tapestries. Its hard to imagine having a cozy dinner for 64 at this table, but the acoustics are so perfect that guests at opposite ends of the table can be easily heard.

Downstairs, 100 servants made this home function for a family of six and their guests. You can visit the kitchens, laundry, baggage room and servants quarters. Even the servants had servants—at least those in higher positions, like the butler.

Also in the downstairs basement you'll find out how the family played. A bowling alley, indoor swimming pool and gymnasium sported what was, at the time, the latest in exercise equipment.

Biltmore is now offering a new Behind the Scenes tour that takes guests to see sections of the house not open to the general public, and where preservation work is in progress.

Allot sufficient time to stroll through the gardens. The Italian, Ramble, Rose Garden, Conservatory, Azalea Garden and the Bass Pond. And top off your visit at **The Winery**. This was part of Vanderbilt's original plan to establish a self-supporting estate. You'll get a better grounding at the Winery Welcoming Center. Plan a few minutes at the Tasting Room where you can sample the wines before you buy.

Biltmore Estate is open from 9:00 a.m. until 6 p.m. daily. Admission for adults is $22.95; for youths 10-15, $17.25. Biltmore is located on U.S. 25 three blocks north of Exit 50 on I-40. (800-543-2961)

ART GALLERIES & ANTIQUING

The **Folk Art Center** is located at Milepost 382, off the

Biltmore House and Garden is a European estate of immense beauty.

Photo by William Russ. Courtesy N.C. Travel & Tourism.

Blue Ridge Parkway, east of Asheville. This craft center is worth a stop if you're taking a day excursion along this nature-scenic highway, and worth making a special trip to visit otherwise.

Over 600 crafts people from 9 southeastern states showcase their work here. The craft shop, **Allanstand**, is named for the 1890 craft shop begun by Frances Goodrich to honor regional arts and crafts. The open two-story building displays work much in the same fashion as a museum, with quilts and wall hangings inching up the second balcony stairway. Fiber works that range from traditional lap quilting to woven jackets are sold alongside functional pottery and furniture. These juried pieces are not inexpensive, but make great gifts.

Whether you're breezing through town or on a leisurely vacation, include **New Morning Gallery** on your agenda. Located in historic Biltmore Village at 7 Boston Way, this unique upper-scale craft gallery offers many one-of-a-kind finds.

Bellagio, located at 5 Boston Way, features artistic clothing and jewelry for those who want something a little different for their wardrobe.

Blue Spiral 1, located at 38 Biltmore Avenue, seems more like an art gallery with contemporary paintings, sculpture and pottery. This down-town gallery includes an indoor sculpture garden.

In addition to the arts and crafts offerings, Asheville has wonderful antique stores. In downtown, **Lexington Park** is a favorite, and you'll find nice shops along Biltmore Avenue.

Accommodations

Just as some people come to Asheville to visit Biltmore Estate, many come to stay at the venerable old 1913 **Grove Park Inn & Country Club** ($$$$). Literally blasted out of Sunset Mountain by E.W. Grove, the resort overlooks the city of Asheville as well as the Blue Ridge and Smoky Mountains.

The view inside is almost as breathtaking as the one outside. Massive stone fireplaces, large enough for a grown man or woman to walk inside, invite you to linger in the common areas. Philosophical sayings are etched into the stone throughout the lobby, and the inn's guest list reads like *Who's Who*. Five different dining rooms, a golf course to be envied, tennis courts, swimming pools, a sports center and a wonderful crafts cottage make this an amalgam of superb vacationing. Grove Park Inn & Country Club is located at 290 Macon Ave. (704-252-2711 or 800-438-5800)

The experience is just as its name, **Freedom Escape**

Lodge ($$), implies—an escape. Not a dress-up place, the first thing you'll want to do is get into comfortable jeans, and women may feel inclined to leave their makeup in the room. Though not as inexpensive as camping, a $52 room with country air and activities is reasonable.

Individuals who want a refresher on life (and this is just the place to get it) are welcome, but the lodge mainly caters to groups. Its specialty is planned excursions to the Smoky Mountain train in Bryson City, the Biltmore Estate, etc. You can swim in the outdoor heated pool, play tennis, fish for trout and bass in the pond that the lodge overlooks, or workout in the gym. Most people enjoy hiking through the woods and fishing in the nearby lake. A buffet brunch and sit-down dinner are both extra ($). If requested when making a reservation, guests will be met at the Asheville airport.

Take U.S. 19/23 north from Asheville to the Flat Creek exit. Turn left from exit ramp, take the first right onto Murphy Hill Road and follow the signs to the Lodge. (800-722-8337)

Richmond Hill Inn ($$$$) may be the most pampering inn in North Carolina. Upon the turned-down bed covers of your four-poster bed you'll find a tiny box of chocolates atop a complimentary book of poetry. Fresh terry cloth robes hang in

Photo by Dawn O'Brien.

Richmond Hill Inn is one of the most pampering Bed and Breakfast Inns in the South.

the closet. There's a hair dryer in the bathroom and a refrigerator on the second floor offers beverages for your enjoyment. High tea, featuring Chef John Dabb's famous maple pecan scones and other light pastries, begins at 4 p.m. each day in the Oak Hall.

Of course, the mansion's original hosts, Pearson and Gabrielle Richmond, liked to pamper their guests, too. When their Victorian home was completed in 1895 atop a hill overlooking the Broad River, they invited all of Asheville's 16,000 citizens for a 4th of July picnic of fried chicken and lemonade. Chicken remains on the menu in the **Gabrielle Dining Room**, but now it's in an apple chutney sauce.

The inn features twin dining rooms: one an elegant room beside a fireplace and grand piano where music from easy listening to jazzy numbers is played, the other, an enclosed verandah that looks out, as writer O'Henry described, "at the dozens of mountains with their heads in the clouds." At dinner, don't pass up the chef's signature Mountain Apple and Onion Soup, which is a zesty twist on onion soup. If you've never tried antelope, you'll love this marinated delicacy, but this is also an opportunity to have free-range veal, which is prepared in several ways, season

depending. A dessert favorite is Cherries Jubilee—a creation of Bailey's Irish Cream and ice cream with hot fudge sauce garnished with bing cherries. Breakfast on the verandah may be anything from a cheese omelet with ham and sweet potato compote to crepes filled with hot fruit or strawberry-smothered waffles. This is one of those dream breakfasts that crosses your mind when staring at a box of cold cereal at home.

Richmond Hill Inn is located 3 miles from downtown Asheville on Richmond Hill Drive. (704-252-7313 or 800-545-9238).

Whether you opt for the llama trek or not, you may want to stay at the luxurious Southwestern-styled **Windsong, A Mountain Inn** ($$$$). Perched atop a mountain, each bedroom looks down into a meadow of llamas. The owners have appointed each Jacuzzi bedroom in a different motif. The Alaska room has a dog sled; the Appalachian room is furnished with crafts and materials of this mountain region. The New Mexico Native American theme of the inn has a homey feel and breakfast is a large deal here—just as you might imagine on a western dude ranch.

Windsong is located in Clyde, about 45 minutes from Asheville. (704-627-6111)

CAMPING

About 8 miles north of Asheville is the **Davis River Campground, Inc.** ($-$$), located on the French Broad River. This small camp has electric and water hookups, plus 4 rustic log cabins with fireplaces. (704-658-0772)

There are two **KOA Campgrounds** nearby. **Asheville East** ($-$$) on Tanglewood Lakes in the Blue Ridge Mountains in Swannanoa has all camping facilities, plus a swimming pool, 2 fishing lakes that don't require a fishing license and a trout stream. Take exit 59 off I-40 west, (704-686-3121). **Asheville West** ($) is located in Candler. Take exit 37 from I-40 west and follow Wiggins Road. (704-665-7015)

Some of the best and most scenic camping is at Mt. Mitchell on the Blue Ridge Parkway at Milepost 355.4. (See information on Mt. Mitchell.)

Dining _____

A great late continental-type breakfast with bagels, sweet rolls and coffee is at **Malaprop's Book Store Cafe**, located at 61 Haywood Street. An old book store, Malaprop's carries the works of many North Carolina authors as well as a good mix of literary interests.

Another breakfast or lunch treat is at the **Blue Moon Bakery** at 62 Biltmore Avenue.

That wonderful aroma of baking muffins greets you the moment the door is opened. You can sit at an old ice cream-type table for lunch of Focaccio bread with dried tomatoes (kind of pizza looking), soft drinks, fruit and sandwiches. The specialty is Granita, a frozen cappuccino or fruit drink.

Also, for good spots for lunch, check out **Chelsea's Village Tea Room** at 60 Boston Way in Biltmore Village or **Deerpark** at Biltmore Estate

For dinner, **Market Place**, now located downtown at 20 Wall Street, is a *tres chic* restaurant that continues to serve some of the most innovative and delicious cuisine around. The lamb and seafood dishes in exotic sauces are prepared perfectly. And desserts, especially the chef's rendering of Tiramisu, is worth many visits to this contemporary restaurant located on a street that looks as if it belongs on a European postcard.

Side Trips _____

LLAMA TREKKING AT WINDSONG

To Get There:
From Asheville, follow I-40 west and take exit 24 onto N.C. 209. From N.C. 209, turn left on Riverside Drive and right on Ferguson Cove Loop. Windsong is located in Clyde, N.C.

Photo by Dawn O'Brien.

This llama for hire.

Share your wine with a llama. That, of course, is after your llama has lugged the wine, shrimp scampi, fettucine and zucchini brownies with whipped cream up and down steep mountain trails and over foot bridges.

Part of the fun is getting to know these gentle creatures who were first native to North America. They migrated to the South American Andes and later crossed over land bridges into Asia where they evolved into the camel. Your inclination is to stroke or pet the silky haired neck of your hiking buddy, but you'll soon discover that llamas are shy creatures. The trek leader explains that llamas are very social animals and will call to each other in a mournful mewing tone when separated.

If you enjoy hiking through the woods crunching leaves beneath your feet and the solitude of graceful Canadian hemlocks and wild flowers in the spring, you'll probably find that leading a llama adds a special dimension to the outdoor hiking experience. Yes, it's naturally great not to be lugging that backpack yourself, but the very act of leading these sure-footed, soft-pawed animals into wilderness areas is a blended experience that you may want to repeat often.

The nice thing about llama treks at Windsong Inn is that you can trek as little or as much as you want. For a more rugged adventure, you can sign up for an overnight camping trip. This can be combined with fly fishing or just sitting around the campfire roasting somemores and talking or listening to the sounds of nature. (704-627-6111)

For More Information:

Asheville Convention and Visitors Bureau
P.O. Box 1010
Asheville, NC 28802
800-257-1300

AAA Carolinas
660 Merrimon Ave., Suite A
Asheville, NC 28804
704-253-5376

BREVARD

The Pisgah National Forest is known as the Cradle of Forestry, and forestry was taught here almost a 100 years ago.

Things To See and Do _____

SLIDING ROCK

From the entrance to Pisgah National Forest, it's about 7 or 8 miles to **Sliding Rock**. Put on a pair of worn out jeans to slide 150 feet down through the icy water's natural cascade. It doesn't cost a dime and is the most invigorating way to cool off and have fun that you can remember. Another cool

Photo courtesy Buncombe Co., N.C. Tourism Development Authority.

One of the area's 250 waterfalls.

wind/down activity is tubing. You can rent tubes at Shorty's, on U.S. 74, and float down the Davidson River.

WATERFALLS

If you're not up to that kind of exhilaration, you can spend the day locating a few of Brevard/Transylvania County's 250 waterfalls. The best way is to take the scenic 79-mile drive that loops through the Pisgah National Forest past camera demanding shots. You could also hike through the designated trails. To make this a truly frugal weekend, fish for you dinner in one of the trout-filled streams. Horseback riding trails through the woods give you one more way to explore the forest. Trail maps are available at U.S. Forestry Service office on U.S. 276.

BREVARD MUSIC CENTER

If you've had enough of communing with nature, check out the **Brevard Music Center**. There is an annual summer **Brevard Music Festival** with international stars. Call the Chamber of Commerce (800-648-4523) for dates or spend a Thursday evening listening to original mountain music and bluegrass at **Silvermont** on East Main Street in Brevard.

*Sliding Rock is a 60-foot slide down a sloping rock formation
that drops into a pool of water.*

Accommodations

BED AND BREAKFAST INNS

The **Womble Inn** at 301 West Main Street in Brevard ($) serves your breakfast on a silver tray in your room, which will make going home hard to get used to. (704-884-4770)

The 1851 **Red House** ($$) was here before Brevard or Transylvania County was established. It has been restored to its former elegance with period antiques, and is well located in Brevard at 412 West Probart Street. (704-884-9349)

For a stay in an 1862 Victorian farmhouse on the edge of the Pisgah National Forest at 151 Everett Road, **Key Falls Inn** ($) will fit the bill with a full breakfast. (704-884-7559)

Now maybe you're thinking—mountains—log cabin. You can bring the family and stay in a log cabin at **The Pines Country Inn** ($$-$$$). It's located at 719 Hart Road in the Pisgah Forest. (704-877-3131)

HOTELS AND MOTELS

The Penrose Motel on U.S. 64 in Penrose, boasts the best rates in the area and is conveniently located 4 minutes from the Pisgah National Forest and 5 minutes from the Etowah Valley Golf Club. (704-884-2691)

CAMPING

For a cheap, but fun family weekend near Brevard, make reservations for a campsite at the **Davidson River Campground** in the Pisgah National Forest, just off the parkway near Asheville. (800-283-2267)

Dining

If you opt not to cookout, the next least expensive dining bet is **Berry's Restaurant** ($) at 935 Asheville Highway, where you'll enjoy country food and Bluegrass on Fridays. The **Carriage House Restaurant** ($-$$) on Country Club Road in Brevard is another good choice, as is **Oh Susanna's** on West Main Street in Brevard. The **Inn at Brevard** ($$$) has great food and the **Raintree** ($$$) is positively exceptional.

> **For More Information:**
> **Brevard Chamber of Commerce**
> **35 W. Main St.**
> **Brevard, NC 28712**
> **800-648-4523**

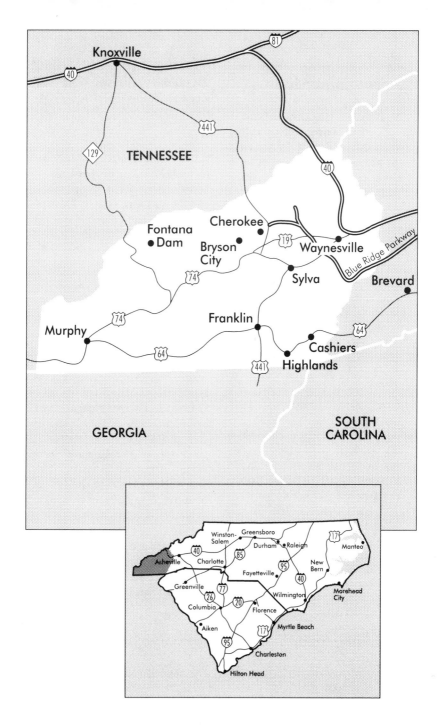

Native American Cherokees, who saw their mountain peaks ringed in a halo of clouds, called them the Smoky Mountains. This former rich hunting ground has become one of America's most visited national parks.

CHEROKEE

> **To Get There:**
> From Asheville take I-40 west to U.S. 19 south to U.S. 441.

Who has grown up in America without hearing about the great Cherokee Indians? It is a story of intelligence, skill, hardship, betrayal, sadness and more recently—success. Today, the 58,000-acre reservation, known as the Qualla Boundary, is a success story that you will discover by stopping at the **Cherokee Historical Association**. Still, in the midst of this little town banded by the magnificent Smokies, it must be said that the level of commercialism in some, but not all, areas of Cherokee is not what you might expect. However, what you would expect—an authentic Indian Village, Oconaluftee—is here.

Things To See and Do _____

MUSEUM OF THE CHEROKEE INDIAN

Worth a visit is the **Museum of the Cherokee Indian** on Drama Road. This is a modern museum that chronicles the events of 10,000 years of Cherokee history through displays of pottery, ancient weapons, tools and other artifacts, along with explanatory audio/visual programs. Admission to the museum is $4 for adults and $2 for children 6 to 12 years of age. (704-497-3481)

OCONALUFTEE INDIAN VILLAGE

Not to be missed is the Oconaluftee Indian Village. It's a reproduction of how the Eastern Band of the Cherokees lived 200 years ago. From the moment you are guided inside, you feel as if you'd walked into a primitive setting. The Cherokee lived in notched log houses chinked with mud, which they copied from the settlers.

It even smells different, perhaps from the potters who mold clay vessels by hand, or maybe it's that fresh straw smell from white oak saplings and river cane that the basket makers strip and use to weave their age-honored patterns. Then again, it could be the smell of burning poplar, controlled to sear into the giant logs for canoes. Maybe it's coming from corn pounded with a mortar, then boiled with hickory ashes, or it may come from the seven-sided Council House with center hole that lets smoke escape from the sacred fire.

Did you know that the Cherokees had a little sweat house where ailing people were placed to sweat out the fevers? This fact should make you happy that you were born some 200 years later. You'll see demonstrations of all the Indian crafts—from-blow-gun makers to bead workers. Admission for adults is $8 and for children 6 to 13, $4. (704-497-2315)

QUALLA ARTS AND CRAFTS MUTUAL

The Qualla Arts and Crafts Mutual is a shop that looks more like a museum. This shop of artisans' works is responsible for keeping alive the authentic arts and crafts of the Cherokee. It is also the only place that you'll find these distinct crafts.

UNTO THESE HILLS

No trip to Cherokee would be complete without attending *Unto These Hills*, now in its 45th season at the newly renovated Mountainside Theater. The summer outdoor drama professionally blends drama, music and dance to unfold the tragic story of how the proud and misunderstood Cherokees were driven west on the "Trail of Tears" from their Smoky Mountain homeland. It also shows how a few remained and, with sympathetic settlers' help, were able to rebuild into a race of productive American citizens. Admission is $9 to $11 for adults and $5 for children. (704-497-2111)

PIONEER HOMESTEAD

Before leaving the area, drive north a half mile on U.S. 441 to the entrance of the **Great Smoky Mountains National Park**. Just inside is the re-creation of the Pioneer Homestead. This is not just a log cabin, it's a

Unto These Hills *is in its 45th season*
at the newly renovated Mountainside Theater.

series of 15 types of buildings that settlers needed to survive in the mountain wilderness. Placed beside a rushing river, the homestead is an interesting and picturesque place to visit and to picnic.

FISHING

Trout fishing in the bountiful streams and rivers on the ancestral lands of the Cherokee Reservation is, for fishing enthusiasts, the best part of the trip. Call for fishing permits and maps. (800-438-1601)

Accommodations

A principal reason that the Cherokee Reservation is such a success is that the businesses are tribal-owned. That includes motels, campgrounds and restaurants.

HOTELS AND MOTELS

Inside Cherokee, the **Holiday Inn-Cherokee** ($$) on U.S. 19 south is a good bet with its North American Indian motif and other convenient services. (800-465-4329)

CAMPING

For camping enthusiasts there are many options. Try the **Cherokee KOA Campground** (800-825-8352) or camp in the **Great Smoky National Park.** (615-436-5615)

Dining

The Holiday Inn's **Chestnut Tree Restaurant** is a good option for dinner.

For More Information:
Smoky Mountain Host of North Carolina
(800-432-4678)

FRANKLIN

To Get There:
Take I-40 west to U.S. 23 south which merges with U.S. 441 into Franklin.

Franklin's claim to fame is the nearby corundum (ruby and sapphire) mines. The prettiest rubies are said to come from India. But that's a hard sell to someone who's just found one in Franklin's Cowee Valley. It's difficult to equal the kind of excitement you feel when that hexagonal shaped red stone winks up at you. You may have spent hours digging out buckets of clay and gunk. Then stood or sat at a trough with fresh spring water circulating through its flume while you sifted dirt and gravel from potential gems. When a vein is hit, you'll find everything from chips to several carats.

The rubies, even in their natural form, are easier to rec-

Photo by Dawn O'Brien.

Franklin's claim to fame is the nearby ruby and sapphire mines.

ognize than sapphires because the sapphires often have a brownish color on the outside that blends in with the other worthless gravel. The clue to it's true identity is in the stone's crystal formation. You can also find garnets (dark red), rhodolite (purplish-red), kyanite (blue) and other beautiful minerals in that bucket of muck.

Things To See and Do

FRANKLIN GEM AND MINERAL SOCIETY

To get the rockhound fever, stop first at the Franklin Gem and Mineral Society located in a recycled 150-year-old jail. The all-volunteer museum is located at 2 West Main Street. This is a small building that is packed with fascinating gems. A display case (in a former solitary cell) now springs into glowing magical colors when activated in the black-lighted Fluorescent Room. A tape explains that it's the rock's impurities that give off energy under a black light.

Upstairs, you'll see models of stone writings from 701 B.C. found in Hezakiah's tunnel in Jerusalem. In this museum you'll find beautiful stones you're probably unfamiliar with and other strange stones in the shape of a ram's horns. You'll also see a 218-pound aquama-

rine and a 48-pound ruby; learn that sapphires and rubies are both corundum and that a ruby isn't a thing in the world but a red sapphire. Admission is free. (704-369-7831)

MINING FOR GEMS

Scores of mines line the area, but most have buckets that have been salted or enriched with a few chips. Some mines use native stones, such as **Mason's Ruby & Sapphire Mine**. It supplies the tools and allow you to dig your own for $8 a day. (Go north on N.C. 28 to the airport sign and turn left; bypass the airport and continue several miles to the mine.) Another good bet is **Shuler's Mine** further north on N.C. 28 (turn off at Cowee Valley Road, known as Ruby Mine Road). (704-524-3551) The mine's largest recorded ruby find weighed in at 163 carats. **Mason Mountain Mine** on N.C. 28 (Bryson City Road) has been run by Brown and Martha Johnson for 28 years. They do enrich their buckets to ensure successful mining, especially for children. Admission is $5 for adults and $2 for children under 12. (704-524-4570)

You can have your rough stones cut into gems and mounted at the **Cowee Valley Lapidary** on Ruby Mine Road.

Accommodations____

Campers can be near the action at the **Cowee Valley Campground** within walking distance of the Lapidary at 168 Ruby Mine Rd. (704-524-2321) Or stay in Franklin at the **Franklin Terrace Bed & Breakfast** ($-$$), at 67 Harrison Avenue. (800-633-2431)

Dining _____

For some good old country food, stop in at the **Sunset** ($). Try **Luciose** for Italian ($$), **Talent's** ($$) for steaks or **Micasa's** ($$) for gourmet Mexican.

> **For More Information:**
>
> **Smoky Mountain Host of North Carolina (800-432-4678)**

FONTANA DAM

> **To Get There:**
>
> Go north on N.C. 28, turn west onto U.S. 74/19 west.

"A little mountain cabin...something in the woods." To many out-of-staters, mountain cabin and North Carolina are synonymous. Urbanites forget the clean fragrance of mountain air invigorated with the scent of pine. At Fontana, visitors appreciate rocking on the front porch listening to the clip-clop of horses' hooves as riders wind through the mountain trails below them. The vegetation here is so lush that you'll get no more than a glimmer of fellow vacationers.

Things To See and Do _____

Sign up for a day of punching through white water rapids on the Nantahala River or a day of tubing on the Oconee River in Tennessee at **Great Smokies Rafting Company** (800-277-6302). Another fun option is doing a half or full day of guided mountain bike cycling (**Euchella Mountain Bikes**, 800-446-1603) through secluded mountain trails and along white water streams. The **Appalachian Trail**, only 3 miles away, follows a wilderness path, providing some of the most beautiful hiking trails in the nation, and you can go at your own speed.

Accommodations and Dining _____

At **Nantahala Village** ($$), located on U.S. 19 west outside Bryson City, the first thing to do before unpacking is—inhale. For dining we'd opt for a delicious meal prepared with fresh mountain vegetables, fruits and mountain stream fish in the **Nantahala Village's** restaurant. Later, build a fire in the cabin's stone fireplace and "veg" out. (704-488-2826)

For More Information:

Smoky Mountain Host of North Carolina (800-432-4678)

BRYSON CITY

To Get There

Take U.S. 74/19 east into Bryson City.

Listen for the train whistle. Just 100 years ago that was the sound that linked the isolated Smoky Mountains to the rest of the nation.

Things To See and Do _____

THE GREAT SMOKY MOUNTAIN RAILROAD

The train carries passengers through the soaring Nantahala Gorge in open-air cars. You'll find that these steep mountains lend credibility to the Indian name "nantahala"— meaning land of the noonday sun. Only the overhead sun can reach down deep enough to play along the gorge's toes. The ride will take you into remote wildflower and fern areas accessible only by foot, almost letting you touch the wilderness with your fingertips. You'll cross Fontana Lake where birds skim the still lake beside floating pontoon boats. From Bryson City it's a 4-hour excursion round trip, but take the train ride to the luncheon destination, then spend the afternoon shooting through white water rapids for a guided return trip down the Nantahala River. Train rides from Bryson City cost $17 for adults and $7 for children under 12 years of age. From Dillsboro, the cost for adults is $15, and $7 for children. (800-872-4681)

WHITE WATER RAFTING

The **Nantahala Outdoor Center** on U.S. 19 west has been providing some of North Carolina's best white water rafting on five Appalachian rivers since 1972. It also has lodging and dining facilities. (800-232-7238)

Accommodations and Dining _____

In Bryson City, the **Randolph House** ($-$$) is a great B & B that also serves delicious dinners. (704-488-3472)

Photo by William Russ. Courtesy N.C. Travel & Tourism.

The Great Smoky Mountain Railway
runs between Dillsboro and Murphy.

For More Information:

Smoky Mountain Host of
North Carolina
(800-432-4678)

CASHIERS

To Get There:

Cashiers is located at the
junction of U.S. 64
and N.C. 107.

Maybe the slowed-down rhythm is due to the 3,487-foot elevation, but in Cashiers, mountains, like people, wake slowly. At dawn, frost coats Rock Mountain's stone face, but as the sun begins to flirt and folks have downed a cup of coffee, a glimmer of activity stirs these mountains to life. Photographers think they've gone to heaven when they wind up the road past Lake Toxaway, and Sapphire Valley into Cashiers where God seems to have put his personal thumbprint. The area is near picture-proof from any angle. It's the kind of place where you wouldn't mind getting lost. Because no matter where you wander—upon the area's longest 411-foot waterfall or stumbling upon a secluded lake (sufficiently cold to discourage skinny dipping), or beside a secreted away golf course—the experience has been a communion with nature that you wouldn't trade for a map.

Things To See and Do

The area is ripe with recreational diversity that spans the four seasons. In the winter, you can ski at **Sapphire Valley Ski Resort**, ride horseback there and along the trails at **Arrowmont Stable & Cabins**. (800-682-1092) It's also a time when you can see more and farther when hiking to the 5,127-foot peak of Yellow Mountain and walk through more wooded trails than anyone has time to count.

Crunching through blankets of leaves, inhale that fresher than fresh scent of pine, because no matter how hard chemists try, they can't duplicate that freshness.

Of course, the earth yields even more fragrances in the spring when the rhododendron and mountain laurel become a visual dazzle. Anglers start getting their fly fishing gear in order for mountain streams, and for those who think that looks like fun but don't know how, the **Orvis Fly Fishing School** (704-743-3768) may be your ticket to a rewarding pastime. With snow runoffs and winter rains, spring is an ideal time to hike to the area's 12 waterfalls. This also holds true for summer and fall.

Summer, when thermometers rise in the lowlands, the

mountains' refreshing cool temperatures bring out tennis players, golfers and campers who know they'll be able to enjoy these sports in comfort.

Fall brings out the anglers again, and is even more popular for leaf color. In fact, when leaves reach their peak, the landscape could not be brighter if it were on fire. So, if planning your waterfall trek in the fall, first drive down N.C. 107 south to the curve, then get ready; the sudden appearance of Lake Jocassee is a stunner. Stop at the overlook where you'll be able to hear the waterfall, which is about a half mile away in Nantahala National Park.

WATERFALLS

The 411-foot **Whitewater Falls**, highest waterfall in the eastern U.S., is the easiest to get to and paved paths make it handicap accessible. Though not as thunderously dramatic as Niagra Falls' plunging waters, Whitewater Falls is higher and the wilderness setting makes its gentler cascade of water more beautiful.

Drift, Rainbow, Turtle, and **Bust-Your-Butt Falls** are found on the Horseshoe River off N.C. 281. **Toxaway Falls** off U.S. 64 east, which passes over the falls, is also easy to reach. And for stalwart souls, **Silver Run Falls** cascades into a pool of chilly water that is deep enough for swimming.

For smallfry, Cashiers' **Sliding Rock** forms a natural waterslide on the Chattooga River. Just past High Hampton Inn on N.C. 107 south and 3 miles into Whiteside Cove Road, **Hurricane Falls** empties into Lake Glenville where there is great fishing. Take N.C. 107

The 411-foot Whitewater Falls is the highest waterfall in the eastern United States.

Courtesy N.C. Travel & Tourism.

north to Norton Road and pass a bridge. You'll find the falls about a half mile down.

LAKES

Spring, summer and fall are the ideal seasons to enjoy the lakes. Glenville Lake, about 5 miles north of Cashiers on N.C. 107 is man-made and covers the former community of Glenville. This lake, with 26 miles of shoreline, offers more recreational water pleasures than most can dream up. And **Jim's Boat Landing** at **Glenville Marina** (5 miles north on N.C. 107) rents canoes, pontoons, speed boats for water skiing (with skis), row boats, and paddle boats. This stocked lake is a premier spot for catching bass, trout, etc. But the entire Cashiers/Highlands area is often referred to as "liquid acres" due to its abundant streams, creeks, rivers and lakes that bear such delicious names as Sapphire, Toxaway, Whisper, Cullasaja and Hampton.

GOLF/TENNIS

You'll find 11 golf courses dotted throughout the area. Most are private, but the two semiprivate courses where you may play, if space permits, are **High Hampton** (704-743-2450) and **Holly Forest** (800-533-8268). The majestic stone face of Rock Mountain looms above Hampton Lake's verdant High Hampton Golf course, making this one of the most naturally beautiful courses around. Holly Forest's course at Sapphire Valley is a scenic wonder as well with water hazards and a waterfall in its midst.

Tennis, too, is a year-round sport but, naturally, sees heaviest activity in the warmer months. The best courts are located in the area's resort centers. **High Hampton Inn & Country Club** allows tennis court privileges (for a fee) to non-inn guests according to availability, but you may also find an open court at the **Community Center**.

BIRD WATCHING

Few places throughout the Southeast afford such bird watching opportunities as does the Cashiers Valley. A total of 149 different species have been sighted here during all periods of the year. In fact, the sport of rock climbing was popular in the area until the Peregrine Falcon, now on the endangered species list, began to nest on Whiteside Mountain. Today, climbers content themselves with hiking through the area's vast network of trails and strenuous climbs to mountain peeks.

If all this sounds too strenuous, take heart. The area abounds with clever shops and includes an antique mall with unusual finds such as a potato dicer, tobacco basket, old snow shoes as well as fine period furniture. Try to imagine a setting more perfect for a symphony orchestra than a knoll overlooking Lake Sapphire with Bald Mountain as a backdrop. This is an annual July event. Call the **Cashiers Chamber of Commerce** for specific dates. (704-743-5191).

Accommodations___

BED AND BREAKFAST INNS

If bed and breakfast inns are what you seek, the **Millstone Inn** ($$-$$$) has one of the most captivating views around, and a handsomely decorated interior as well.

RESORTS

"Anyone for bingo?" asks a friendly guest as you're getting your room key at **High Hampton Inn & Country Club** in Cashiers. A huge fire roars in the stone fireplace, and you note a few guests busy with a puzzle, while others meander from the inn's rustic dining room.

The dining room offers a "wow" view that overlooks the lake and vast stone-faced Rock Mountain behind it. Each day the inn serves three huge buffet meals that let you choose from a vast array of good, nourishing regional dishes. The dessert table's lopsided homemade cakes look a lot like what comes from most of our kitchens, which adds to this inn's down-home flavor and makes it a temptation for us to overindulge.

A visitor is almost guaranteed to find some activity to his or her liking. The lawn below is set up for croquet and the International Croquet Festival is held annually in mid-October just down the road on N.C. 107 south at the **Chattooga Club**. There are wonderful hiking trails around the base of Rock Mountain where you can picnic, and High Hampton Inn has guided hikes to various waterfalls. You can rent a mountain bike at the **Gathering Place** below the Pro Shop, and give your calves a real workout. You can even join in a llama trek up Rock Mountain by signing up in the lobby. White water rafting down the Chatooga River, whose headwaters begin at High Hampton, is another thrill-packed option.

And if this area is a beacon for photographers, it is no less so for "wannabe" artists. Watercolor classes are available for both children and adults just by signing up. The activity list goes on and on. Television is not included in the "go see," neither in your room nor in the lobby, and for many, this holds great appeal. Telephones aren't included either, except for two in old tin-lined phone booths in the lobby. This is a place that encourages the lost art of getting to know people. With its appeal to old-fashioned values, the High Hampton has our vote.

High Hampton Inn ($$$ including meals) is located 1 1/2 miles from Cashiers on N.C. 107 south. For reservations, call 800-334-2551.

The **Greystone Inn** in Lake Toxaway, former home of socialite Lucy Camp Armstrong Moltz, has been redesigned as the "final destination in paradise." Tastefully decorated in understated elegance, it is certainly the place to forget about any problem that ails you. Greystone is the kind of resort that you could quickly acquire a taste for. The inn overlooks Lake Toxaway and the staff fusses and pampers you just as you've always thought you deserved but never got at home.

Golf, tennis, sailing and water skiing are chief activities, but lying in the hammock also has great appeal. The inn's bedrooms are spacious and most come with fireplaces and huge Jacuzzi bathrooms. Here, you can stash your worries. Just one price ($$$$) includes everything. (800-824-5766)

"Don't think about it—jump," your instructor encourages. (This could take the edge off your "comfort zone.") "Hurl yourself forward and grab for the trapeze. Swing out...then slowly come back down to earth. Don't worry, the harness will hold you." Those are the last words you hear before challenging yourself to what the instruction book calls, self-discovery at **Earthshine Mountain Lodge**. It's a little akin to rock climbing. But you look down at the horses in the meadow below and wistfully consider the group who took the morning horseback ride into the woods. You look back over to Earthshine Lodge's deck. People are drinking coffee and reading, and you imagine they're looking to see if you're really going for it. You close your eyes, leap forward, grab for the bar, swing suspended in space like a free-fall for one awesome moment, then float down to the cheering crowd below.

Your bedroom, with private bath and overhead loft, looks out on the meadow. While lying in a log bed upon an antique quilt, you hear the rhythmic chirp of country crickets. This reminds you of grandmother's place. It's hard to say why. The quilt is old—the lodge is new. In fact, the aroma of fresh, unfinished pine walls surround you. And grandmother's place didn't have a waterfall 1 3/4 miles away, either. You may have helped feed the horses, put the chickens up and gathered eggs (as children do at Earthshine) or sung songs after dinner, at grandmother's, but seldom did you enter into square dancing.

A lot of guests don't go to ecologically sensitive Earthshine for the activities, they prefer doing nothing more than reading on the lodge's front deck overlooking the Blue Ridge Mountains. Earthshine becomes an awakening experience not easily forgotten.

Earthshine Lodge has 8 rooms. Three meals per day and horseback riding is included for $80 per person, $40 for children. The lodge is open year-round. Call for directions. (704-862-4207)

Sapphire Valley Resort ($$$-$$$$) at 4000 U.S. 64 west in Sapphire is another gorgeous, full-service resort. It features both a heated outdoor and indoor pool as well as a spa and sauna with an exercise/weight and games rooms. You can ski, ride horses, fish, play tennis and golf and enjoy its superb restaurant. (800-533-8268)

CAMPING
Singing Waters Camping Resort ($) is located 10 miles north of Cashiers on Trout Creek Road off N.C. 107. Hammer the stakes for your tent in

Photo by Dawn O'Brien.

Ecologically sensitive Earthshine Lodge overlooks the Blue Ridge Mountains.

the shade trees next to Trout Creek. This campground has hot showers, heated bath houses, laundry facilities and more than enough fishing, swimming and hiking to please any outdoor lover. (704-293-5872)

Dining

Did you ever get so hungry grocery shopping that you couldn't wait to eat? That is not a problem at **The Hot Rocks Cafe at the Market Basket**. ($$-$$$) This restaurant is a gourmet/health food/classy grocery store. You can pull out a chair right beside the baby grand piano, listen to nightly entertainment and order something phenomenal from its seafood and vegetarian cuisine. Also provided is one of dining's newer wrinkles—hot rocks at your table to cook your own dinner. Most guests get a bang out of this fat-free cooking, but for those of us who go out so that someone else can have all that fun, dinner is prepared for you. Mountain trout is (to be expected) sensational, but the pastas and bean dishes are equally good. With deadpan voices, waiters announce that the desserts are not "decalorized." Take that warning seriously. The cafe serves dinner only, and brown bagging is allowed. The Hot Rocks Cafe is located 1 block past the intersection of U.S. 64 and N.C. 107 on 107 south.

Photo courtesy N.C. Travel & Tourism.

In the Cashiers area, a spring-fed lake reflects a picture-perfect image of a scenic golf course and Rock Mountain.

White Goose Cafe at Oakmont Lodge ($$), located a few blocks north on N.C. 107 is open for breakfast, lunch and dinner. Before you come inside this former barn, walk through the outdoor museum of farm tools. It's like strolling through memories of mountain living. You can sit on a bench or relax in the hammock and watch the white goose for which the restaurant was named. She still swims in the pond just beyond the restaurant's porch with her seasonal brood. Children are offered fresh biscuits to feed Cashiers' best fed ducks.

Inside, you'll see pounds of fun memorabilia such as a brass plate advertising a shave & haircut—$.25. A big stuffed bear plays oldies on the player piano. Crab cakes are this cafe's signature menu item, but lamb chops score high, too. For lunch, homemade soups and sandwiches. play well with the brownie sundae. Brown bagging is allowed.

Winslow's ($$$) is located on U.S. 64 east at Laurel Terrace. This restaurant's chef gets the nod for providing the most original gourmet dinners in Cashiers.

Brown Skillet ($), located on N.C. 107 north, is perfect for those watching their pocketbook, but not necessarily their waistline. The good old country food includes fried chicken as a specialty. Brown bagging is permitted.

For More Information:
Cashiers Chamber of Commerce
Box 238-S
Cashiers NC 28717
(704-743-5191)

HIGHLANDS

To Get There:

Highlands is located at the intersection of N.C. 106 and U.S. 64.

Pull over at the **Whiteside Overlook** on U.S. 64 west about 5 1/2 miles before you get to Highlands. Dismiss the fact that you're on a highway because mountain views don't get much prettier than this.

Cradled on a mountain top plateau, Higlands, at 4,118 feet, is a little higher than Cashiers. About 60% of Highlands remains in the Nantahala National Forest. In 1875, two intrepid entrepreneurs, Samuel T. Kelsey and Clinton C. Hutchinson, decided to build one central commercial center for the U.S. They took a map and drew a line from New York to New Orleans, and a intersecting line from Chicago to Savannah. Those lines converged at the Higlands plateau. The men then came to the area and purchased the plateau from the Dobson family. However, it took little time to realize that their scenic land parcel, cool and devoid of disease threatening fevers, was better suited for tourism. They sent flyers to surrounding states advertising rooms for $1.25. The rest, as folks say, is history.

Downtown Highlands is a lively mix of chic shops, crafts, historic inns, economical-to-expensive restaurants, art galleries, a library, outdoor outfitters, a condiment store, an auction house like Blowing Rock's, a nature center, a gas station that also sells antiques and (best bargain in town) a resale shop. This tiny hamlet exhibits a cultural bent by enticing visitors to its Highland Playhouse professional summer stock theater, annual month-long summer Highland Chamber Music Festival and the Highlands Forum, a center for the study and debate of current critical international issues. Art galleries abound too; one shares the same building as the library. Best of all, a 20-minute hike from the Nature Center on Horse Cove Road will take you to the Continental Divide, a.k.a. Sunset Rocks, which overlooks the town.

Highlands, not a throwback to the '30s, is family oriented, which may be the deciding lure for affluent retirees. The day after Thanksgiving, lo-cals congregate downtown for carols, Biblical Christmas readings, tree lighting, Santa's visit and fireworks.

Highlands and Cashiers are both pretty little towns where you can feel safe walking the streets. No one can ever remember a murder or mugging in either area—a boast not every small town can claim any longer. Crime is said to be pretty much nil because the areas are off the beaten path. Don't everybody pack at once.

Highlands' shopping blooms with variety, but there are two unique shops you won't want to miss. **The Condiment Shop** is at the corner of Church and 4th Street. (Highlands hasn't felt the need for store numbers, yet.) There's nothing about this 1925 building that prompts you to go inside. Undecorated, the simple interior's shelves are adorned with hundreds of local condiments. Farmers and other folks scout Georgia's and North Carolina's valleys, mountains and vegetable gardens for wild to cultivated fruits and vegetables which they bring here to be processed. The Condiment Shop transforms pumpkins, watermelons, cucumbers, tomatoes, corn, peppers, wild grapes, blueberries, muscadine, crabapples, figs, strawberries, etc., into pickles, relishes, jams, jellies, conserves, preserves and anything else the owner has a mind to create. The prices aren't expensive and owner, Louis Edwards, can spin more Highlands history for you than anyone around.

Sweet-toothed people will want to stop at **Sweet Treats** at **Mountain Brooks** on 4th Street. Two ice cream or yogurt flavors—vanilla or chocolate—are blended with your choice of fruit, syrup and nuts to produce your favorite ice cream.

Things To See and Do _____

The recreational activities for both Highlands and Cashiers are similar with a few exceptions. You'll be hiking, mountain biking, horseback riding, boating, fishing, tubing, hunting, golfing, camping and skiing in different but equally scenic areas. However, in Highlands you're closer to both white water rafting and panning for gems in Franklin.

WATERFALLS

On U.S. 28, just 2 miles south of Highlands, cascades **Satulah Falls** and you can see **Lower Satulah Falls** from the overlook a half mile further south. Good hikers, undaunted by steep climbs, can follow the 1-mile foot trail down to **Glen Falls**. A series of 3 falls drop approximately 60 feet each on the east fork of Overflow Creek in the Blue Ridge Valley. You'll find this falls off N.C. 106, 3

Photo courtesy N.C. Travel & Tourism.

Mountain biking has grown in popularity in the North Carolina mountains.

miles south of town. It won't take too long to seek out the 18 **Kalakaleskies Falls**, all within a 1/4 mile of each other. These smaller falls are off U.S. 64/28 west, 2 1/2 miles northwest of Highlands on the Cullasaja River. **Bridal Veil Falls**, located 3 miles from Highlands on U.S. 64 west, is a particularly interesting waterfall as you can drive behind it. **Dry Falls,** just past Bridal Falls, is a true misnomer. You can walk behind the falls, but you will get sprayed a bit. The **Cullasaja Falls** on past Dry Falls lies parallel to the road in the Cullasaja River Gorge. It has a 250-foot cascade, which puts it in the not-to-be-missed category for waterfall aficionados.

GOLF

If you want to play golf in Highlands, the public course is at **Sky Valley Golf Club**, located 13 miles from downtown off N.C. 106 near the Georgia state line. (704-746-5302)

SKIING

You can ski at **Ski Scaly Mountain**. The area has a rope tow and double chair lift, plus snow making equipment. (800-342-1387)

BIKING

Mountain bike rentals and maps are available at the **Mountain Bike Depot**, located on E. Main Street in Highlands

and at Candy Basket in Cashiers.

FISHING

If you would like a guide to take you to special fishing areas, try **The Fish Hawk of Highlands** (704-526-9256), or **The Main Stream Outfitters**, (704-526-5649), or **Highland Hiker** (704-526-5298). You can get equipment and teaching along with the best places to find good fishing.

TUBING

One of the most inexpensive things that you can do to have fun is tubing on the Cullasaja. Tubes are available from the **Cullasaja River Campground**. (704-524-2559)

RAPPELLING

If you would like to try your hand at mountain rappelling lessons, contact **Mountain Down Tours**. It also offers overnight camping and guided hikes. (704-526-3063)

HORSEBACK RIDING

In the warmer months you can switch skis for horses and ride the trails on Scaly Mountain. **High Country Riding Stables** is located 8 miles southwest of Highlands on N.C. 106. (704-526-5710)

Photo by Lavidge & Assoc.

The scenic mountain golf courses, high in the Blue Ridge Mountains,
are both challenging and beautiful.

TENNIS/SWIMMING

You can play tennis or swim at the **Highlands Parks & Recreation Department** and also at **Sky Valley.** For court reservations and pool times, call (704-743-5302).

SHOOTING

Plum Orchard Creek Sporting Clays and **Wingshooting School** at 26 East Wright Square, provides a challenging course, shooting instruction for all levels and gun rentals. (704-526-5649)

Accommodations___

BED AND BREAKFAST INNS

The Old Edwards Inn ($$-$$$), located on Main Street, is the kind of place where you can sit out on the balcony in the summertime and watch families come out of the ice cream shop below. It's quiet enough, even in the center of downtown, to read one of the books from the inn's library and write a few post cards outside. The rooms in Highlands oldest (1880) inn have recently been renovated in the Country Manner style. Colonial paint colors, wall stenciling, wall coverings of that era and antique furnishings make this a comfortable place to prop up your feet for a weekend or longer. A continental breakfast that features homemade rolls and strawberry butter is served in the Central House Dining Room as well as the best of Southern-styled lunches and dinners. Great seafood dishes are another draw as the restaurateurs spend their winters managing a coastal restaurant. (704-526-5036)

The Highland Inn ($$-$$$), located across the street from The Old Edwards Inn has a similar personality, with its own rustic dining room that also offers an extended continental breakfast. Lunch and dinner are similar to the cuisine at its neighbor inn because it is managed by the same people. Higland Inn has an upscale appeal with comfortable country touches and both inns are on the National Register of Historic Places. A rather special amenity is its "Highland Nightcap." This inn can accommodate children and has a few rooms suitable for handicapped guests. (704-526-5036)

A few blocks down Main Street will bring you to **The Phelps House Bed & Breakfast Inn,** ($). Although the bedrooms and baths, decorated to reflect this 1885 inn's history, are not large, its full breakfast is: eggs, hotcakes, country ham, sausage, grits and biscuits. A great bargain! (704-526-2590)

HOTELS AND MOTELS

Mitchell's Motel ($), located on N.C. 28 and N.C. 106, is an even more economic bargain. For over 50, years the Mitchell family has been a prominent part of Highlands history. This rustic stone and log motel is surrounded by forests and a small lake, yet within walking distance of downtown. It, too, is a family-oriented type of place where guests like to gather in the lobby to play games or just sit by the fire and talk. A continental breakfast is served in the lobby each morning. Two bedroom cottages with fireplaces and kitchen facilities are also available. (704-526-2267)

CAMPING

Cliffside Lake and **Van Hook Glade**, are both located in the Nantahala National Forest. **Cliffside Recreation Area** ($) is located 1.5 miles off U.S. 64, 4.4 miles west of Highlands. (704-526-3765) There are 12 campsites for tent camping with tables and a bathhouse that includes showers. A permit is required for fishing in the lake (obtained at Reeves Hardware and Rexall Pharmacy in Highlands).

At **Van Hook Glade** ($) there are 17 family camping units, each equipped with a parking spur, fireplace, table and tent space. The parking spurs will also accommodate small trailers, and the facilities at Cliffside are available for your use. Skitty Creek is almost equidistant between the two camping areas and is often used as a route to Dry Falls. Take the turnoff just before Cliffside. (704-526-3765)

Dining

Hildegard's Restaurant ($$$$), on East Main Street has 6 differently decorated and accented dining rooms. This authentic German restaurant serves wonderful Bavarian-style potato dumplings and Black Forest cake.

Paoletti's Restaurant, ($$$$), on East Main Street, presents the greatest Northern Italian food.

For something a bit different, a rustic old mill that serves gourmet French cuisine, such as duck in a lingonberry-wine sauce, is the **Frog & Owl Cafe** ($$$), located on Buck Creek Road. It has great desserts, too.

The Mountaineer Restaurant ($) is where locals go for breakfast to read the paper and catch up on town news.

You can order a catfish sandwich from the **Hilltop Grill** ($), located "on the hill" on 4th Street. This old-fashioned grill has good milk shakes and other sandwiches as well.

For More Information:

Highlands Chamber of Commerce
P.O. Box 404-C
Highlands, NC 28741
704-526-2112

OTHER POINTS OF INTEREST

West Virginia

Mother nature put her energy into scenic beauty when she painted West Virginia. Tall, craggy mountain peaks covered with snow and skiers in the winter and rushing white water rivers dotted with rafters in spring, summer and fall make West Virginia a challenging getaway at any time of the year.

For More Information:
West Virginia's Travel and Tourism Department
800 CALL-WVA
(Including reservations for state parks and bed and breakfasts)

NEW RIVER GORGE

To Get There:
Take I-77 north to Exit 48, then U.S.19 north.

Things To See and Do

WHITE WATER RAFTING

Three of the most challenging rivers in the world for white water rafting are located in West Virginia: The New, The Gauley and The Cheat. When thousands of gallons of whipped white waters are coming at you, you learn fast who is in charge—Mother Nature. Your guide yells to everyone to dig harder in angling the raft. You punch into the foaming froth expecting your muscles to bulge and soon realize this is no passive roller coaster ride. You've got to do your part—fast. The instruction and safety video (which any good white water rafting company will insist you watch before beginning) helps, but it can't relate the power surging through you, dredging up energy you didn't know was there. It can't explain the exhilaration you feel riding the rapid through that bucking torrent that sails across your face.

Rafting is exciting, but there are definite safety measures that must be followed. It is essential that you take instruction from a qualified rafting guide. Children over the age of 6 may raft with their parents on the Upper New River; children over 12 may raft the lower sections of the New and Gauley.

"The Gauley Season" only lasts for about six weeks in the fall when water is released from an upriver reservoir. Only experienced rafters over the age of 16 should participate! If you're planning on going during the season, make your reservations well in advance.

There are many good rafting companies in the white water area. Our trip was with **Rivers Resort**, (800 TRY-RIV-ERS). The reward at trip's end is two wooden nickels you can redeem back at the **Red Dog River Saloon** for a beer or soft drink. This is also where you relive your experience, not only with fellow rafters, but in a video shot of your trip. Duplicate videos are made for rafters to purchase. Other well known rafting companies are: **Class VI Runners** (800-252-7784); **North American River Runners**(800-950-2585); and **Wildwater Expeditions Unlimited** (800-982-7238).

ROCK CLIMBING

On a good day (and some bad, too), the lure of sheer rock cliffs at Seneca, around Summersville Lake and along the bare canyon walls of the New River Gorge, compel climbers to test their skills. Akin to rafting, the sport attracts four types of people: thrill-seekers, spiritual-seekers, nature-seekers, and those who just want to be out in the open and have fun. It, too, builds self-esteem and team work. Fitness and good nerves are obvious requirements, but that's not enough. This sport, like rafting, definitely requires training. If this is a turn-on sport for you, consider looking into Tom Wendell's **Hard Rock Climbing Services**. (304-574-0735)

MOUNTAIN BIKING

In almost any season, but especially spring through fall, biking through West Virginia's fabulous state parks is just a peddle away from a heavenly experience. Rugged mountain bikes do best in these terrains, and if you don't have your own, you can rent one at **Ridge Rider Mountain Bikes** on Keller Avenue in Fayetteville, West Virginia. (304-574-2453)

Accommodations

Most white water rafting companies have camping available. If you choose Rivers, you can rent a rustic cabin or a campsite. Prices range from a special $49.95 (includes tent camping, continental breakfast and a pasta dinner) to $300 for a 3-day kayak clinic with camping and steak dinners. Horseback riding, float trips and other in-

White water rafting on the New River.

terests can be worked into some packages. Rafting equipment can be purchased and wet suits rented at its new outfitters store. Take I-77 north to U.S. 19 north toward Beckley. Look for Fayette Station Road and turn left at **Rivers Resort Complex**. (800-TRY-RIVERS)

The **Hawks Nest State Park** ($$), a rustic lodge that overlooks the New River Gorge, rents rooms by the day and takes reservations up to a year in advance. The lodge's dining room ($-$$) operates daily and offers breakfast, lunch and dinner. A tram transports guests to the gorge where paddleboats are rented. From the New River Gorge Bridge, take U.S. 19 north to U.S. 60 exit (about 5 minutes away) and take a left to Hawk's Nest near Ansted. (304-658-5212)

Fourteen miles from U.S. 60 near Rainelle is **Babcock** **State Park** ($$, 304-438-3004), where 1 and 2 bedroom log cabins with open fireplaces are sprinkled down throughout the canyon on the creek or scenic overlooks at the mountain's top. You can also tour the defunct Glade Creek Grist Mill here.

The White Horse Bed & Breakfast, ($$-$$$) is located at in Fayetteville, (about 5 minutes away from rafting). Upon entering this lovely, Greek Revival bed & breakfast inn, a guest remarked: "Holy cow— this is like a miniature Greenbrier." Although done in early 1900's antiques, this old grande dame is a lot more laid back. Owners, Cleon and Jane Vosler rescued the home from overgrowth and neglect and restored it themselves. You'll love the sun room filled with overflowing greenery, but you'll love Jane's full breakfast even better. (304-574-1400)

Dining

Enders ($-$$), located at 107 Keller Avenue, is a particular favorite for kayakers and rafters who know what it's like to be upended in the water. Lunch runs the gamut from pasta to Tex-Mex and dinner is equally diverse ranging from hamburgers to steak.

Smokey's ($-$$) on Ames Heights Road in Lansing, West Virginia, is another favorite choice of rafters.

ALLEGHENY MOUNTAINS

To Get There:
To Snowshoe/Silvercreek from Charlotte, N.C., take I-77 north, then I-64 east to W.V. 92. Go north to W.V. 39, then west to U.S. 219 north for 26 miles. From Triangle/Greensboro, go north on U.S. 220 to I-64, then west to W.V. 92, then same as above. (Maps are misleading, U.S. 219 north from I-64 is difficult during winter.)

Things To See and Do

SKIING

Would you like to know the feel of soaring like an eagle? That is how many skiers feel on **Snowshoe and Silvercreek's** (304-572-5252) long runs. Without actually taking "air" as some of the "hotdog" skiers do, gliding with grace down either of the resort's two mountains puts definition to the state's slogan, "Almost Heaven, West Virginia".

With the Silver Creek acquisition in 1992, Snowshoe is now two big mountains with more than enough skiing for everyone...beginner to expert. The gentler (easy) slopes and trails of Silver Creek fit beginner and intermediate skills. The sight of Snowshoe's famous Cupp Run's 1500-foot vertical drop over 1 1/2 miles is the intermediate and advanced skier's dream run. Most skiers take a little breather to psych themselves into attempting this exciting slope that ski champion Jean Claude Killy rates, in the *Book of Lists,* as the best racing slope in America. The resorts have 50 slopes, and 11 ski lifts speed up waiting time, which means that you get a lot more skiing time. It's true, you are never too old to learn how to ski, but the best time is to start as a child. Both resorts offer **Children's Ski Schools, Child Care Centers, Adult Training Centers** and **Rental Facilities.**

And though the resorts were created for skiing, they have become year-round resorts. From late spring through fall marks the time to come equipped with camera, knapsack and golf clubs.

BIKING

You can rent a mountain bike at the **Snowshoe Mountain Biking Center** located at either Silver Creek Lodge or at the bottom of the mountain next to the Inn at Snowshoe. (304-572-1000 ext. 165) This area has been described as "the Rockies of the East and a playground for both novice and expert mountain bikers." The resort has over 75 miles of scenic backroads and you can take a spin over to **Cass Scenic Railroad State Park** (23 miles away). (304-456-4300) Here, you can take a day to ride on a train pulled by a turn-of-the-century Shay locomotive to the second highest point in the state, Bald Knob, which is 4860 feet above sea level. Catch its live theater production that showcases the history of Cass, a restored logging community complete with country store.

GOLF

Summer months are the most popular times to play golf at Snowshoe, although some golfers get in as much spring and fall time as possible at Gary Player's 1993 **Hawthorne Valley Golf Course**. This 18-hole, par-72 course is accented by spectacular mountain vistas, and each hole is distinctly unique, with the front nine and back nine so different that they appear to be from two different courses. (304-572-1000 ext. 197)

Staff photo.

A view of West Virginia's Allegheny Mountains from one of Snowshoe/Silvercreek's 11 ski lifts.

TENNIS

If tennis is your game, the **Hawthorne Valley Tennis Center**, near the Hawthorne Valley Golf Course, offers 7 Har-Tru courts.

HORSEBACK RIDING

Near the resort's entrance, you'll find **Mountain View Stables**, which has guided trail rides and a number of stimulating activities for horseback riders of varying skills.

SIGHT-SEEING

Sight-seeing is another beckoning draw to this region. Besides the breathtaking scenery along the highways, you can visit the state's many state parks where camping and cottages provide overnight, weekend and weekly stays. In Pocohontas County, take in **Droop Mountain Battlefield State Park, Pearl S. Buck's birthplace**, the **Cranberry Glades** (a bog similar to the tundra found in the North), or explore **Beartown**, which is an intriguing walk through supernatural rock formations.

Accommodations

At Snowshoe/Silvercreek, you can stay at one of the inns' lodges or in a simple or elaborate condominium. At the base of the mountain, **The Inn at Snowshoe** offers an indoor pool, two large Jacuzzis and an exercise room. For a "no frills" economy stay, **Spruce Lodge** ($$$), next to Skidder Slope is the way to go, but if it's in your budget, try the **Inn at Whistlepunk** ($$$$).

Dining

Shoeshoe's many restaurants include the **Red Fox Restaurant** ($$$-$$$$), adjacent to the Inn at Whistlepunk, noted for hearty mountain cuisine and gourmet delights and the restaurant's lounge, **Yodeler's Pub** ($-$$) is neither too rowdy nor too mellow. You can dress as casually as you like for dinner at **Goodtime Bobby's Restaurant** ($$$-$$$$) amid antiques and stained glass. The **Skidder Restaurant** ($$-$$$) offers slopeside dining in a lodge-like atmosphere. Families often like dining at **Brandi's Restaurant** ($$). An economical and quick way to dine is at **Shaver's Centre**, which has several types of self-service places. For those ready to howl some more, there's no better place than the **Comedy Cellar** that highlights the best known comedy performers around.

For More Information:

**Pocahontas County Tourism Commission
800-336-7009**

Index

Symbols

A

N

O

Q

S

U

V

W

Y

Z